Becoming
Brazilian
How to Work, Live and Love like a Brazilian

Editora Appris Ltda.
1.ª Edição - Copyright© 2021 do autor
Direitos de Edição Reservados à Editora Appris Ltda.

Nenhuma parte desta obra poderá ser utilizada indevidamente, sem estar de acordo com a Lei nº 9.610/98. Se incorreções forem encontradas, serão de exclusiva responsabilidade de seus organizadores. Foi realizado o Depósito Legal na Fundação Biblioteca Nacional, de acordo com as Leis nos 10.994, de 14/12/2004, e 12.192, de 14/01/2010.

Catalogação na Fonte
Elaborado por: Josefina A. S. Guedes
Bibliotecária CRB 9/870

W784b
2021

Winter, Thomas Augustin
    Becoming Brazilian: How to Work, Live and Love like a Brazilian / Thomas Augustin Winter. - 1. ed. - Curitiba : Appris, 2021.
    319 p. ; 23 cm. – (Coleção geral).

    Inclui bibliografia.
    ISBN 978-65-250-0803-5

    1. Brasil - Identidade cultural. 2. Brasileiros. I. Título. II. Série.

CDD – 918.1

Appris editora

Editora e Livraria Appris Ltda.
Av. Manoel Ribas, 2265 – Mercês
Curitiba/PR – CEP: 80810-002
Tel. (41) 3156 - 4731
www.editoraappris.com.br

Printed in Brazil
Impresso no Brasil

THOMAS AUGUSTIN WINTER

Becoming
Brazilian

How to Work, Live and Love like a Brazilian

FICHA TÉCNICA

EDITORIAL	Augusto V. de A. Coelho
	Marli Caetano
	Sara C. de Andrade Coelho
COMITÊ EDITORIAL	Andréa Barbosa Gouveia (UFPR)
	Jacques de Lima Ferreira (UP)
	Marilda Aparecida Behrens (PUCPR)
	Ana El Achkar (UNIVERSO/RJ)
	Conrado Moreira Mendes (PUC-MG)
	Eliete Correia dos Santos (UEPB)
	Fabiano Santos (UERJ/IESP)
	Francinete Fernandes de Sousa (UEPB)
	Francisco Carlos Duarte (PUCPR)
	Francisco de Assis (Fiam-Faam, SP, Brasil)
	Juliana Reichert Assunção Tonelli (UEL)
	Maria Aparecida Barbosa (USP)
	Maria Helena Zamora (PUC-Rio)
	Maria Margarida de Andrade (Umack)
	Roque Ismael da Costa Güllich (UFFS)
	Toni Reis (UFPR)
	Valdomiro de Oliveira (UFPR)
	Valério Brusamolin (IFPR)
ASSESSORIA EDITORIAL	Evelin Louise Kolb
REVISÃO	Thomas Augustin Winter
PRODUÇÃO EDITORIAL	Lucielli Trevizan
ASSISTÊNCIA DE EDIÇÃO	Marina Persiani
DIAGRAMAÇÃO	Daniela Baumguertner
CAPA	Daniela Baumguertner
COMUNICAÇÃO	Carlos Eduardo Pereira
	Débora Nazário
	Karla Pipolo Olegário
LIVRARIAS E EVENTOS	Estevão Misael
GERÊNCIA DE FINANÇAS	Selma Maria Fernandes do Valle
COORDENADORA COMERCIAL	Silvana Vicente

This book is dedicated to:

Josie Winter, my mother, for helping me to learn to read and write, in memory of my father, Tom Winter, who told me his adventures of South America as a child.

Acknowledgments

Many thanks to Vasser Baily, Lucielli Trevizan and Emilie Winter, for helping to edit this book and giving advice. To Marco Santos who gave much advice on the finer points of Brazilian meats and grilling techniques. To Sirlene Ribeiro for advice on Minas Gerais and Brazilian Culture in general. I want to thank my publisher Appris in Brazil for publishing a book in English. Finally, Wagner Santana who introduced me to the books of Laurentino Gomes, whose histories of Brazil helped me in understanding Brazil and support the main thesis of this book.

Contents

PART I

Introduction: The Way of the Brazilian 13

Chapter One
Being a gringo is great,
but do not pay the monkey 27

Chapter Two
How to Behave Like a Brazilian 35

Chapter Three
Brazilian Exceptionalism & Practical Information 63

Chapter Four
Being Brazilian Through Food and Drinks 75

Chapter Five
Brazilian Relationships 139

Chapter Six
Brazilian Faith and Spirituality 155

Chapter Seven
Knowing Brazil though its Celebrations 163

PART II

Chapter Eight
The Problems of Brazil, Blame the Portuguese 197

Chapter Nine
Jeitinho and Malandragem: Underclass Survival Skills 219

Chapter Ten
Corruption and Impunity 233

Chapter Eleven
Social Inequality and Racism 245

Chapter Twelve
Criminal Violence in Brazil 271

Chapter Thirteen
Destruction of the Amazon 289

Epilogue/Conclusion: Going Home 307

Bibliography 309

PART I

Introduction: The Way of the Brazilian

A man on Bicycle with Flowers - Ivonaldo Velosa de Melo
Source: author's private collection

If you are reading this book you likely already have or will have a connection to Brazil. It could be that you will travel to or work in Brazil, or it could be that you are in an intimate relationship with a Brazilian. Whatever your reason, you will be in for a fun time. As you read this book and start your path to being Brazilian, I encourage you to keep an open mind and take some precautions. Brazil will not be like your home country, and if you want it to be, you will be sorely disappointed. Trying to compare Brazil to your home county will never allow you to embrace Brazil on its own terms, and as a result, you will long for your home country without understanding Brazil.

I have lived and worked in many countries but chose Brazil as the country to raise my children and dedicate most of my career. I have seen most foreigners adapt, love, and embrace Brazil, but I have also seen some foreigners who could never adapt and went home bitter, without completing their assignment. If you are going to live and work in Brazil it is important to realize that cultural differences are real, and you need to accept them as such. This seems like an obvious statement, but for someone who has never lived in a foreign country, their only frame of reference is their home country. It is natural and normal to view other cultures through a prism of your own cultural values. This paradigm of looking at another country though the values of your own culture will likely cause you to have what is called "culture shock." Culture shock is very real, but it can be avoided or minimized though learning and understanding the society you are living in. Culture shock impacts your moods and views on living in a foreign country. You may have feelings of excitement and elation followed by feelings of depression and anger. This is normal and you will likely cycle through these feelings of excitement and depression for a few months as you adjust to your new culture. Maybe you will be frustrated that things do not work just like they do at home. Many times, these feelings are brought on by petty things. One may wonder why there are no seedless oranges in Brazil or where your favorite cereal is. These feelings may even cause you to want to leave and go home, divorce your spouse, or just make yourself miserable. Though these feelings are normal, they are also avoidable. Brazil is a wonderful country, but you need to accept it as it is and embrace Brazilians as they truly are. The primary reason I wrote this book is to help you learn to be Brazilian and to learn to embrace and love your Brazilian experience.

Brazilians like to describe their country as if there were two Brazils. One way Brazilians think about their country is economic, another way they think about Brazil is geographic. Locals say that Brazil is a mix of Switzerland and Ethiopia, meaning that it is a country of haves and have nots. This is true; there is large scale inequality. The economic inequality comes from Brazil's history of slavery juxtaposed with prosperity. This prosperity in Brazil stems from an abundance of resources, as well as Brazilian optimism and inventiveness. Another common way Brazilians like to look at their country is geographically. Brazilians distinguish the North and Northeast regions of Brazil from the southern regions of Brazil.

In this view, Brazilians put Rio de Janeiro as a dividing line. From a cultural point of view there may be some validity to this idea as well. Brazilians who make this distinction, tend to believe that the northeast is the center of true Brazilian culture. This view holds that southern Brazil is full of European immigrants, and therefore, are not sincerely Brazilian. Some southern Brazilians also have strong views of northern Brazil as well. It is true that most European immigrants settled in southern Brazil. However, slavery was practiced throughout the country and Afro Brazilian influences are everywhere in Brazilian culture. Furthermore, as we will see in this book, both northern and southern Brazil had an history of regional rebellion, and all Brazilians from their great mix of cultures have contributed to Brazilian culture. It is exactly the mixture of people and ideas, that makes Brazil such a great place to live.

From a cultural viewpoint Brazil is much too large and complex to divided into just two parts. Northern Brazil does have a different feel than the south, but that does not really make the south less Brazilian. Brazil is not as simple as black as white. It may surprise people to know that more Japanese live in São Paulo than any other city outside of Japan. Likewise, who would guess that the biggest Oktoberfest outside of Germany is in Brazil? This Oktoberfest is held in a town that looks like it could be in Bavaria. Brazil also has had large immigrations of Italians, Arabs, Turks, Ukrainians, Polish, Germans, and many other counties in addition to the Portuguese that colonized Brazil. Certainly, Afro-Brazilian culture is stronger in the North and North East. For a good part of Brazil's history, slaves made up around half of the population found in most places in Brazil.

The final way of looking at Brazil geographically, is coastal versus the interior. For most of Brazil's history the lion's share of the population lived on the coast. This leads to a Brazilian paradigm of the urbane Brazilians living in coastal cities versus the rural farmers and ranchers living simpler lives in the interior. The interior of Brazil, in addition to its long-established mining industry, is now also a powerhouse in agriculture. Today, the fastest growing cities are in the interior of Brazil. Not only does this trend of migration to the interior promote prosperity for Brazil but it also unfortunately puts pressure on its ecology, including the Amazon rainforest.

Despite all these contrasts, there exists a common Brazilian identity and culture superimposed on regional differences. In this book, we will learn these common cultural mannerisms and take time to visit the various regions of Brazil to understand the history of each region that makes Brazil such an interesting place to live. Brazil was unified from very distinct regions under the Brazilian monarchy. This monarchy was imported from Portugal but separated from the home country to unify Brazil. It is the history of this European monarchy that makes Brazil unique to all the other countries in the western hemisphere. This unification of the regions of Brazil was not without violence and many parts of Brazil continued movements for independence until the 20th century.

Today, Brazilians are in the middle of another historical battle between law and order and crime and corruption. Brazilians are facing a decision. Do they reform their bloated government or follow the paths of Venezuela and Argentina and suffer continual economic crisis? Brazilians must also address their history of slavery that created societal inequalities. Unless social inequality is addressed, education and opportunities are improved, the crime and violence that plague Brazil will continue. Finally, Brazil needs to address how it will grow and balance these internal needs against the needs of the world to protect the Amazon basin.

Your first impression of Brazil will likely be how green it is. Not just light green like grass is green, but lush dark greens of every shade that go on and on and on. No matter how or where you arrive in Brazil, the impression is green. Now close your eyes and imagine a wonderful tropical paradise, with green jungle hills and flowers in the trees of all colors. Waterfalls flow through the jungle down to white beaches. Hills reach up to the sky and roads cross down the hills to the sea. Imagine this: In the hills you see a shanty town with little, boxy, red-brick houses stacked on top of each other. Suddenly you see a man riding his bike down a winding road. In one hand he has a beer, in the other hand he has a cigarette, in another hand he gives a thumbs up sign, smiling from ear to ear. He is juggling a football ball with one foot and his girlfriend is holding onto the bike seat for dear life. He is driving on the wrong side of the road, into oncoming traffic, and everything is just fine! *Tudo bem*! *Fica tranquilo*! (It's all good! Be cool!). That is being Brazilian!

If there is one single trait the Brazilian prize, it is optimism. If you are late and your train takes off without you, it is OK! There is another train is 20 minutes and we can hang out and talk. Brazilians are incredibly positive; if you have a problem, we can fix it! If your car is broken, your neighbor Dona Maria can give you a ride to work on her motorcycle! You do not know her? She is great you will be great friends! You lost your license to drive for too many traffic tickets? I have a friend who can fix that for you!

Your husband or girlfriend left you? Take advantage of *Carnaval*, it is only a few months away and you will meet new people and your partner will be begging to have you back after *Carnaval*! Even if you have a problem that you believe cannot be fixed, you are still living in Brazil so anything can happen! It is all very calming in a strange way.

Brazilians famously say that God is Brazilian. When I first heard this phase prior to the 2003 movie of the same name, I took the phrase to mean that God was Brazilian because he made a country without any natural disasters. Brazil has no earthquakes, or tornados. In Brazil it rains a lot, but that is better than droughts. When it does flood, usually lack of planning and infrastructure are to blame, so hard to pin that on God. There are no blizzards or ice storms in Brazil. When the temperature dips slightly below freezing, it is national news. TV reporters get dressed as if going to Antarctica. They step on the ice to prove it is solid and show everyone how they can see their own breath! With no earthquakes Brazil has no tidal waves. Brazil had only one small hurricane with 90 mph winds in 2004, in its entire history! Brazil's problems are made by people, not by God!

Most of my career has been working in Brazil, and my children are Brazilians. I even cheer for the same football team which remains, unknown and unrecognized, between the first and second division. Suffering for your football team is not an exclusively Brazilian problem, it just feels that way! I have lived and worked in many countries all over the world, but my path continues to take me back to Brazil. I had a career which required me to travel throughout South America, and having an American passport means you must obtain a visa for every trip between these countries. As I traveled a great deal throughout South America, I took advantage of the fact that my children are Brazilian, and fulfilling the requirement to be a dual national, I got my Brazilian passport. I did, in fact, become a Brazilian!

A series of serendipitous events brought me to Brazil. Some 35 years ago, I was living in the middle of Paraguay. I was a Peace Corp volunteer living close to the road, the road that intersected Paraguay from East to West. It was a simple existence living with the campesinos, eating mandioca and beans and bathing in a creek that flowed down to this road. If I needed to travel anywhere, I could walk to road and take the bus going east to arrive at Asuncion, the capital of Paraguay. This was during the dictatorship of Alfredo Stroessner, whose military government had a nasty habit of torturing and tossing out of airplanes people they did not like. For this reason, the US embassy gave Peace Corps volunteers special identity cards so we would not be picked up by mistake. We were advised to shave our beards, as beards were communist. Red was also the color of the dictator's political party so you could where red, however blue was the color of the token opposition. So, the rule was, no blue and no beards, because of course only communists wore those things. Because the Peace Corps is an extension of the U.S. government many of us were paired with Paraguayan Government employees who would use red bandanas at times in support of their dictator. Everybody thought everybody else was a spy. The country had been under a state of military siege for 30 years and there was a midnight curfew. With all this going on I did travel east to Asuncion, many a time.

I love the Paraguayan people and speak some Guarani to this day, which helped me a great deal in researching this book. Many historical figures, places, and words used in Brazilian Portuguese come from Tupi Guarani which is like the Guarani spoken in Paraguay. Due to the state of siege imposed by Stroessner at that time, there were limits to how much fun you could have if you were a twenty something. You needed to sneak around the city to avoid the military and the police after midnight, but only two establishments stayed open after midnight. One was the "Playboy Club," which seemed to have an unspoken political immunity, and the second was a hot dog stand that sold beer. We always kept our US Embassy cards with us to help us get out of trouble if we ever got caught.

That was what it was like taking the eastbound bus in Paraguay. If, however, I took the bus west, I would arrive at the city of Presidente Stroessner. From there you could take a city bus that would cross the border and arrive in Brazil, in the city of Foz de Iguaçu which is where the second largest waterfall is the world is located. Even though Brazil had only just recently been liberated from its own horror of military dictatorship, there was something in the people that always spoke to freedom and adventure. Brazilians, perhaps like the Italians, really are not made for military dictatorships. Brazilians like the good life, and as we will see in future chapters, are not particularly good about following the rules that their government makes in overabundance. The Brazilian clubs and parties were the best. The people the friendliest the women the most beautiful, and it was a country yearning to be free. There were great rock bands, nightlife, and all types of music! You could do anything, be anyone. Brazilians would go out to dinner when the curfew was beginning in Paraguay. Even though Brazil had only recently become a democracy after years of military oppression, the Brazilian people were just naturally born to be free. I remember one of my first trips in Brazil seeing a strike of a bank by the employees. The red flags of the left and the union were there, but instead of violence there was a band playing samba music top of a bus for the striking bank employees. There was food and dancing in front of the closed bank. Compared to the police beatings and tear gas that I had seen in Paraguay, Brazil was the place to be! Brazil was to be the country of the future. I write this book to welcome the reader to the possibilities of this great country.

There is no other country as dynamic, exiting, dangerous, loved by the world, and as free as Brazil. Every day is an adventure. It is a country which I have made my home. This book is to make the stranger feel at home at work or at play here. It may make Brazilians reflect on some of the idiosyncrasies of being Brazilian. For Brazilian readers, they may find my views on their culture as social commentary and laugh. There is no moral message here. Whatever is written in this book is written with love for the people and the country of Brazil.

This book is not a travel guide, it will not list the best restaurants or hotels. This book could be a travel aide, to help the visitor get a deeper understanding of Brazil and a richer experience when traveling to the various regions of the country. I prefer to think of this book as a living aid, for those visiting and working in Brazil. I call it a living aid as my hope is that you will learn to become a Brazilian in how you live and work while you are in Brazil. The term living aid is useful to people who want to have a great time in Brazil. Think of this book as a living aid for your time in Brazil as the book is intended to help you live in Brazil as if you were Brazilian and not a traveler.

As you are navigating Brazilian culture, you will at times be in a situation that does not seem correct. Perhaps it will be a comment you made that brought an unintended reaction, or something that you have done. It could be you could not find the brand of food or clothes that you use. It could be that you ordered a California Roll at the Brazilian Sushi Bar and found they use mango instead of cucumber. It could be what you think is an avocado and what a Brazilian avocado is are in fact two different fruits. Worse still is that the Brazilians like putting sugar and not salt on their avocado. At these moments you will feel strange and disoriented. This feeling of disorientation is a sign of culture shock. You need to be prepared to stop at this moment and reflect that you are no longer in your home culture, but you are in Brazil. This is the moment that you need to read this book and learn to embrace Brazil and being Brazilian. Even today my friends call me a gringo and of course I correct them, but the point really is, if you can become Brazilian in attitude and actions, you simply will have a much better time.

This book will help the stranger learn how to navigate Brazilian culture:

- Tips and pitfalls for working and traveling in Brazil.

- What is Brazilian time?

- Tips on Safety.

- Normal Brazilian etiquette, customs, and manners to avoid being rude.

- Why it is not cool to show the OK sign?

- How to make a *Caipirinha*.

- What is the difference between *moqueca capixaba* and *moqueca baiana*?

- What are the three variation of the Brazilian man-to-man hug?

- How to make friends and find love in Brazil.

- You will learn why what Brazilian call French Bread, *pão francês*, has nothing to do with the bread in France.

- What is a *Malandro*?

- Why Brazilians have a complicate relationship with rules? What is *Jeitinho*?

- What is the Brazilian National dish and where did it come from?

- How to dress and act on the beach.

- Afro-Brazilian influences on New Year's in Brazil and what foods are served and why Brazilians never serve turkey on New Year's.

And much, much more.

Brazil is said to be the country of the future, but that future never seems to arrive. Brazil continues to have problems in governance, inequality and education that have continued since Brazil was a colony. Brazil has so much going for it. It has the most abundant freshwater in the world in its rivers. Brazil is the largest country in Latin America. At 8.5 million square kilometers (3.2 million square miles) and with over 208 million people, Brazil is the world's fifth-largest country by area and the fifth most populous in the world. Its capital is Brasília, and its most populated city is São Paulo. The federation is composed of the union of the 26 states, and the Federal District. It is the largest country to have Portuguese as an official language and the only one in the Americas; it is also one of the most multicultural and ethnically diverse nations, due to over a century of mass immigration from around the world.

Bounded on the east coast by the Atlantic Ocean, Brazil has a coastline of 7,491 kilometers (4,655 mi). It borders all other countries in South America except Ecuador and Chile and covers 47.3% of the continent's land area. Its Amazon River basin includes a vast tropical forest, home to diverse wildlife, a variety of ecological systems, and extensive natural resources spanning numerous protected habitats. Besides the well-known Amazon rainforest, Brazil has the Pantanal in Mato Grosso do Sul as well as the Mata Atlantic rain forest along the coast from Rio to Parana. All this biodiversity is the subject of significant global interest and debate regarding deforestation and environmental protection.[1]

Brazil in the 9th largest economy in the world with a significant agriculture and mining sector.[2] As a huge country it has many regional differences but there is a common Brazilian culture. Each region has its own identity, and this book will explore some of these regions, but mostly it is meant for the reader to adapt quickly to the common Brazilian culture. Brazilians do not identify themselves as "Latinos" they see themselves as Brazilians. First the language is different. While Brazilians can generally understand Spanish, the reverse is not so true. Portuguese sets Brazil apart. Second, Brazil is huge, a colossal country, that is why it could surprise foreigners how little English is spoken outside the main cities. All Brazilian seem to be studying English, but few Brazilian speak it. Finally, Brazil has a unique history that sets it apart from the rest of Latin America.

---

[1] Wikipedia, "Brazil". Available in: https://en.wikipedia.org/wiki/Brazil. Access in: 13 nov. 2020.
[2] *Ibidem.*

This book in written in two parts. Brazil 1.0 which is intended for the traveler or businessperson to become acquainted with the customs, culture, food, and other topics to make travel or business trip more fulfilling. This section is designed to teach the visitor how to act and interact with Brazilians. Brazilians are a very social people and hold visitors in high esteem. Being a gringo or foreigner puts you automatically in an elevated social class. Brazilians are curious about the world and they look forward to meeting foreigners. The word gringo, as you will find out, is not an insult in Brazil. Rather being a gringo should give you many chances to interact with Brazilians if you chose to do so.

The first part of this book is to help this interaction with Brazilians by giving the reader a base of knowledge about Brazil. Also included in Brazil 1.0 is a background on customs, cross cultural communication, as well as an overview of the regions, celebrations, food, and drink, so that the reader has a fuller understanding of Brazilians and a little help to act like them or at least understand them. Brazil is a large country, and each region has its own differences, but rather than simply repeat stereotypes which Brazilians have for each other, this section give you an introduction to each region's celebrations, history, and food to give a deeper understanding of each region.

Trying to explore the regional differences of Brazil through foods, music, and celebrations allows the reader to add to the experience of a particular region in Brazil without falling into typical Brazilian stereotypes. Brazilians, like other people, make jokes about Brazilians from other regions. Some of these regional stereotypes are funny, however others could be misinterpreted or misunderstood to be insulting. Brazilians are fun loving, but their humor can at times, seem rough or insensitive. These Brazilian stereotypes used to describe each reason are not always flattering. As I hope to emphasize the positives of Brazil in the first part of the book, an exploration of the regions of Brazil will prominently feature the food, drink, and celebrations of the different regions. My hope is by seeing each region this way the reader can come to his own conclusions.

In Brazil 2.0 we will look at the major problems that Brazil still needs to overcome to fulfill its potential to be the country of the future. If you are reading this book you likely will spend some time in Brazil, and if you spend time in Brazil you hopefully will want to see Brazil's future improve. All Brazilians recognize that Brazil has serious problems, and many recognize that they are in a critical point in Brazilian history where Brazil must try to address these problems. What I will argue in Brazil 2.0 is that the major problems faced by Brazil today are related to their history as Portuguese colonies which later were united under an Empire. When the Portuguese ruling family fled Napoleon to arrive in Brazil, they set in motion the only European monarchy in the western hemisphere. The unification of Brazil under a monarchy instead of a republic retarded Brazil's development as a democracy and weaken the institutions of government that have allowed corruption and lawlessness to continue. This is not an obvious conclusion for Brazilians to reach. Being gringos, allows us to look at Brazil from outside the paradigm of Brazilian history.

Brazil is unique in Latin America to have had its own monarchy. One main theme of this book is that the arrival of the Portuguese monarchy made Brazil a victim of its own history. The country was so dependent on slavery that there was little internal sympathy for abolition. The Portuguese crown depended on the money of slave traders. Slavery was the one policy that would unite both republicans and monarchists. There were a few attempts to create an independent republic in Brazil but all failed as they were crushed by the monarchy. This really set Brazil back in its development and has left the country with weak democratic institutions to this day. For while Europe and the rest of the Americas were overthrowing their monarchs to set up democracies, Portuguese monarch and court arrived in the 15 separate colonies of Brazil. The colonies of Brazil were not unified by revolution but under an emperor instead. The Brazilian population in 1808 was mostly illiterate. Portuguese colonial policy had banned the printing press from the region.[3] Portuguese colonial policy also discouraged travel and trade between the Brazilian colonies. Roads connecting the various colonies were discouraged.

Due to this history, Brazil was never able to live through and realize the ideals of enlightenment and democracy that needed to create strong social institutions needed for a strong and just society. Brazilian colonies instead of rebelling against a monarchy, became the center of a monarchy. When the Portuguese royal family escaped from Napoleon in 1801 to Brazil. thousands of newly destitute aristocrats and others in the court arrived as well.[4] To provide a historical context of the size and perhaps comment on the corruption of the Portuguese government, it is notable

---

[3] GOMES, Laurentino. *1808*: Como uma rainha louca, um príncipes medroso, e um corte corrupta enganaram Napoleão e mudaram a Historia de Portugal e do Brasil. São Paulo: Globo, 2014, p. 59,

[4] *Ibidem*, p. 62.

to compare to the change of capitals in the United States which happened around the same time. In 1800 the new United States moved its federal government from Philadelphia to Washington D.C. At the time of the move, the Federal Government had only 125 full time employees to govern a similar sized country.[5]

When the monarchy was finally overthrown in 1888, instead of a popular revolution, the government was replaced with what was basically a military government, supported by an oligarchy. The overthrow the monarchy happened so quietly that the most Brazilians did not even realize that the royal family had left. As we will see, these events, delayed the development of Brazilian institutions and society for more than a hundred years, and only now, after multiple failed attempts, are Brazilians seeing the need for reform of their social institutions. In the second part of this book, we will see that the major problems of Brazil started with Portuguese colonial policy to Brazil, and the arrival of the monarchy in Brazil when they arrived to escape Napoleon.

Though Brazilians do not directly blame Portuguese rule for creating the major problems in Brazil today, Brazilians have an ambivalent and complex attitude to the Portuguese and Portugal. On one hand they recognize that Portugal has a major impact on Brazilian culture. Many Brazilians are proud of their Portuguese heritage and still share Portuguese food and holidays. However, in popular culture, Brazilians make fun of Portuguese in jokes and music. Besides imitating Portuguese accents, Brazilian jokes about Portuguese are common. In all the jokes, the Portuguese are mocked for not being intelligent. Likewise, the memory of the royal family is not complementary. In common folklore, the first king of Portugal to arrive in Brazil, Dom Juan, was very fat and ate chickens from the sleeves of his coat. He is famous for not bathing and being afraid of crabs and thunder. His queen, Dona Carlota, is remembered to have been ugly and unfaithful.[6] The presence of the monarchy in Brazil likely preserved the union of Brazil and kept the regions from unraveling into separate republics but that does not make Brazilians nostalgic for their former king. Throughout this book we will see that regional tensions that existed during the monarchy, exist in Brazil to this day.

---

[5] Available in: https://www.history.com/this-day-in-history/president-john-adams-orders-federal-government-to-washington-d-c. Access in: 04/03/2021.

[6] GOMES, Laurentino. *1808:* Como uma rainha louca, um príncipes medroso, e um corte corrupta enganaram Napoleão e mudaram a Historia de Portugal e do Brasil. São Paulo: Globo, 2014, p. 74.

In the second part, Brazil 2.0 discusses deeper cultural topics to gain insight into why Brazil is Brazil. Brazil is a country blessed by nature and a wonderful melting pot of races and culture, but cursed by ineffective institutions, and a history of neglect, exploitation, and corruption. In 1835 Alexis de Tocqueville, a Frenchman, while traveling the United States wrote, "Democracy in America," a social commentary on that country with the European perspective, comparing the new country to the old world of Europe. I will try in Part 2 of this book to modestly try to do something similar. Brazil is in a unique moment in its history and like de Tocqueville did in his book, sometimes it is easier for someone outside the culture to make observations impartially. I hope the commentary will help Brazil move forward from these difficult times. It will touch on Brazilian topics of history, politics, corruption, inequality, and legal and tax reform in the hopes that we all really can transform Brazil be the country of the future. Only by taking an honest look at the shortfalls of Brazilian institutions can we break the cycle of oppression, corruption, and impunity that rob the Brazilians of their potential.

At times I will use a word or phase in Brazilian Portuguese or slang, or I will use the Brazilian Portuguese to convey as idea specific to Brazilian culture and thought. When I use a Brazilian Portuguese word it will be in italics. As stated, before the Brazilians have a love-hate relationship with the Portuguese and this extends to the language. While there remains an academic intellectual love of the Portuguese language, yet incorrect usage and spelling is common even among the educated. Brazilian Portuguese has evolved. Academic Portuguese language is very structured and has not really changed for hundreds of years. However, the people's language of Brazil is Brazilian Portuguese, which is dynamic and has mutated into a means of expressing things unique to Brazil. Even within regions of Brazil there are phases and words specific to an area. These differences in the lexicon are quite well known to Brazilians and it can be challenging to write about being Brazilian without using them. When I use one of these words, I will give my best effort to capture the meaning in English, but I will feel free to use the Brazilian Portuguese and English word interchangeably. The Brazilian language reflects the country and dynamic. The original Portuguese language from Portugal is conservative and stale. Today it is difficult for Brazilians to understand the Portuguese of Portugal. This theme of a dynamic Brazil meeting a conservative corrupt and decadent Portugal will be a common theme repeated in this book.

Chapter One

Being a gringo is great, but do not pay the monkey

A Casa do Pedrinho
Source: https://acasadopedrinho.com/pagando-mico-junto-com-o-filho/. Access in: 09/21/20

There is no better country to be a foreigner, whether it be for a short visit or a long work assignment, than Brazil. Brazilians love foreigners and will go out of their way to make them feel welcome. Maybe that is one of the reasons why everyone in the world loves Brazil. Brazilians, like the United States, is a country composed of immigrants. They are curious about other countries and have been historically exposed to various cultures, which is perhaps another reason why you never need to feel isolated or alone in Brazil. It is like the song of the Liverpool football team; in Brazil you never need to walk alone.

Visitors may be surprised and offended that they are called *"gringos"* by Brazilians. However, this term does not have a negative connotation in Brazil and is often used in an endearing manner. The term *"gringo"* is used to describe anyone who is not Brazilian, not just North Americans. It is as simple as that and no reason to be offended. You will automatically have a higher social status than you likely had in your home country by being a *gringo*. Brazilians will be interested in you and what you have to say. Brazil, more than most countries, is tolerant and accepting of other nationalities and ethnicities. Being a *"gringo"* in Brazil makes you interesting. Instead of ignoring you or avoiding you, Brazilians will engage with you and invite you out. If you tend to be social and friendly, you will likely make many friends during your trip here.

In this book, we will cover the basics of Brazilian behavior and a background on Brazilian culture. This will be your guide on your road to become Brazilian. This will help you overcome cultural differences, but you still need to be ready to embrace being Brazilian. Brazilians have wonderful customs and behaviors that are useful to learn. Brazil is also a huge country with a wide variety of religious beliefs, customs, ethnicities, food, and celebrations. To know Brazil and Brazilians, you need to know every region and their own histories. Certain core values and behaviors are common to all Brazilians, but to really know the country, you need to treat each region on its own terms. Brazil is an extremely rich and complex culture and to try to attempt to cover the entire country with overview misses to much of the richness of each region. It is too easy to fall into the same generalizations and stereotypes that Brazilians have about each region of their country. Following chapters will examine the different regions history and customs, so you know what to expect, without being too simplistic. After all, Brazil did not start as one country, it started as many different isolated regions. These regions became a unified state only after undergoing intrigues, conspiracies, revolts, and violence. Remember to fully understand and appreciate the richness of Brazil's cultural heritage, it is imperative that you spend some time in each region.

Jogo do Mico: A Brazilian Cultural Allegory

Pagando mico (which in English means "paying the monkey") is the Brazilian expression for making a fool out of yourself. Before we learn how to act Brazilian, let us spend some time on reviewing what behaviors need to be avoided while in Brazil. For a *gringo*, making a fool of yourself is more common and easier than most foreigners would like to imagine. Brazilians in general enjoy joking about some of the more famous gaffs. This may not at times be politically correct humor, but it is Brazilian humor, nonetheless. Brazilian make fun of each other all the time, so do not be surprised if they make fun of you if you do something embarrassing. These remarks are not ill-willed, but if you are new to this, it may sting at first. This part of the book is to help you avoid making a fool of yourself when in Brazil.

When doing something embarrassing, Brazilians will say you are paying the monkey or *pagando mico*. Brazilians like to fit in, and when you do not fit in, you are *pagando mico*. The history of how this saying came about gives a certain insight into Brazilian culture.

The phrase *"Pagando Mico"* or (pay the monkey) comes from the children's card game called Jogo do Mico or (Game of the Monkey) created in the 1950s.[7]

In the game, Jogo do Mico, all the cards have animal figures, and the player must form pairs with the male and female of each species. When you form a pair of animals both male and female you put the pair of animals down on the table and continue to do so until you have no more cards in your hand. But in the deck, the little monkey (mico) has no pair. The mico has no male or female mate, but the all the other animals have a mate. Therefore, whoever finishes with the monkey card in their hand loses – that is, he pays the monkey. The person left with the mico card who does not have a pair. He loses, and everyone else wins!

Pagando Mico is a wonderful allegory and morality tale for Brazilian culture itself because it identifies certain Brazilian qualities. Brazilians are very social. Relationships are very central to their way of life. Brazilians are all individuals without the need to flaunt their individuality. Of course, they want to be successful and some like to be leaders, but they like it most when everyone is getting along, or working as a team, or having fun at a

---

[7] Available in:https://super.abril.com.br/mundo-estranho/qual-a-origem-da-expressao-pagar-mico/#:~:text=Ela%20vem%20do%20baralho%20infantil,ou%20seja%2C%20paga%20o%20mico. Access in: 09/21/20.

party. There is little formality in daily interactions in Brazil. There is a form of formality, in situations of social hierarchy such as at private clubs, at work, or in a restaurant. There exists a difference between who is serving and who is the client. Outside of these structured formal social situations, Brazilian generally interacts in the same fashion, without pretext of social class. For example, you may be at a restaurant with your children running around or on an airplane with a baby crying. In these times of stress Brazilians of all social classes come together and just make things work out. The waiter at your table may take time to play with your child, the stewardess on the airplane may offer to hold your crying baby until you are ready to take the baby back. On your next international flight to and from Brazil, stop to observe if flying economy, that if families or couples are given separated seats on the airplane, Brazilian will rearrange their own seating to accommodate families and couples automatically!

Brazilians also want to fit in and be cool. They want to be like the other animals in the game that have a pair. They do not want to be the little monkey all alone! In fact, is hard to translate, "I want to be alone" to Brazilian Portuguese. When you translate, I want to be alone in Portuguese *"quero estar sozinho"* it has a sad tone to it. It is hard for a Brazilian to understand why you would want to be alone. Being alone is like wanting to be sad to a Brazilian ear.

Fortunately, it is easy to be accepted in a group of Brazilians. Brazilians will either invite you to join them in a social setting, or you can easily meet and strike up conversations with them. There is nothing wrong with acting like a foreigner in Brazil. I will repeat, that Brazilians think very highly of gringos. Have you watched the animated film about the girl from Minnesota who has one of the last blue parrots who must get back to Brazil to save the species? Gringos are rarely portrayed badly; they are just simply awkward. This chapter is just to give the reader a few quick steps to being Brazilian.

Try not do the following in Brazil or you will end up paying the monkey:

- The OK sign is not OK. It is vulgar. Use the thumbs up sign to say everything is OK. *Tudo bem*!

- Brazilians will offer you little cups of coffee in many circumstances. Just take the coffee! Refusing the little coffee is awkward.

- Avoid eating food with your fingers. Brazilians rarely eat food with their fingers, and if they do, they use a napkin or a toothpick to avoid touching the food. If you think it is time to use your fingers to eat food, watch what the Brazilians do.

- Avoid talking loudly! This may have something to do with expressing your individuality or thinking that by speaking loudly you will somehow help your hosts understand English. No, speaking English loudly will not help and talking loudly can be a real turn off in Brazil. To be honest I have also seen Brazilians do the same thing in Portuguese. Brazilians sometimes try to speak loudly to you in Portuguese thinking you will understand Portuguese better. Try to keep your volume to the level of your hosts.

- Do not wear green and yellow together for a social function! These preppy colors may work in New England, but they are the colors of the national flag and football team. Everyone may use these colors to watch the national team play, and if going to an event to watch the Brazilians play this is a great idea, however just showing up in green and yellow at any other time is looked at very strangely.

- Do not go to the beach in shoes or street clothes! Once again this may be fine in Holland, England, or Nantucket but leave those shoes at your hotel! Everyone uses sandals at the beach, or they walk barefoot. There are some famous brands of sandals with a large variety of styles. You can buy these sandals easy all over the coast of Brazil. If you are not ready to use speedos or thongs, your regular swimsuit will do fine.

- Avoid being critical of Brazil even if the Brazilians you are with are critical! Brazil has lots of problems that we will discuss in greater detail in the second part of this book, but Brazilians are also immensely proud of their country. This is a tricky situation. Never start a conversation with a criticism of Brazil and be wary of being critical of Brazil even if your hosts bring up some topic. The conversation could turn quickly against you, with the Brazilians defending their country. In general, try to avoid this topic unless you know your Brazilian host intimately.

- Do not drink too many caipirinhas! Brazilians love to party and likely started at a younger age than you. They enjoy a good party better than most, but Brazilians consider it a turn off to see someone physically drunk. Brazil is not a culture where drinking till you drop is encouraged. Drink until you are happy and no more!

- Do not confuse Brazil with other countries, especially Argentina. Argentina is the rival of Brazil in football. The capital of Argentina is Buenos Aires, and the capital of Brazil is Brasilia! They do not eat tacos in Brazil and the Brazilians you are likely meeting have nothing to do with cutting down the Amazon unless you are working in the lumber industry in the Amazon which is thousands of miles from the major cities on the coast!

- Keep both hands on the table while eating or drinking. Hiding your hand under the table on in your lap are poor table manners.

- After eating, do not say you are full, which is sounds crude to a Brazilian. Brazilians never say they are full, they say they are satisfied, which is *"Estou satisfeito"*

- Never burp at the table! Get up and go to the bathroom. This is extremely rude.

- Personal hygiene standards are higher in Brazil: stay clean, use clean clothes, shower at least once a day, and brush your teeth. Brazilians are very hygienic and are known for taking two baths a day. They really do brush their teeth three times a day. It will come as a surprise that Brazilians expect foreigners to be less hygienic, but while you are here, it is nice to stay clean.

- Dress well and in clean clothes. Brazilians are judgmental about appearances.

- Brazilian toilets and toilet paper are not the same as in other countries. If you keep flushing paper in the toilet it will eventually clog. That is what the trash basket is for.

- Brazilians are not Hispanic. Avoid making the comparisons. Brazilians will look to Europe, particularly France or the United States for intellectual influences before looking to Hispanic America. Brazil is an Atlantic facing country.

- Racism is a serious offence. We will discuss social inequality in a specific chapter. More than half of all Brazilians are of African descent, and almost all are of multiracial. Brazilians have an extraordinarily complex and nuanced attitude towards race and social class. Stay away from this subject. If a Brazilian makes a comment that seems racist, do not join the conversation, Brazilians have a complex history with race and slavery which you may not understand at first.

- Football is a huge pastime and Brazilians are passionate about it. You need to be careful in making comments. Before joining a conversation about football, understand what team your Brazilian friends cheer for. Most Brazilians have strong attachment to their teams and hate their team's rivals. Try to understand what teams rivals are to avoid big misunderstandings. For example, if the Brazilian national team played badly, it is acceptable to say that they played bad, but you would never say the Argentine team played well, or worse say the Argentine team is better than Brazil!

- Feel free to dance Samba at Carnival but avoid dancing samba pointing up and down with your arms in the air. This may have something to do with western cultural ideas on personal space, but please do not to this, you will really stand out as a gringo. Dance samba with your arms to the side.

So now that we know some of the major mistakes that a foreigner makes, lets now study some of the basics of Brazilian behavior. Like all humans, Brazilians are no different in judging people on first impressions. It has been my experience that Gringos make simple mistakes by not being sensitive to Brazilian behavior. These mistakes are not intentional. It is normal to assume that all people and cultures are the same, or that the differences are insignificant. This is a mistake. While Brazilians hold Gringos in high esteem and will continue to be nice to you despite your social lapse or faux pas, these mistakes could make business deals and social interaction less successful.

Unlike other parts of the world, relatively few Brazilians speak English. From the number of English schools, it would seem like every Brazilian is studying English, and yet surprisingly few Brazilians speak it. Most Brazilians do not have many opportunities practice their English and they will try to practice with you. The visiting Gringo should use this opportunity to start up conversations and get to meet Brazilians. A sure way to get on the good side of all Brazilian is to let them talk English to you and compliment to them on their English. Saying something positive about the Brazilian's English will make them happy and is an ideal ice breaker for social interactions in Brazil.

Brazilians love foreigners. Trying to follow Brazilian cultural rituals will help you a great deal with your experience in Brazil. So, when someone offers you coffee, take it. If a Brazilian is late, be patient. Try not to eat with your fingers and do not criticize Brazil to Brazilians. Follow these rules and you will do fine.

Chapter Two

How to Behave Like a Brazilian

Roda de Samba by Carybé (1916)
Source: *Bahia Já*, 2021

Personal Space, Greetings, and Interactions

One of the first things you will notice when you are in Brazil is that your personal space may feel smaller. North Americans and Western Europeans have what I call the "thumb in the ear" rule. I did not invent this concept, but I have seen this rule in demonstration in cross cultural orientations for multinational organizations working in Brazil. However, I cannot find a reference to give credit to who ever invented it. The closest reference I could find was work by Edward T. Hall in what is called *Proxemics* or the study of *personal space*.[8] The distance of the thumb to the ear, which Hall defines as personal space, is a close approximation of 1.5 feet. This means that people in many cultures avoid being closer than the distance of one person's extended arm into the thumb into another person's ear! See picture.

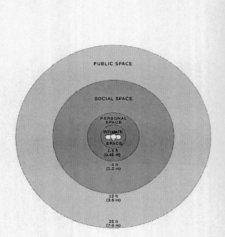 

Proxemics
Source: author's collection and Wikipedia

Try the following experiment: When talking to someone from your own country, try to stand closer to them than the *thumb in the* ear rule will allow. Ignore how you feel, keep standing close to them, and keep talking with them as you step closer. It is likely that you will see this person look extremely uncomfortable and try to move back or walk away. In most North American and European cultures, we do not like having our personal space invaded. We keep this distance in our daily interaction, and we feel

---

[8] Available in: https://thereader.mitpress.mit.edu/understanding-personal-space-proxemics/. Access in: 09/15/ 2020.

uncomfortable if people transgress this space. However, not all cultures feel this need, and Brazilian culture is one of them. Brazilian culture does not recognize your need for personal space, at the same time it will not understand your desire to be alone!

Brazilians have a smaller area of personal space, or perhaps they do not have any limits of personal space depending on the given circumstance. This means that interactions and conversations may occur a lot closer than what you are used to. Most groups and gatherings are very warm and inclusive. They do not think anyone should be alone and cannot understand why someone would like to be unless they are studying or working. If you must stay a weekend in a hotel in a strange city, just let a Brazilian know and more likely than not, help you find something thing to do. If you are working in Brazil and tell your coworkers, one of more will likely make plans for you so that you are not alone and included in something. Take advantage of this. The best way to get to know Brazil is being with Brazilians. By the way, the reverse is true. If you have a Brazilian coworker in your home country, invite them out to do something. Gringos get the reputation of being cold and aloof, so put in the extra effort to include and engage Brazilians. It will be worth it!

You could be surprised that your personal space may be invaded even in a work setting. If you are new to the country or traveling for work, you will likely receive the standard western handshake. It could be just as likely that you could be greeted with a hug if you are a man or a kiss on the cheek if you are a woman. Brazil is a large country with a diverse population, so it is quite common of Brazilians to categorize themselves through region and socio-economic status. Unfortunately, Brazil also suffers from classism, so how you dress and appear will impact how you are judged in Brazil. The following standard greetings in Brazil are universal by both region and social class:

Basics rules of Brazilian Greetings

It is important in a business or a social situation to greet everyone individually and look each person in the eye. In a group or social situation, the person or couple arriving is expected to greet each person walking around the and great everyone, prior to sitting at a table or starting a meeting. If you arrive and just greet the boss or the people you know, wave to everybody else and sit down, it is impolite. The same is true in a social situation. If you are arriving at a small party or gathering at a restaurant, you do not greet only the people you know, but you obligated to greet and introduce yourself to the people you do not know. Upon leaving or finishing a meeting, you are expected to bid farewell to each person individually. It is rude to do otherwise.

Brazilian Greeting: Women to Women and Women to Men

When two Brazilian women meet in a social situation it common for them to exchange a kiss on both cheeks. However, they do not touch lips to cheeks, nor do they touch cheeks! This is supposedly done not to mess up each other's make up.

Source: author's collection

When a man and a woman meet in Brazil, it is also common exchange two kisses on the cheek. Once again you do not plant your lips on the cheek, but rather this time both people touch cheeks! Why women giving kisses to each other do not touch cheeks while men and women giving kisses do touch cheeks is a mystery.

Becoming Brazilian

The number of kisses you give depends upon the different states and regions in Brazil. To make things even more complicated, in some state where the custom is to give two kisses, they will add an extra kiss and say "Three kisses to get married" and this can take you by surprise! As a general guide to numbers of kisses that are by custom giver per region: refer to the map below. The best thing to do is watch the Brazilians and follow their lead. There are worse things in this world than getting an extra kiss!

Brazilian greetings: how many kisses per state
Source:https://www.reddit.com/r/Brazil/comments/2bwuu6/brazilian_greetings_how_many_kisses_per_state/

This kissing greeting is independent of age, social class, race, or geographic region in Brazil. Because the number of kisses is hard to follow, the best thing to do is follow the lead of the Brazilian kissing you. There is nothing implied in these kisses and you will end of kissing a lot of people. You could kiss your lawyer or doctor in Brazil, and it would not be strange. After a while you get used to it. There is nothing implied, it just a greeting.

39

Kisses in Text messages

In text messaging, Brazilians may also finish a text that says *"Beijos"* or *"Bjs"* (which means "kisses") or *"abraço"* (which means "hugs"). Now you may jump to the conclusion that a Brazilian is being forward with you, but in most cases you would be wrong. These endings in test message or emails are not uncommon. Avoid jumping to incorrect conclusions if you see emails or messages in the workplace ending with "Bjs" or "Kisses". This is simply the text messaging or an email extension of the Brazilian greeting.

Women Social Interactions

Something that is not uncommon between women especially in the interior of the country is for women to walk arm in arm or hand in hand in public. See Pictures. Again, there is nothing for the foreigner to read into this. This is simply a sign of friendship and not an indication of a romantic relationship.

Source: author's collection

While men and women holding hands in Brazil is a sign of a romantic relationship, women walking arm and arm with a man is sign of a close relationship but not necessarily romantic.

Greetings with children

Children in Brazil run the show and are highly valued in Brazilian society. When introduced to children, you will gain greater acceptance by the family members by calling yourself *"Tio"* (which means uncle) or *"Tia"* (which means aunt). If kids or teens call you *"Tio"* or *"Tia"*, it is a sign of respect.

Under some situations, especially in traditional catholic families, you will see children asking for a blessing prior to leaving a social event. However, this is reserved only for family. In this situation usually prior to leaving a social situation, a child or teenager will ask for a blessing from the most senior relative, put their hands together and says *"Bença"* (which means blessing) and the relative makes the sign of the cross as a priest would do.

Common verbal greetings include *'olá'* ('hello'), *'bom dia'* ('good day'), *'boa tarde'* ('good afternoon') and *'boa noite'* ('good evening' or 'good night').

Brazilian Greetings: Men to Men, 3 types of Brazilian hugs, and other greetings.

Besides the standard handshake, there are three standard men to men hugs that you may see in the office but certainly will experience all of them in social situations.

Greeting 1: Extension of the handshake

This is the least intimate of the men to men hugs. In this greeting the men shake hands and put the other hand on the shoulder of the other man. After shaking hands both hands are released. See below:

Source: author's collection

Greeting 2: Tummy Tap

This is the intermediate intimate hug and one of the most difficult for foreigners to get used to. In this hug each man puts his arms around the shoulder of the other man, and they tap each other's belly and after a few taps both hands are released. You can imagine that this takes some getting used to if you are not prepared! See below:

Source: author's collection

Greeting 3: Bear hug

This is the most intimate greeting between men. It is the standard bear hug with various degrees of tapping each other's back and sometimes swaying side from feet to feet. Sometimes greeting 1 or 2 can turn into greeting 3 and after a few taps on the back both hands are released.

Source: author's collection

Greeting 4: Cool handshake

Usually in situation where you are playing sports or in a bar with younger men, you may come across an alternative handshake. In this handshake both men extend their open hand at a 45-degree angle, slap lightly each other's open palms and close with a fist pump. See pictures below:

Source: author's collection

Source: author's collection

Brazilian Greetings: Public displays of affection

It is common for couples of all ages to show affection. Foreigners may be surprised to see how much public displays of affection are frequent and unapologetic. Whether you are in a shopping mall, a beach, on the street, or at a night club, Brazilians are comfortable and openly express affection. It is normal for couples, to make out publicly. Public displays of affection is normalized and socially accepted in Brazil.

The Brazilian Goodbye Ritual

Brazilians also have an exceptionally long and elaborate way to say goodbye. As with greetings, it is equally important that you say goodbye to every single person when you leave a place. In a business situation it is enough to simply shake hands, give hugs, and briefly chat with everyone. You must remember that business relationships are built on trust in Brazil and saying goodbye correctly is as important as greetings to build a solid business relationship.

It is in social situations where goodbyes can take much longer and may even seem like a ritual. Let us take an example: You and your friends finish dinner in a restaurant, pay your bills and decide to leave. You get up from your table and everyone talks, hugs, and kisses each other to say goodbye just as you have learned in this chapter. Remember you must hug or kiss and say goodbye to each person in the group, without ignoring anybody. You walk out on to the street and start to talk again. Someone decides to call a cab, or the valet arrives with the car. Everyone says goodbye, hugs, and kisses again to everyone else, and then the couple that gets in the cars drives off. The remaining group stays together to talk and when the next car arrives, everyone says goodbye and hugs and kiss again. This continues until everyone has left have left. Brazilians take their personal relationships seriously, and therefore you need to be patient when it is time to say goodbye to avoid being rude.

Brazilian Hand Gestures

Brazilians are a very expressive people. They also have a variety of hand gestures and signals for nonverbal communication, of which all are understood throughout every region. These hand signs are fun to learn and easy to incorporate in your daily life. If you get a chance to use one of these signs correctly, you will get a good laugh from your hosts, and they will appreciate how well you know their culture. Here are a few of the signs to familiarize yourself with:

- The American "OK" sign does NOT mean OK in Brazil. It is quite vulgar hand sign in Brazil. It means to *stick it*. Yes, think about the hand sign again, and you can understand where that connotation came from! Brazilians who know you will laugh and Brazilians who do not know you may take offense.

Source: author's collection

- The equivalent of the OK sign in Brazil is the thumbs up sign.

Source: author's collection

- The Full sign: The hand pointing upward four fingers facing front and moving back and forth is the sign for full. The context can be that there are in too many people, a lot of food, there is a long line, etc.

Source: author's collection

- The hurry up sign: This sign takes practice to do correctly. Touch your thumb to your middle finger and shake your hand back and forth. If you can get a snapping sound from your fingers (like snapping your fingers) you have this sign mastered.

Source: author's collection

- The bad driver sign: Barbers are associated with bad drivers in Brazil. In Portugal during the late middle ages, barbers not only cut hair and shaved beards but did surgery and pulled teeth. This is why barbers have the red, white, and blue pole. In Brazilian culture, however, these medieval barber surgeries and teeth pulling did not work out so well for the clients. After the 15th century the name *"barbeiro"* started to get used to refer to someone or something not well executed. Later in Brazil *"barbeiro"* also became associated specifically with a bad driver. Therefore, the sign for a bad driver is when you take your four fingers and run them up and down your jawbone as if you are shaving! See below:

Source: author's collection

- The talking nonsense sign: also known as *Papo Furado*. *Papo* is the skin below your jaw, but it also means to chat. *Furado* means there are holes in it. This sign says not to believe what someone is telling you. The fingers of one hand, palm down, moves up and down touches the skin under the jaw. See below:

Source: author's collection

- I am not interested sign: With both hands facing backwards, clap one hand to the back of the other hand, going back and forth changing hands. See below:

Source: author's collection

- Something is particularly good sign: Grab the earlobe and rub. See below:

Source: author's collection

- I want the bill sign: When you are at a restaurant and need to get the waiter to bring you the bill, look at the waiter and hold out one hand and pretend to write with the other hand. In future chapters on food dining and table manners you will understand that dinning sometimes takes a long time, and if you are hosting, this is good way to end the night out.

Source: author's collection

- "We are screwed" sign, also known *se foder*: This is a strong sign and crude language, but it also is common. You use this to describe when something bad happened to you, not when you want something bad to happen to someone else. The word is a swear word so be careful about saying it in public.

Source: author's collection

- I am cheap, you are cheap, or we do not have money sign: The hand sign is used to signify a cows hand (*mão de vaca*) or old bread (*pão duro*), as in I am so cheap I eat old bread. Clench your fist.

Source: author's collection

Becoming Brazilian

- I am done, it is over, or done for the day sign: Spread your hands out low like an umpire in baseball moves to say you are safe at home.

Source: author's collection

Brazilian Idiosyncratic Phrases *for everyday use*

Brazilian Portuguese is full of sayings and idioms that are immediately understood by the listener. These sayings not only share a common meaning, but also a cultural experience. Some of the sayings are humorous when taken literally. Other phrases are wise. Either way, learning and using a few of these will help you be more Brazilian.

Gringo: There is no country more welcoming to foreigner than Brazil. The term *gringo* is not a pejorative word in Brazil, and it does not refer specifically to people from the United States. A *gringo* is a foreigner (in Portuguese, *estrangeiro*) with no negative connotation. On the contrary: Brazilian hold all foreigners in high esteem. An example of this was during the last world cup: it became fashionable for Brazilians to dress in the uniform of other countries and use a fake accent in the attempt to be more attractive.

Rapadura é doce, mas não é mole não: Rapadura is a sugar cane candy made from boiling molasses to a solid form is sweet, but it is not soft. Figuratively, this phrase means that life is sweet, but it is also hard. You can pretty much use this phrase for almost anything good or bad in life and you will get a sympathetic understanding and knowing expression from any Brazilian. If your car breaks down, you can use this phrase. You get a raise at work you can use this phrase. Brazilians will identify with your feelings and understand you as if you were Brazilian.

O olho do dono engorda o boi: The phrase literally means: the eye of the owner make the cattle fat. Figuratively, it means that if you want things to turn out well, you got to do it yourself.

Saudades: There is no literal translation for this word, which is a great source of pride to Brazilians who love the idea that they have a word that cannot be directly translated to other languages. Figuratively, the word means to miss someone or something. But *saudades* is a noun and an object, *not* a verb. *Saudades* does not necessarily have to be for a person but can also be used for a place or memory. You can have *saudades* for a beach, or playing sports, or being young. You have *saudades* to say that you miss someone (which in Portuguese, would be: *eu tenho saudades*). *Saudades* is the feeling of missing someone or nostalgia, not the act of missing someone. It can also have a melancholic tone to it, but not always. It could be a feeling for your family when you are away, like homesickness, but it can also be the feeling you have when you realize your children are grown up. It could be the feeling when you remember of a long-lost love. Unlike missing someone, or homesickness, *Saudades*, can be a good feeling, because you have loved and lived.

Fica frio: Literally it means to stay cool, but figurately it means to stay calm.

Pisar na bola: Literally, this means to step on the ball. I suppose this comes from stepping on the ball and ruining a game of football, because figuratively this means something got messed up or someone let you down. Example: My brother *pisou na bola* and forgot to buy the tickets for the show tonight.

Pão duro: Literally means hard bread. Brazilians commonly buy their bread daily, which is fresher. Therefore, if you buy day-old bread you are cheap. Figuratively, *pão duro* means being stingy with money.

Pagar o Pato: Literally means, to pay the duck. We have already learned that *pagar mico*, pay the monkey, means to do something embarrassing. In this case, *pagar pato* is sort of like bad karma. Example: a young person parked his car in a disabled parking spot and when he came back his tire was flat. He paid the duck!

Cara de Pau: This literally means stick face or wood face. Figuratively, this means someone who acted shamelessly and took some advantage of a situation or someone else. Example: your manager takes credit for the research and work you did. He was *cara de pau* for doing that.

Abacaxi: This literally means pineapple, perhaps because a pineapple is a hard to eat. To have a *abacaxi* means a problem. I took the pineapple (*peguei abacaxi*) means, I got the problem. Similarly, *descascar o abacaxi*, which is peeling the pineapple, means to solve the problem.

Viajar na maionese: This literally means to travel through the mayonnaise, but figuratively it means to be confused, to be daydreaming, or you are making no sense.

Bicho vai pegar: In Brazil the equivalent of the boogie man for the children in Brazil is called *bicho papão*. Therefore, the saying figuratively means that someone is going to have a problem, or someone is getting into trouble.

Soltar a Franga: This literally translates to let go of the chicken. Figuratively, it means to have fun and to let loose.

Encher Linguiça: This literally means to stuff sausage. Figuratively it means to talk a lot about meaningless or unimportant details.

Puxar Saco: This literally means to pull the bag, but figuratively it means to be a sycophant and a flatterer.

Legal: This literally means legal, but figuratively it means something is good or cool.

Matar dois coelhos com uma cajadada só: Literally means to kill two rabbits with one hit. Figuratively, it is the equivalent of "killing two birds with one stone".

Chutar o pau da barraca: This literally means to kick the tent pole. Figuratively it means to let it all fall apart, to give up, to be reckless and not care.

Quebrar o galho: This literally means to break a branch. Figuratively, it means to fix something short term or cover for someone in a temporary fashion.

Acertar na Mosca: This literally means to hit the fly. Figuratively, it means you hit a bulls eye or hit the target.

Gostosa: Literally, this means tasty or delicious, but figuratively it means someone attractive and sexy.

Brazilian Time

How to manage your work and personal relationships without losing your sanity

Einstein must have been Brazilian! The concepts of time are extremely relative in Brazil. In the northeast of Brazil, time seems to move slower than a thousand kilometers south in São Paulo. What is confusing is that while some events start on time, particularly when it comes to transportation schedules, games, and movie screenings other event do not, such as doctors' visits television shows and most social event. A professional football game will start on time, but your scheduled hospital surgery will be late. Doctors commonly mark your appointment 30 min early to make sure you come on time, but it could be that they are late themselves as well! If you are scheduled for surgery, the doctors will require you to come in an incredibly early time. Be prepared that no one for your surgery will arrive until they know that you have shown up. Weddings are also notoriously late with neither the Priest nor the Bride arriving on time. However, if there are a series of weddings at the same church, the weddings may start relatively on time. Live concerts and shows tend to start late too, especially if there are a good reason, like "it's raining". Even television shows may not start on time and can run late for unexplained reasons. On the other hand, for social occasions, you need to plan to arrive late. If you arrive at a dinner party on time, you likely will find your host or hostess in a towel and not even dressed for her own party. Strangely is rude for arrive for a party on time! Let us not pay the monkey!

The General Theory of Brazilian time relativity

In general, Brazilians of the northeast and from Rio are famously less punctual then Brazilians from the South and São Paulo. People in São Paulo do try to be on time for business functions, but on the flip side, traffic is so unpredictable that at times it is impossible to arrive at the correct hour. Normally people will notify if they are running late for business functions in these regions. Bahia is famous for being laid back, but in my personal experience, at least for business, I have found it one of the better places to work for punctuality. Although this might feel frustrating, you cannot take this personally; it is not about you! If your business meeting is late, it is highly likely the person who was supposed to see you was also in a previous meeting that started late.

One way to try to improve the odds of a meeting not being delayed too much is to notify that you would like the meeting to take place in *"tempo americano"* (aka, "American time"). This signals that your 10:00 AM meeting will have a start time at 10:00 AM sharp, not 10:15 or 10:30. Be aware that this likely will not work perfectly, but by saying *"tempo americano"* your meeting may just be just a little late, if not on time.

For social situations, plan to arrive *at least* 30 minutes after the announced start time of the event. As a rule of thumb, you can delay less if you are meeting at a restaurant than if you are going to someone's house. Another thing to note is that, unlike parties and dinners in other countries, Brazilian gatherings do not have a definite end time. To end a party at a given time is a peculiar and confusing idea to a Brazilian! Brazilians have asked me many times how people in the United States can plan an ending time for a party. I try to explain that the ending time of a party is done for practical purposes, such as letting the guests know what they should go home. This still leaves the Brazilian mystified. Social situations tend to also start and end at a much later time: dinner could start anywhere from 8-10 PM, night clubs only really open their doors around midnight. The suggested times of lateness are still relative to the region of the country. When in doubt, feel free to ask questions to whoever you will be meeting up with on how late you need to be to a social function.

General rules on how to navigate Brazilian time

- Be punctual to all business functions. You are there to work, and you make a good impression if you are on time -- even if your hosts are not.

- Recognize that there are still legitimate reasons for delays in Brazil. Traffic, weather, other delays are all valid reasons for being late. For the most part, it is still socially acceptable and reasonable to be 30 minutes late.

- Brazilians try not to stress about being late when they cannot control the events, and you should too.

- Do not take it personally if Brazilians are late, it is a habit and culturally acceptable. It is not about you.

- Never schedule back-to-back meetings. Schedule 30 minutes breaks between meetings. A break between meetings helps you avoid being late during the day.

- For social engagement, purposely arrive late. Do not try to be on time unless the host explicitly said *"tempo americano"*.

Social Etiquettes and Table manners

Brazilian etiquette and table manners differ in some ways from other cultures. These are subtle differences, but the reader should be aware of these points not only when visiting Brazil but also when hosting Brazilians outside of Brazil.

"Yes" means yes, "no" could mean yes, and "thank you" means no, thank you

When you offer drinks or dishes to guests in most places, everything is straight forward; yes means yes and no means no. In Brazil this is more subtle. If a Brazilian comes over to your house, and you offer them something, many times the guest will politely say no, or thank you which means no, but is still expecting you to understand that they are "just being polite", and you would offer it a second time or a third time around, they will then accept your offer. The exchange may sound something like this:

Host: Welcome to our home. Can I get you anything to drink?

Guest: No, thank you, your house is lovely.

Host: Why thank you, we just had it redone. Are your sure you would not like a beer?

Guest: I really do not want to be a bother, thank you for asking.

Host: Really it is no bother, please, have something to drink.

Guest: Actually, it was so hot today; I would love a beer.

Host: Here is one, nice and cold.

You can begin to understand the potential complication for cross-cultural misunderstanding. Imagine how many Brazilians who really were thirsty or hungry never got served trying to be polite in another country. I will now add another detail to the mix. Many of us were taught at a young age to eat everything on our plate, to be polite. In Brazil, it is quite the opposite: Brazilians will purposely leave a bit food on their plate, to show that they are full and content.

As a young man on my first trip to Brazil, I was invited by my girlfriend to eat lunch with her family on a Saturday. This is a major event in a relationship, and I was determined to make a good first impression. As it was a Saturday (which is also known as "Feijoada Day"), the family was gathered around the table and we were ready to eat *feijoada*, the traditional black beans and meat stew. My first serving was an enormous plate of black beans, rice, pork chops, bananas, and oranges. I cleaned my plate, as I was taught to do.

When my girlfriend's mom saw that I cleared my plate entirely, she immediately thought that I was still hungry. She said, "please have some more feijoada" and I replied back "no, thank you. I am good!". She looked puzzled and said, "I insist, please have some more". I responded, "No really, I am quite satisfied". Frustrated with my response, she grabbed my plate and said "We have plenty of food! Eat!". Now having been served a second plate of food, I tried my best to not insult my girlfriend's mom, and cleaned my entire plate again, but now I could barely eat the last bite. However, being a good young man from Oklahoma, and not wanting to be rude, I finished the second serving.

Seeing my plate empty again, my girlfriend's mom immediately said, "would you like another serving?". I said "No, no. I am full". She responded, "Please I insist!". There was no way I could eat anymore, and now I was the one who was frustrated with the situation. After all, I was trying to be polite, confused why no did not mean no. So, I stood up from the table and in desperation shotted, "No! No! No more food, I cannot eat anymore!"

This at least got my girlfriend's family attention, but then everyone went silent! We were having one of those awkward moments, of cross-cultural miscommunication. I was paying the monkey. Finally, I was saved by one my girlfriends sisters' husband. He was a big man from Rio Grande do Sul (southern part of Brazil with a big German settlement), and he made a joke, saying that he had no idea how such a little American guy could eat so much! The silence was broken, and everybody had a good laugh. After that day, I learned my lesson: never clear your plate if you are done eating!

Brazilian Table Manners

The Brazilians you meet in business situations will have impeccable table manners. Brazilian table manners are based on the continental style of eating but with a few differences. Unlike Americans, Brazilians do not switch knives and forks as they eat. The knife remains in the right hand, and the fork remains in the left. Once in use, the utensils should not return to the table, but stay on the plate. When eating is paused, some Brazilians will cross knife and fork at angles on the plate, fork tips pointing down. When the meal is finished, the knife and fork are laid parallel to each other horizontally across the center top of the plate - make sure they do not cross each other. Americans and Europeans usually leave their utensils parallel at an angle on the plate to indicate that they are finished. Like most of the world, you still use the utensils working for the outside in. Salad Forks and knifes are found outside forks and knifes for the main course. Make sure to leave your utensils on the plate, so salad or soup utensils are cleared with the salad or soup plates. Once a utensil is in use it should not return to the table. As mentioned before, Brazilians typically leave some small amount of food on the plate to indicate they are satisfied. Waiters at restaurants will be looking for signs to tell them when it is time to take your plate away.

The fork and knife at the top of your plate is meant for dessert. Bread many times is not served with butter and there may be no bread plate. In this case, place the bread on the side of the main plate.

In Brazil just as in other countries it is rude to eat with your elbows on the table, however your hands should always be on the table. Brazilians do not put their hands on their lap or anywhere not that is not seen.

Brazilians almost never eat food with their fingers. It is considered unhygienic

If it is at all possible to use a knife and fork, Brazilians will always opt to use them. Foods that other cultures would eat with their fingers such as watermelon, chicken wings, pork ribs, beef ribs, and pizza are still eaten with knife and fork. Sometimes you will see Brazilians eating sandwiches and hamburgers in their hands, but they are careful to always use a napkin or paper wrapping around.

Dinning Etiquette for seating

It is rare to have pre-determined seating at a dinner party, and there no rules to separate couples at a dinner. However, there is a custom to have the most important person sit at the head of the table. If you are invited to a restaurant, the host may sit at the head of table. Usually the host pays the bills at the restaurant, but it is always good manners to offer to pay. Sometimes a person of higher social rank pays the bill. If it is an informal get-together, the bill is usually split. One thing you may notice when dining out in Brazil, is that the women always dress up for dinner, and many times men are much more casual.

Other table manners to keep in mind

- Pass plates to the left.

- Keep your hands on the table, do not place elbows on the table, do not put your hands on your lap during dinner. Remember to not change hands with your knife and fork, so rarely are you only eating with your fork.

- Absolutely no burping or blowing your nose at the table. If you need to, get up and go to the bathroom.

- Toothpicks are used both to avoid using your fingers to touch food, but it is also used to pick your teeth (while still using a napkin to cover your mouth).

- Use your napkin to wipe your mouth after you drink or eat.

- Coffee is usually served after dinner. Heads up, it is strong coffee, and it is rarely decaf!

- The most common toast is *"Saúde"* (which in English, means health).

Chapter Three

Brazilian Exceptionalism & Practical Information

This chapter is dedicated to useful and practical information related to Brazil for your visit or long-term stay. Everyone knows that Brazil is the only country in the western hemisphere that speaks Portuguese, but Brazil is so big that it can set its own rules in other areas as well. This chapter is dedicated to useful topics that are unique to Brazil and will impact your day-to-day life.

Beaches are the Great Equalizer

Brazil is a country of fantastic beaches and a unique beach culture. In a country of tremendous social inequality, beaches are one of the few democratic spaces. Beaches cannot be privately owned, and public access to all beaches in guaranteed in the constitution. The beaches are the one place where rich and poor, people of all racial and socio-economic backgrounds are equal and can interact with a game of beach football or volleyball.

Though Brazilian law states that the beaches belong to the government and cannot be sold to private individuals, you may still find some resorts or hotels that take advantage of the geography to give you the feel of a private beach. If you are going to come to Brazil, I highly encourage you to not hide away in a resort, but rather explore the range of beaches the coast has to offer. This provides a rich experience for the visitor and a great way to learn about Brazil. Each region and each beach will have its own infrastructure. Some beaches will have restaurants and music and extensive infrastructure, while others are more remote with perhaps only people selling food and drinks from coolers. Some beaches are in the middle of cities, while others are secluded and almost abandoned.

Unless you are going to a truly remote beach, there really is not a good reason to take a lot of stuff with you. You will usually find most beaches have local businesses that can provide you with chairs, umbrellas, food, and drink. It is somewhat unusual to bring your own chairs, umbrellas, and coolers, when there are locals who make a living making your beach experience a pleasure. This is a great way to support them.

Megabarracas em Fortaleza
Source: https://s3.amazonaws.com/media.viajenaviagem.com/wp-content/uploads/2015/07/megabarraca-fortaleza.jpg. Access in: 03/25/2021

Brazilians use the word *"barraca"*, which literally means shelter, but at the beach it refers to a local business with a kitchen and employees, that will provide you with chairs, umbrellas, food, and drink. Sometimes these *"barracas"* are primitive, in other beaches they can be extravagant, with entertainment or sports areas. The basic rule at a *"barraca"* is that you buy your food and drinks at the same stand that is providing you the chairs and umbrellas. You pick your "barraca" and the umbrellas and chairs are there for you use as long as you want. The servers bring you food and drink and you pay your bill at the end of the day. There is no need to bring your own chairs or umbrellas if there are locals whose job is to make your beach visit a pleasure. When you go to a *"barraca"* you are supporting a local business, and it is fun and inexpensive.

Small business at the beach
Source: *Montar um Negócio*

If you want to dress like a Brazilian on the beach here are the basics. Everyone uses flip flop sandals, so never use shoes on the beach, not even tennis shoes. Women dress in small bikinis, but they will also use one pieces bathing suits at times. Brazilian women wear something called a *canga* that is extremely useful. A *canga* is a colorful piece of fabric, like a beach sarong, that can be made to wear like a dress or skirt. Besides protecting from the sun or used as a wrap, a conga can be used instead of a towel to lie on the beach or to help carry items.

Men wear a swimsuit called a *sunga* which is a square tight-fitting bathing suit. They might also wear surfer shorts. If you feel uncomfortable wearing a sunga, surfer shorts are a great option.

On the beach people play football, paddle ball, or a totally Brazilian game called *foot volley,* in which players kick and head a volleyball over a net using their feet, not their hands.

Woman on *canga*
Source: author's collection

Footvolley at Leme beach
Source: https://www.flickr.com/photos/80487073@N00/11506805964. Access in: 03/12/2021

The democratization of the beach experience in Brazil is shared by many people selling all types of goods on the beach. People sell clothes, sun hats, corn, beer, ice cream, and much more. The interaction is quite informal: they come to you, you go to them, try on stuff, and if you like it, you buy it. Many people make their living by this informal trade. Not only are you supporting others when you buy their products, but it is unusual for Brazilians to bring their own food on to the beach, and rarely a portable grill. In summary, there is no reason to take lots of stuff to the beach, it is already waiting for you there. Brazilians have a saying, *"tenha um boa praia"*, or have a good beach!

Language, Brazilian Portuguese, and "Portanhol"

The language spoken in Brazil is Portuguese, however Brazilian Portuguese is quite different from the Portuguese of Portugal. If you speak Portuguese from Portugal, you will find it hard to understand Portuguese from Brazil due to local expressions, idioms, and slang, along with the accents of each region. The Portuguese spoken in Rio de Janeiro is likely the closest accent to Portuguese from Portugal. Rio was the Capital of Brazil during the period where the court of Portugal moved to Brazil. This likely impacted the Rio accent.

If you are a native Spanish speaker you will also have some difficulty understanding Brazilian Portuguese due to the variety of vowel sounds in Brazilian Portuguese versus the strict vowel pronunciation found in Spanish. Brazilians will likely have an easier time understanding a native Spanish speaker if they speak slowly. Brazilians are used to a variety of accents and many have contact with Spanish speakers as the country is surrounded by Spanish speaking countries.

What will surprise and perhaps frustrate most foreigners is how few Brazilians speak English. It seems that almost everyone in Brazil has studied English, but few Brazilians speak it. Curiously, some Brazilians are able write English but are still not particularly good at speaking it. This seems puzzling but it also is a sign of Brazilian exceptionalism. Like the United States where few people speak a second language, Brazil is huge and isolated from English speaking countries and surrounded by mostly Spanish speaking countries. All Brazilians know that speaking English is a way to advancement and they may take English classes in school, but they do not have the opportunity to practice speaking English so many are embarrassed to try. Most Brazilians do not have the opportunity to learn it. While you are in major cities and hotels you will be fine speaking English but as you move away from the major cities you will no longer be able to rely on English to communicate.

If you are a non-native Spanish speaker or a native Spanish speaker who regularly travels to Brazil, you will be able to communicate in an unofficial language called *Portunhol*. *Portunhol* is a universal language of Latin America, used by multinational corporations and tourists alike. It is not a written language but a common spoken language between people of South American countries. We, as English speakers, often do not learn a second language because English is so universal. *Portunhol* however, is a useful unofficial language in South America. It works because the languages are close enough that you only need to modify a bit of pronunciation and learn a few words of the other speaker's language, then you can create a common language. Especially when you are a meeting with participants from multiple countries in South America with no English-speaking participants, the meeting will be conducted in *Portunhol*.

Gas (Petrol) Stations and Fuel Options

Many things in Brazil are different just because they can be! Similar to the way that the United States refuses to adopt the metric system and continues to use English weights and measures even after England abandoned it, Brazil has adopted or invented certain practices and stuck with them until they are standard in Brazil even though it is standard just for them. In the area of fuels for transportation, Brazil is a leader of innovation. How you fill up your car at the gas station, can create some challenges for folks who are visiting or moving to Brazil.

The first thing you will notice is that no one fills their own car. There is no self-service in Brazilian Gas Stations. Gas station workers will likely stop you from filling your own car with fuel and may even think you are a thief for doing so! There is always a gas station attendant to put fuel in your car. Although not required, the station attendants will offer to check you oil, water, and air pressure. A tip is not required, but it is appropriate to tip for good service.

Additionally, instead of seeing just gas or petrol, it will seem that you have a wide variety of fuels and you will need help knowing what fuel to use and when. Many cars and especially taxis have been modified to run on natural gas, in addition to gasoline. The tanks for the natural gas are usually hidden in the trunk or under the back seat. Almost all cars, including rental cars, run on any combination of gasoline (petrol) or ethanol alcohol. Brazil is a huge producer of sugar, and most sugar mills can process a mix of sugar and ethanol. The gasoline (petrol) at the pump already includes 30% ethanol and you cannot buy pure gasoline in Brazil; it simply does not exist. Brazil began using ethanol as a fuel after the first oil crisis. The Brazilian government imposed to use ethanol as a fuel, and forced this requirement, so the car manufactures needed to redesign engines to run on this fuel. In the beginning, these engines were hard to start in cold weather and required preheating the fuel before ignition. Overtime, these engines improved and now, even in countries with low or no mix of ethanol with gasoline, these engines are still standard. Any car that has the word "flex" on it can thank Brazil for the development of this engine. You may see the word Flex at cars in your home country, and these too could run on pure ethanol if available. Flex engines is a great example of Brazilian exceptionalism.

You will notice the price of ethanol is always less expensive then petrol. Petrol however burns more efficiently, so you drive further on a liter of petrol than you will on a liter of alcohol. The rule is if you can go a distance on a liter of petrol, you will go only .80 that distance on a liter of ethanol. So, when deciding between buying petrol (30 percent Ethanol) or 100% ethanol, look at the price of Petrol and multiply by .8.

Are you wondering if this is the same ethanol that is in your Brazilian cocktail the *caipirinha*? The answer is chemically speaking, yes, it is! However, the fuel is an almost pure industrial ethanol with trace amounts of methanol mixed in to stop you from trying to drink it. At the same time, you should be suspicious of what is being sold as petrol. Petrol stations that do not come from recognized firms should be questioned. Many private gas station owners have been known to mix other products with their gasoline (petrol) to make it cheaper. The petrol and ethanol pumps should have a clear tube on the side that shows that the fuel has at least the correct density. Only buy fuel you do not trust in an emergency, and just enough to get you to the next station. Bad fuel will hurt your car.

Another fuel is diesel. There are two grades: S10, which is for cars and SUVs, and S5, which is for large trucks, but can sometimes be found in small stations. The size of S5 diesel dispenser is too big to fit in a car or SUV. Brazil is a leading producer of biodiesel. Both grades of diesel are mixed with biodiesel which is produced in Brazil from a variety of crops.

Electricity and Standards: Or Standards that nobody follows

Brazil is blessed with its immense natural resources and access to water. In fact, before sustainability became fashionable, Brazil was producing most of its electricity using hydroelectric power. Brazil is one of the major producers of electricity from water. What is curious, and somewhat confusing, is that it never standardized the use of 220- or 110-volt power. As a very loose rule of thumb, the big cities in the south use 110 volts, while the north and coasts use 220 volts. According to the Brazilian standard a 220-volt outlet will be red, while a 110 outlet will be white, but even this standard is rarely followed. What is even worse, if you try to look behind your outlet, you will likely not be able to see any standard colors in the wiring. All of this to say: you need to be careful as you go around the country when you use electronics. Make sure you always ask and/or carry an outlet adapter. Many hotels have outlet adapters for a guest to use, and almost all hardware stores carry adaptors that will adapt US and European plugs to Brazilian outlets. Many of the electronic products sold in Brazil have switches to change the voltages.

Before 2001, Brazil did not have a standard electrical outlet, so hardware stores would sell both US and European outlets. They also manufactured outlets that were a combination for both. By some estimates, there were as many as 10 different outlet types! However, in 2001, a unique standard was created and somewhat enforced exclusively for Brazil! One of the most irritating problems with these standard outlets is not only do they not fit with any other standard in the world, but the outlets themselves come in two sizes depending on the amount of energy an appliance needs. At times you will buy a product like an electric heater or vacuum cleaner and realize that the outlets in you are apartment are too small a diameter. Why didn't Brazil adopt a universal standard? Because it is Brazil! It is big enough of a country and has an industrial policy to manufacture inside the country to get away with it. Brazil is the only country in the world to use this outlet!

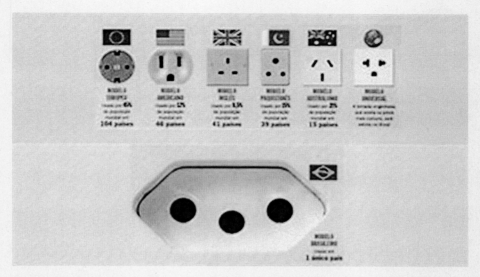

Electronic items. What type of power outlets should I expect in hotels in São Paulo and Rio de Janeiro?
Source: *Travel Stack Exchange*, 2015

Money, Banking, Credit and Debit Cards

One of the most impressive traits of Brazilians is their ability to adapt. What many people do not realize is just how advanced the Brazilian banking system became because of hyperinflation of the 1970-80s, and how inventive Brazilians were to adapt to it. With inflation roaring at 1-4% per day, it was critical to receive and transfer funds quickly, cheaply, and reliably. It is exceedingly rare to see payments by check. Brazilians was one of the first countries to develop a cheap method of electronic payments to adapt to inflation. Due to this, it also means that there were bank clearing systems with specific standards.

When you wire funds from your own country, you will find that this is an expensive process. Not only do you have the standard wire fees but also most backs take a spread for handling wire transfers. On the other hand, making electronic payments in Brazil is very inexpensive. Traditionally, when you make a transfer or payment to accounts within the same bank, this is called a DOC and cost next to nothing. If you must make a payment to a different bank, this is called a TED and the cost is a few cents more.

The central bank has now created a new standard called "Pix" that works with bank applications on your phone and cost nothing.

If you are living in Brazil, you will commonly find a bar code on your invoices. This is called a *boleto*. You will find that all ATM machines have laser scanners or the bank application on your phone can also read and pay these barcodes. To pay bills, you simply put the bar code below the laser scanner or camera and you ring up the payment. For the company issuing the bill, the electronic file from the bank automatically matches the information on clients billing system and can be programmed to collect interest for late payments. This process is light years ahead of some other countries, which is also why checks are rarely used in Brazil.

This includes travelers' checks. Therefore, when coming to Brazil, make sure to bring dollars or euros in the form of cash, as well as your credit card. Credit cards get very favorable exchange rates. Some hotels exchange currency but also not at a good rate (hot tip: most hotel rooms have safes, so use them).

When trying to exchange currencies, it's important to know that the official FX rate established by the government is the PTAX rate. It is based on the previous spot transactions of banks for the previous day. Note that this is the only FX rate that matters for official financial transactions while you are in Brazil (another example of Brazilian exceptionalism). The exchange house located in shopping malls are usually more competitive than those in airports or hotels. These rates are sometimes published as tourist rates which can be more or less advantageous to the official rate. To see if a FX rate is good or not, try to reference both the PTAX and published tourist rates. At times you can get better rates than the central bank PTAX rate exchanging cash, but it should be close to the official rate.

The advantage of bringing a credit card is that ATM machines will convert at a favorable FX rate your credit card transactions into cash. You will find that Master Card and Visa are most accepted. Outside of major cities, you have more trouble finding stores and restaurants that accept them. However, there are always ATM machines around that can be used to withdraw cash. When you make purchases with your credit card you will also receive a favorable exchange rate to your home currency.

If you are going to live in Brazil, you will need to open a bank account. To open an account, you will most likely need to show proof of work, a work visa, and a RNE or a national identity for foreigners. It is close to impossible to pay bills for an extended period without a local bank account. Make sure you also bring money from your home country. Instead of doing a wire transfer, which is expensive a bureaucratic and the funds must clear the central bank, you can look at an alternative money transfer service. These services are widely used by Brazilians outside Brazil who want to send money back to their families. These tend to be less expensive, but you need to make sure they are dependable.

Personal Hygiene

This is hard to tell foreigners this, but when they come to Brazil, many of them lack hygiene in the eyes of Brazilians. This could be surprising to hear if you are coming from a first world country, but after spending enough time in Brazil, you will understand. It is common knowledge that one should brush their teeth and floss after every meal, shower once a day, wash their hands with soap before and after every meal, but most *gringos* do not follow these rules.

Brazil however is the champion of handwashing and teeth brushing. It seems as if this has always been the habit for Brazilians. My guess is that this habit was influenced by the native population before the Portuguese arrived. In Guarani, the word for stranger or foreigner is *"Pe Nee"*: *Pe* means foot, and *Nee* means smelly, therefore, *smelly feet*! Think of the impact a Spaniard or Portuguese taking off his boots would have had on the native population! The early Brazilians must have taken up the habit of bathing because travelers in the 18th century commented on how often Brazilians bathed. It must have been a great shock to the Brazilians to see the lack of hygiene among the Portuguese aristocrats. The Portuguese still held onto beliefs of the middle ages that bathing brought disease and therefore bathed rarely. It is said that King Dom João VI only bathed once in Brazil to cure a medical condition from a tick bite.[9] The poor king however was also frightened of crabs, so the only way he would take a bath was to enter a barrel of water with holes to allow the sea water in.[10]

Another legend concerning hygiene and the arrival of the Portuguese Aristocracy to Rio de Janeiro in 1808. The entire Portuguese court counting close to 15,000 people were all packed into wooden sailing ships. Invariably

---

[9] Available in: https://diariodorio.com/breve-historia-dos-banhos-de-mar-no-rio-de-janeiro/. Access in: 06/06/ 2020.
[10] *Ibidem.*

there was an outbreak of lice, which broke out among the aristocratic women, including the queen of Portugal. As a result, many of them including the Queen, had to shave their heads. While the King of Portugal made a side trip to Salvador, Bahia, the rest of the court proceeded to Rio de Janeiro. The arrival of the Portuguese court was an amazing event for the *Cariocas* as the people of Rio de Janeiro are known. The women of Rio anxiously waited for the Portuguese Aristocrats to disembark. Unknown to them, an infestation of lice on the trip had forced the queen Carlota of Portugal, her daughters and many of the aristocratic women to shave their hair.[11] As a result when these women left their ships to arrive in Brazil, the women from the ships wore turbans to cover their bald heads. This caused a curious reaction among the awaiting *Cariocas*. Many of the Brazilian women noticed how the Portuguese women had shaved their heads and wore turbans to hide their lack of hair. The Brazilian women, seeing the turbans, decided that this must be the latest fashion and began to wear turbans too.[12]

Brazil is the second largest market of consumers of cosmetics and personal hygiene products. Brazilians of all social economic backgrounds take their hygiene and appearances very seriously, and most want to look and smell nice. You will notice most Brazilian bring their toothbrush to work. We all know we are supposed to brush our teethes after lunch, so it would seem obvious that we would bring or toothbrush to work. In Brazil, they practice what they preach! Brazilians, especially women, take great care of their fingernails and toenails. Fortunately pedicures and manicures are inexpensive and easily available. Brazilians judge others by their appearance, so take advantage of these services while in Brazil.

---

[11] GOMES, Laurentino. *1808:* Como uma rainha louca, um príncipes medroso, e um corte corrupta enganaram Napoleão e mudaram a Historia de Portugal e do Brasil. São Paulo: Globo, 2014, p.134.
[12] *Ibidem*, p. 135

Chapter Four

Being Brazilian Through Food and Drinks

Brazil is a large country with many regions and each region has its own peculiarities. If we simply try to classify Brazilians by their respective regions, Bahia, São Paulo, Rio, Northeast, and Rio Grande do Sul, we may tend to just think of Brazilian stereotypes rather than explore the true difference of each region due to its own culture and history. Brazilian food is varied by region due to local history and environment. The point of this book is to introduce you to Brazil, and we have largely covered the common culture in Chapters one, two and three. In this chapter we will get to know each region though its food. I cannot think of a more pleasurable topic.

The best way to know the regions and people of Brazil in though the food and culture of its regions. Because of regional differences, Brazilian food is diverse and a wonderful way to get to know the local culture while you are traveling. Brazilians perpetuate certain stereotypes for each region, that are widely shared and usually funny. Given the size of Brazil it is natural that Brazilians would categorize Brazilian food based on ingredients that are native to the region. But there are other influences also incorporated thanks to the rich history of immigration to Brazil from Africa, Europe, and Japan. Many fruits, vegetables, and oils are unique to Brazilian cuisine, and much of it was adapted from food of different cultures. In this chapter we will learn about the regions of Brazil though the food and drink. Every region of Brazil has a unique and rich history. Here we will give an overview of each region and a brief overview of its food and drink of as you travel Brazil. Like other countries food is central to many social interactions in Brazil. Social customs and manners also will be covered when they are different or unique to Brazil.

Brazilians have names and terms for the people of each region. Brazilians self-identify by their region and certain regions are famous for certain characteristics. Some Brazilians have historical prejudices for certain regions of Brazil. Most Brazilians are proud of the region in which they grew up.

Brazilian Food

The National Dish: Feijoada

Feijoada is the national dish. Really it is not just a meal but an event! At least every Saturday, and in many parts of the country on Wednesday as well, restaurants and households all over the country prepare this dish.

Feijoada
Source: *Recepedia*

Feijoada is a black bean stew with jerked beef, salted pork loin, bacon, sausages, and leftover bits of pork. It is served with collard greens, rice, orange slices, *mandioca* or cassava, cassava flour, spice sauce, and other various side dishes. It is omnipresent in Brazil on Saturdays. Alberto Santos-Dumont, an aviation pioneer who is celebrated in Brazil, used to prepare this dish in Paris early in the twentieth century. This dish has deep roots in Brazilian culture.

If you look up *feijoada* on the internet you will see that modern writers suggest that the dish is just a modification of bean stew dishes in Portugal. Most Brazilians, including myself, overwhelmingly dispute that their national dish comes from Portugal. Brazilians' relationships with Portugal are complicated. Rather than a Portuguese origin, Brazilians believe that the origins of Brazil's national dish, feijoada, stem from its history with slavery. Slaves would supposedly craft this hearty dish out of black beans and pork leftovers given to them from their households' master. These leftovers included pig feet, ears, tail, and other portions seen as unfit for the master and his family. This was cooked Saturday which was the slave's day of rest and eaten by all the slaves. For my Brazilian friends it is far more likely that *feijoada* was invented by some unknown cook who was a slave from Pernambuco, Brazil than be adapted from a meal from Portugal. That this Brazilian national dish came from slaves is the belief of most Brazilians. Brazil has references to the meal *feijoada* in newspapers and other printed documentation as early as 1827, long before the slaves were free. I prefer to believe what all my Brazilians acquaintances believe that this dish was created by slaves. It is true that the Portuguese do have bean-based stews, but the Portuguese uses white beans, not black beans, and side dishes were not as varied nor as locally specific to Brazil. *Couve,* as this green vegetable is called in Brazil, is like collard greens, which is common to the soul food of the United States. The inclusion of cassava or *mandioca,* as well as the cheap cuts of meat such as pig tail, tongue, and cheeks suggest that this plate was created by the poor. Furthermore, the suggestion that the idea that *feijoada* came from Portugal diminishes the impact of slaves on such an important part of Brazilian culture.

As the story continues, one day the slaveowner tried this dish with the slaves and found it so delicious that he also began to eat it on Saturdays as well. The first written references to this dish are published in newspapers from Northeast Brazil, so I will assume that a slave cook in the Northeast should be credited for this invention. A noted early mention of the national dish from Pernambuco was in an article published On March 3, 1840, in the Journal of Pernambuco. Father Carapuceiro published an article in which he said,

> "In families where the true gastronomy is not known, it is usual practice and starts to convert to *feijoada* the fragments of the dinner of the eve, (leftovers) to what they call the burial of the bones [...] They throw in a large pot or cauldron remnants of turkeys, roasted piglets, bacon and ham hocks, besides good amounts of dried beef, in Ceará, everything goes from blending with the indispensable beans: everything is reduced to a grease!"[13]

The subtext of Father Carapuceiro's writing is that *feijoada* is not from the educated classes (Portuguese) but instead was created by the lower classes where "true European cooking is not known!" Do not be put off by this description.

Feijoada is delicious, but it is rather heavy. This may also explain why *feijoada* is prepared on Saturday. Today Brazilians of all classes all over the country enjoy this dish made by slaves. Enjoy it with friends, have a *caipirinha* and take a nap!

Mandioca, Farofa and Farinha

Mandioca, or cassava in English, is ever present in Brazilian food in all regions. You may already be familiar with Mandioca as the starch used to make tapioca pudding. However, *mandioca* root is often served as a side dish at Brazilian meals just as potatoes are in other countries. Potatoes of course came from Peru, but they were adapted for cultivation in Europe, and *mandioca* was not. *Mandioca* is like the potato of Brazil. Potatoes are also served in many Brazilian dishes, but *mandioca* was cultivated by the Brazilian natives and *mandioca* is indigenous to the area, easy to grow and common. It takes time to cook as the skins must be removed and the root boiled until soft. It tastes like a potato, with a slightly different texture.

---

[13] GASPAR, Lúcia. *O Carapuceiro*. https://pt.wikipedia.org/wiki/Feijoada_%C3%A0_brasileira Viewed 12/07/2020 (Translation is my own).

Mandioca
Source: ATI-GEL Vegetais Congelados

Farinha and *farofa* are side dishes made from the starch of the *mandioca* plant. *Farinha* is the starch from the mandioca after drying it, and *farofa* is *farinha* that is toasted in a pan, usually with salted meat, or beans. The recipe varies from place to place, but both are eaten as a side dish or added on top of a meal.

Farofa
Source: https://www.tudogostoso.com.br/receita/163102-farofa.html. Access in: 03/25/2021

Caipirinhas, the national drink

Três caipirinhas diferentes
Source: *Guia da Cozinha*, 2019

If *feijoada* is the national dish, then *caipirinha* is the national drink. The traditional *caipirinha* is made with *cachaça*, which is a sugar cane distilled spirit. *Cachaça,* which is also sometimes called *pinga*, is made by fermenting the sugar cane juice and then distilling. The best cachaças are aged in a variety of wooden barrels, some native to Brazil. This aging gives a wide variety of flavors to *cachaça*. The traditional caipirinha is made with *cachaça*, sugar, lime, and ice. It is important to use only Brazilian sugar when making a *caipirinhas*. In fact, if you like *caipirinhas* and want to make them at home, you need to bring Brazilian sugar back with you. Brazilian sugar is finer grained than international standards. This allows the sugar to dissolve in the *caipirinha* when it is mixed. If you try to use regular sugar you will have a strong drink with a thick layer of sugar crystals on the bottom of the glass. You must use Brazilian sugar to make a caipirinha.

Many years ago, the upper-class Brazilians outside the state of Minas Gerais would make their *caipirinhas* out of rum, vodka, or sake, but over the last decade there has been a resurgence of interest in *cachaça*. *Cachaça* and rum are both made from sugarcane, but they have different industrial processes. In the case of rum, sugarcane is boiled down to molasses. Sugar crystals are filtered, and water and yeast are then added to allow fermentation of the liquid. It is then distilled to become rum. Rum is usually aged in oak barrels for years and then bottled.

Things You Didn't Know About Cachaça, Brazil
Source: *The Culture Trip*, 2018

With *cachaça* however, the sugar cane juice is fermented and then distilled. Good *cachaça* is distilled in batches and industrial *cachaça* is distilled in columns in a continuous industrial process like the process for making industrial alcohol. The industrial *cachaça* is the cheapest and unfortunately the most common in the United States, but there are literally hundreds of artisanal *cachaças* that have a wide variety of flavors and make great *caipirinhas*! Artisanal *cachaças* are made in batches like a whisky, not in an industrial process. *Cachaça* is generally stored for a shorter time then rum and is stored in a wide variety of wood barrels. Rum is mostly stored in oak barrels. Some *cachaça* makers use oak, but many others use native Brazilian wood barrels, such as *bálsamo* or *jequitiba* to add flavor. The use of local barrels using native woods makes some of the finest *cachaça* with a wide array of flavors. In the last decade, the

Brazilians have gained a greater appreciation for this spirit. So, ask for your *caipirinha* to be made with *cachaça* and let your host know that you want to try a good one. Besides being a good conversation starter, this will save you a bad headache as there are few worse hangovers than those that come from drinking bad *cachaça*.

Caipirinhas are classically made with limes, but many fruits being are used now instead of limes. Mangos, kiwis, tangerines, lemons, maracujá are only some of the alternatives, so experiment and see what you like. Be careful, *caipirinhas* taste great but they are stronger than you think.

Brazilian Exceptionalism through Food

Brazilian food is as varied as its people. There are some idiosyncrasies that a newcomer should be aware of when dealing with food. Here are some of things unique to Brazil with regards to food.

Bacalhau Codfish or similar fish

While the Portuguese did not invent *feijoada*, they did influence Brazilian diets with North Atlantic cod. With an abundance of fresh local tropical fish, the importance of salted codfish to Brazilians could be a mystery to a *gringo*. During the colonial period, most ships arriving to Brazil brought salted cod in their provisions. The Portuguese have been eating cod since the 1400's. As Portugal was a sea faring nation, it brought this tradition to the shores of Brazil. *Bacalhau* codfish is not fresh, nor in all cases is it truly codfish due to cost, overfishing, and popularity. Other North Atlantic fish of similar types are also salted and dried and sold as cod. All this North Atlantic fish arrives in Brazil salted and dried. When you look for *bacalhau* in the supermarket it is packaged, salted, and not refrigerated. *Bacalhau* is very expensive, and it is time consuming to prepare as it takes a while to get the salt out prior to cooking. It needs to soak in water for hours and the water needs to be changed frequently to remove the excess salt. There are many ways of preparing this fish. Brazilians consider this a delicacy, so it is served at special holidays. It is a requirement for Christmas, New Years, Good Friday, and Easter, but is eaten year-round.

Lemons and Limes

When Brazilian refer to *lemons*, they mean limes. What we call lemons are called *Sicilian lemons*. *Limões (limes)* are used in all types of food, and of course in the famous *caipirinha*.

Passion Fruit and Maracujá

Maracujá tastes and looks like passion fruit but the skin is yellow instead of blue. Passion Fruit and maracujá belong in the same family of fruits. The *maracujá* has a sourer taste. Passion Fruit is not well known in Brazil.

Passion fruit (Maracujá or Fruit de la Passion)
Source: *AZ Martinique*

Avocados and Abacates

Brazilians have two varieties of avocados. The larger variety native to Brazil is called an *abacate* which as a smooth light green skin. The smaller variety, just as here, is called an *avocado*. In Brazil it is more common to eat the *abacates* with sugar as a dessert.

Abacate e avocado
Source: *Veja Saúde*, 2018

Pão Francês is not French Bread

Brazilians call the bread they eat every day fresh from the baker *Pão Francês* which translates to French bread. But the delicious *Pão Francês* bears little resemblance to French baguettes. Brazilian *Pão Francês* has an incredibly soft center unlike the chewy bread in France. *Pão Francês* must be bought fresh each day at the local bakery. You can find what we call French bread at most bakeries as well, just ask for a *baguette*.

Coração de Galinha or Chicken hearts

Sooner or later you will be exposed to cooked chicken hearts. This is a common appetizer that Brazilians love to start off a *churrasco*. Once you get over the appearance chicken hearts are not too bad.

Coração de frango
Source: *Frigorífico Origem*

Exotic fruits

Brazil has many fruits that you cannot find anywhere else. Many can be found in your Brazilian supermarket or in the Municipal market. Here are some worth trying:

Açaí: Outside of the Amazon region you will never see this fruit in its native state. In the Amazon it is served as a warm thick juice with tapioca. Açaí fruit does not travel well, so outside of the Amazon is it served as a cold dessert. If you go to Brazil, you will notice that açaí is absolutely everywhere. There are cafés and shops dedicated to the açaí, selling anything from açaí ice cream to fruit bowls, and it is served with a variety of toppings. The health benefits are well known as it is a powerful antioxidant. It is usually mixed with *guaraná,* which is a nut from the Amazon loaded with caffeine. Eating acai gives you an energetic happy feeling when you eat it.

Jabuticaba: This fruit is common in Brazil. Many *gringos* find it unusual because the fruit grows on the trunk of a tree. This fruit has the appearance of a darker and larger blueberry. All parts of the fruit are edible, but the sweet flesh is much more pleasing to one's taste buds than the sour skin. *Jabuticaba* is another superfruit that is abundant in Brazil. It cannot be exported it because the berries stay fresh for only a few short days after being harvested. You cannot even find it in Brazil's supermarkets. People grow it in their yards and make them into jam.

Fruta do Conde: If God made candy this would be it. This fruit almost has the taste of bubble gum or cotton candy. *Fruta do conde* has a soft skin and multiple soft, sweet, white sections that you eat. It's like you are eating healthy candy!

Cupuaçu: This fruit, like *Açaí*, comes from the Amazon rainforest. You will find this fruit served as a dessert in many of the same places that sell *Açaí*. *Cupuaçu* is a very strange-looking fruit resembling huge kiwis on the outside. They weigh around 1 kilogram (2.2 pounds) each. Cupuaçu has a white-colored pulp with a seed pod in the center. Its scent can be described as that of pineapples and chocolate at the same time. Some people think it smells like bananas. But don't let that scare you. Like other Brazilian fruits, *cupuaçu* is a superfruit, rich in nutrients. It contains numerous antioxidants, vitamins, and amino acids. It has a tangy flavor with a hint of chocolate aftertaste.

Seriguela: This little fruit is starting to show up as a snack outside its native Northeast Brazil where it is extremely popular. *Seriguelas* are eaten with their skin on; their small size makes it impractical to attempt removing the skin prior to consumption. This yellowish fruit tastes and looks like a miniature mango and is very juicy. Brazilians like to enjoy *seriguela* on its own as a snack or in juices or ice cream.

Coffee: *Cafezinho, Café com leite, expresso*

Brazilians have an intense relationship with coffee. Coffee is an old and essential part of Brazilian history and traditions. Brazilians like their coffee strong. It is typically served in small cups. Do not ask for coffee as it is served in the United States. It does not really exist, and most Brazilians do not like it. They refer to regular American coffee as *"chafee"* or tea-coffee because it is so weak.

You will usually be offered *cafezinho* prior to a meeting or after a meal. You will be offered *cafezinho* if you are waiting to see your lawyer or your bank manager. In some cities your profession dictates which coffee bar you will frequent to drink your midday coffee. Journalists go to one coffee bar, lawyers to another, and doctors to yet another coffee bar. *Cafezinho* is not espresso. *Cafezinho* is strongly brewed coffee strongly sweetened with sugar and served in a small cup. In a modest shop this might be a paper cup, or in an upscale office it could be served in a china cup. Because drinking coffee is a normal part of business and most social functions, accept the *cafezinho* if it is offered. You do not have to drink it if it is too sweet.

Expresso, or espresso in English, is distinct from *cafezinho*. *Expresso* comes from an *expresso* machine just like they have in Italy, whereas *cafezinho* is a strong filtered coffee normally served sweet. *Expresso* machines are quite common even at simple lunch stands, so if you want an *expresso* you need only ask for it. The new *mini-expresso* machines are also now immensely popular in Brazil.

Café com leite is another common drink usually served at breakfast. As the name says, this is coffee with milk, usually served with hot milk and sugar. Sometimes it is served from separate pots of hot milk and hot coffee, or it can be premixed, usually with sugar. Children at even a young age drink coffee with milk, this is not considered unusual.

Food from the South: Rio Grande do Sul and Gauchos

One of the proudest regions of Brazil is the South which consists of Rio Grande do Sul and Santa Catarina. The people of this region, even if their ancestors came in later waves of immigration, consider themselves *Gaúcho*, a type of Brazilian cowboy from long ago. Even today you will still find Brazilians wearing this typical *Gaúcho* clothes and eating typical *Gaúcho* food.

If you have had any Brazilian food before coming to Brazil it is likely you dined at a Brazilian steakhouse. This food originated in Rio Grande do Sul, the land of the famous *Gaúchos*. *Gaúchos* descended from Europeans and indigenous Brazilians. *Gaúchos* are breed a of tough, brave, and foolhardy people of honor, comparable to American cowboys. *Gaúchos* are known for their skills with horses and cattle. In Rio Grande do Sul, all of the people even urban dwellers are considered *gaúcho*. The traditional *gaúcho* roamed from the Pampas of Argentina though Uruguay to Rio Grande do Sul. Interestingly, many Brazilian *Gaúchos* are of Spanish descent and many come from the Azores. This seems reasonable since the region where *Gaúchos* inhabited spanned from Northern Argentina to Southern Brazil. This land was largely lawless and controlling rule was disputed. Only in 1756 with the victory over the Guarani Indians did it fall under Portuguese control. *Gaúchos,* and to a lesser extent the rest of the southern region of Brazil, have an independent impulse. Multiple wars were fought in 1836, 1893, 1923, and lastly 1930 to secede the Rio Grande do Sul and southern region of Brazil from the rest of the country.

Gaúchos
Source: *Encantos de Santa Catarina*

The *Gaúchos* from Rio Grande do Sul have a popular reputation in Brazilian culture. Most of them really are very honorable, tough, and macho, comparable to the America cowboy. However, unlike the American cowboy, the *Gaúchos* are thought to be so extremely macho that the rest of Brazil loves to make fun of them, making jokes about their masculinity. This of course makes the *Gaúchos* angry which is the point of the joke! This twisted Brazilian of sense of humor is not very subtle but is classically Brazilian.

When the *Gaúchos* herded their cattle, they would normally eat beef. They would cook the sides of beef on sticks or their swords over an open fire for long hours. Brazilians still cook beef this way, and it requires tending a fire for many hours to slowly cook the meat. This tradition leads to the Brazilian barbeque or *churrasco,* and the *churrascaria* or Brazilian steakhouse.

Churrasco

Churrasco is the name of the social event of cooking the meat. *Churrasco* also refers to the preparation of the meat just as barbecue describes the same in the U.S. Neither word refers to a type of sauce! *Churrasco* is popular in most regions of Brazil. A *churrasqueira* is the type of grill Brazilians use to grill there meat, and these are found in built into many homes and apartments. This suggest how important *churrasco* is to Brazilian culture. Brazilian barbeques are a far more elaborate affair than the typical American equivalent of grilled hot dogs and hamburgers on a bun! Any Brazilian *churrasco* will serve many different cuts of meat which are cooked on skewers over an open fire.

Churrasco is a common Brazilian social event and if you are invited to one you should go. *Chrurrasco* is the name of the type of grill used to prepare the meat. Today most houses and apartments have *churrascos* built into the common areas to facilitate this type of entertainment. Although most common in the south, if you get a group of men together anywhere in Brazil, there will always be one or more men that are more than happy to spend the entire time minding the fire that cooks the meat. The meat consists not just of beef, but also chicken, pork and various sausages. You can still find *churrasco* cooked over open-pit fires just like the *gaúchos* originally did, but this is typically called a *fogo de chão* (literally "floor oven.") As opposed to an American grill these are open pit fireplaces with skewers and other instruments needed for cooking the meat. Because *churrasco* is so important to Brazilians, these grills are almost standard to most houses or apartments in all parts of the country.

A Brazilian *churrasco* is a grander affair compared to the American barbeque because there are so many different cuts of meat and salads served. Many salads as well as meat are washed down with beer and *caipirinhas*. Like most Brazilian events there is no time for specifically starting or ending a *churrasco,* they just go one until the meat or beer or fire stops.

If you find yourself in Brazil for a short trip and have not been invited to anyone's home for *churrasco*, you should go to a *churrascaria* or Brazilian steakhouse which tries to imitate this custom. In most *churrascarias* you get your salad from a buffet with a large variety of food: salads, cheese, and dishes of every sort. After helping yourself to side dishes you sit down at the table with a disk, one side green and the other red. Turn the disk over to indicate if you want more meat. Green means bring meat, red means do not bring meat. When the disk is green waiters will bring a large variety of meat.

Brazilians cut their beef differently than other countries, therefore it is difficult to make exact comparisons to cuts from other countries. This will give you an introduction to the most important cuts of beef in Brazil.

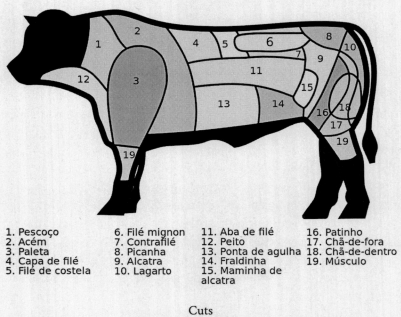

1. Pescoço
2. Acém
3. Paleta
4. Capa de filé
5. Filé de costela
6. Filé mignon
7. Contrafilé
8. Picanha
9. Alcatra
10. Lagarto
11. Aba de filé
12. Peito
13. Ponta de agulha
14. Fraldinha
15. Maminha de alcatra
16. Patinho
17. Chã-de-fora
18. Chã-de-dentro
19. Músculo

Cuts
Source: *Wikipedia*

Picanha: This cut does not exist in the United States. This muscle is cut across the round, the rump and the loin. Most countries consider this cut to be a lower grade. Brazilians however take the entire muscle and come up with a cut of beef that they prize more than any other. The difference is that the *picanha* has a layer of fat around it which when cooked correctly on the *churrasco* makes the meat tender and flavorful.

Picanha
Source: *iG*

Filet Mignon and *Contrafilé:* These cuts are identical to their international equivalent. Brazilians do not eat T-bone or porterhouse steaks, but the filet mignon is the most tender smaller side of those cuts. The contra file is the loin steak on the other, larger side of the T-bone. The *contrafilé* is very popular in Argentina, so sometimes this cut will be referred to as it is called in Argentina, *bife de chorizo*.

Alcatra: This is my personal favorite and another cut of beef that does not have an American equivalent. Once again, instead of cutting across the sirloin, it is the cut below the *picanha*. It is best to call it part of the top sirloin. It does not have fat wrapped around it but alcatra is just as flavorful.

Alcatra Bife
Source: *O Açougue*

Fraldinha: As Americans cut across the muscles to butcher the beef into primal cuts, Brazilians separate the muscle, so there is no equivalent of *fraldinha*. This cut of meat is leaner than picanha without the layer of fat for grilling. Although this cut is not identical, it is similar enough to call this a flank steak or a bottom sirloin.

Maminha: This is close to the equivalent of the bottom sirloin or tri tip roast but a tender sirloin. As the meat is cut differently the meat is more tender than a sirloin and is as flavorful as *alcatra*.

Costela: This is the same cut as beef ribs and prepared similarly to slow-cooked barbecue beef ribs, but without the barbecue sauce. The entire beef rib is cooked for hours and served with *farofa*, cooked mandioca starch, and a vinaigrette or with Argentine Chimichurri sauce. The meat tends to be fatty but very tender due to the slow cooking. Brazilians have many ways to cook beef ribs.

Costela Fogo de Chão
Source: *Panorama do Turismo*

Cupim: *Cupim* is the bump on the back of brahma cattle. As Europe and North America have few brahma or zebu cattle and brahma crossed cattle you could be unfamiliar with this cut of beef. Brazil is hot country and Brahma cattle and brahma crossed cattle are common in the hotter regions. This cut also requires slow cooking. It is very tender and somewhat fatty. Worth trying while in Brazil, but it has a unique texture. To be honest, for gringos this can be an acquired taste.

Cupim
Source: *Globo*

Regional Drink, Chimarrão a local ritual

Chimarrão is the name of a strong caffeinated tea, rich in antioxidants, that comes from the leaves of the *yerba mate* tree. Originally drunk by the Guarani Indians in Paraguay, its popularity spread through regions of Paraguay, Argentina, Uruguay, and all the states of southern Brazil. In Brazil is it drunk with hot water and can be shared communally. By communally, I mean everyone shares the same cup and straw. If you are in southern Brazil, invite yourself to join in the ceremony of drinking *chimarrão*.

Cerimônia do chimarrão
Source: *Barão Erva Mate*

The chimarrão or mate tea ceremony

There are certain rules to preparing and drinking *chimarrão*. Similar ceremonies exit in other countries that drink *chimarrão*, or *mate* as it is called in Spanish. To avoid making this too complicated we will focus on how *chimarrão* is drunk in Brazil and just note that there are slightly different words and ceremonies in the other countries where *yerba mate* is drunk.

The cup or gourd that hold the *yerba mate* that your group will drink is called a *"cuia"*. The metal straw is called a *bomba*. Preparing *chimarrão* is tricky. Mate comes from the leaves of a tree and these dried leaves are processed and sold in bulk. You drink tea made with the loose leaves, and the first sip you need to be careful not to get a mouthful of *mate* dust in your mouth, also the water is hot, but never boiling. The preparer holds the *cuia* filled with loose *mate* tea and carefully puts the *bomba* in the *mate*. Everyone who is going to drink *chimarrão* sits in a little circle (this is called the *roda de mate*) with the preparer taking the first drink. The first drink of *chimarrão* is usually strong and may have some dust. The preparer may take a second drink ensuring the *bomba* is not clogged and the temperature is correct. When the preparer is satisfied that the *bomba* is not clogged and *chimarrão* is flowing well, he fills the *cuia* with hot water and passes it to the person sitting to his left using his right hand. When it is your turn to drink, do not move with the metal straw or *bomba*, as that is an easy way to clog the *bomba* and mess up the ceremony. When it is your turn, just drink the tea in the *cuia* until the water is gone and pass it back to the preparer with your right hand. The preparer will refill and pass the cup to the person on your left. In this way the *chimarrão* passes among the circle and eventually back to the preparer who will drink in his turn. During this ceremony people make small talk. People can join and leave the circle as they want. To tell the preparer that you do not want any more *chimarrão*, simple say *"obrigado,"* or thank you, and he will know not to serve you again. You do not need to leave the circle, and you may continue with the small talk, but you will not be served in the next rounds.

    Pagando Mico: Things Gringos should not do drinking *chimarrão* with a group of Brazilians.[14]

1. Do not ask for sugar.

2. Do not make comments that you think this is not hygienic.

3. Be sure to drink all the tea in the *cuia*, it would be strange to send the *cuia* back half full!

4. Do not grab for the *cuia* when it is not your turn.

5. Avoid touching the *bomba* because you can clog it. If the Bomba is clogged ask the preparer to adjust it.

Things to do, Places to go

    Tour the Wine Country. There are fun vineyards in the southern part of the country that love to receive visitors. While Argentina and Chile are better known for their wines, Brazil is producing better wines each year. The region is a mix of vineyards, sub-tropical rainforest, and waterfalls.

---

[14] Availaible in: https://www.baraoervamate.com.br/cerimonia-do-chimarrao/. Access in: 10/3/21.

Serra Gaúcha
Source: https://www.decanter.com/wine-travel/south-america/brazil-wineries-serra-gaucha-413347/. Access in: 03/25/2021

Food from the Southern States: Santa Catarina and Paraná

Like Rio Grande do Sul, Santa Catarina and Paraná have a largely European population, but they do not share the Gaucho culture. On the other hand, there is a wide variety of German, Arabic, Italian, Swiss, Ukrainian, and Polish communities that each have their own traditions and ethnic foods. Also, the south of Brazil is colder in the winter than other parts of Brazil. In some parts of this region as well as Rio Grande do Sul, the temperature can fall below freezing. This cold weather has influenced this part of Sothern Brazil's cuisine. Winter of course is in June in South America, and European settlers in the south brought hot spiced wine, fondue and *quentão*, which is a hot spiced *cachaça* drink to warm you on cold nights. This region is also home to large pine nuts that grow on the *araucaria* pine tree native to the region. These nuts are heated and eaten during the winter, especially for the June festivals we will discuss in a later chapter.

Another dish of note from this region is *siri*. *Siri* is a small crab that lives on the beaches of Southern Brazil. Eaten as an appetizer, the *siri* is caught and the meat is mixed with farina and various herbs and spices, baked and usually served in the crab's shell. This is a typical appetizer can be found from the beaches south of Rio and are less common north of Rio.

Regional dessert Sagu

Sagu de vinho
Source: *Coisas da Léia* (coisasdaleia.com.br)

Sagu or *sagu de vinho* is a typical desert of the southern region of Brazil. It was created in Rio Grande do Sul. Some of the best wines in Brazil are made in this region. the word *sagu* comes from the Malayan word *sago*. In South Asian cuisine, sago palms are the source for starch which is extracted in little round pearls to be used in cooking. The Spanish and Portuguese empires stretched around the globe in the 15th century and brought with them the technique to extract the starchy pearls. It was discovered that similar pearls could be extracted from the Brazil's native cassava, or *mandioca*. *Mandioca* was eaten by Brazilian natives and later also by the European immigrants that arrived in southern Brazil. While the Brazilian natives extracted the starch from the *mandioca*, later waves of Italian and German immigrants are likely responsible for this dessert which is *sagu* with wine and cloves. The little balls of starch are the same used in the dessert Tapioca in other countries. Not to be confused with Brazilian Tapioca which is a totally different dish.

Things to do, Places to go

Oktoberfest

Oktoberfest is not a Brazilian holiday and it is not celebrated throughout the country, but it is a big festival is in Blumenau, a city in Santa Catarina. In fact, the Oktoberfest in Blumenau is the largest Oktoberfest outside of Germany. This city in southern Brazil was built to look like a town in Bavaria by Brazilians of German heritage and Brazilian that want to pretend they are German in October and drink beer. There is a large German population in Southern Brazil, which makes it ideal for Oktoberfest. Other cities in the south have Oktoberfest but the party in Blumenau is the biggest in Brazil and one of the biggest in the world. It is also incredibly fun because Blumenau, built with German architecture, adds ambiance to go along with the German food and Brazilian-German people. The festival is filled with German Brazilians dressed as if they have arrived from Bavaria, German folk dancing, and plenty of beer accompanies authentic German food. It is like being in Boston for Saint Patrick's Day. Everyone is German during Oktoberfest in Blumenau.

Oktoberfest
Source: *CVC viagens*

Florianópolis: Is the island capital of Santa Catarina. This region has some of nicest beaches in Brazil. The entire area around the city of

Florianopolis is exceptional for surfing and there are also areas for diving. You should go there in the summer, between December and May, because by Brazilian standards it is cold in winter. Many people from Argentina and Uruguay also summer here.

Foz de Iguaçu: In the state of Parana on the border with Argentina and not far from Paraguay is one of the wonders of the natural world: the water falls of Iguaçu. The name Iguaçu comes from the *guarani* word *Y* (pronounced like a nasal "eh") for water and *Guazu* for big. It is a good name for the second largest waterfall in the world. It is similar in size to Victoria falls in Africa and quite a bit bigger than Niagara Falls. Instead of tourist traps like you see at Niagara Falls, you are surrounded by large expanses of the *Mata Atlantic,* Brazil's other major rainforest. While most *gringos* know of the Amazon rainforest, fewer know that the coast of Brazil was once covered with a second rain forest call the *Mata Atlantic*, which held even greater biodiversity than the Amazon even though the Amazon is much bigger in size. The park of *Foz de Iguaçu* is in the state of Parana on the border with Argentina and near Paraguay. This park perhaps the best and largest example of the Atlantic rain forest. The Atlantic rainforest has even larger biodiversity than the Amazon, unfortunately a large amount of this forest was destroyed for human settlement.

Foz do Iguaçu
Source: Tripadvisor, 2021

Food from the Bahia and Victoria: The center of Afro Brazilian Culture

As you pass the brightly colored buildings, you can hear the drumming in the hills. You walk down the cobblestone road heading towards the sounds coming from the plaza. Maybe it is the singing coming from the capoeira circle, or it could be the slightly off 3/4 beat of the *forró* music as the dancing couples sway intricately in the bar. It could be the frenetic *axe* music and dancing on the beach. It could be a percussion band from the shanty town below. It could be the sing song accent of the locals, and their blending of words and phrases. No matter which it is, you are not in Kansas anymore. You are in Bahia! The land of tranquility.

If São Paulo is the financial powerhouse of Brazil and Rio is the beautiful city, Bahia is the cultural center of Brazil. This is the region where Pedro Alves Cabral first set eyes on Brazil in 1500, when his boat was blown off course from his intended destination of India. Bahia was the first area colonized by the Portuguese and the last to join the Brazilian Empire as its elites stayed faithful to the Portuguese. Salvador was the first capital of Brazil before Rio, and the first city visited by the King of Portugal when he fled to Brazil in 1808. It was the center of the African slave trade, and Brazil has the dubious honor of being the last country in the western hemisphere to liberate its slaves in 1888.

Bahia is a celebration of African influence. African culture is celebrated in Bahia through its music, dance, religions, celebrations, and customs. Bahia takes great pride in its culture. The Afro-Brazilian culture is celebrated in Bahia and impacts all of Brazil. Bahians maintained much of their culture in the face of oppression by the Portuguese, Catholic Church, and military governments. Afro-Brazilian cultural influences eventually permeated music, dance, language, art, and of course the food of Brazil. Even the names of many locations and plants in the region come from Indian languages. Today the people of Bahia and Victoria are free to practice their religion and customs and are proud of their African heritage. Bahia and Victoria are states where the culture of the oppressed vanquished the culture of the oppressors.

Before discussing the obvious influences on food, here are a few other ways in which the Afro-Brazilian culture vanquished the culture of the oppressors. When the Portuguese arrived in Brazil, the foreign germs they inadvertently brought with them largely wiped out the native population and with it the local religion. Due to the resulting labor shortage, the Portuguese brought slaves from West Africa to work on the sugar plantations and mines. The Portuguese forced conversion to Catholicism for all the slaves. According to official census, today only a small portion of the population practices these African religions. But the Afro-Brazilians adopted certain symbols of Catholicism. The slaves remained faithful to their African gods simply by praying to the Catholic saints as well as *Candomblé*, and *Umbanda "Orixás"*, which they associated with Catholic saints interchangeably. The most famous example of this is the Virgin Mary, which was adopted by Afro-Brazilians to represent Our Lady of the Navigators who protects fisherman, and is associated with *Iemanja*, the goddess of water. They share the same celebratory feast day, New Year's Day, in Brazil, also a holiday of obligation for Catholics. The catholic image of Jesus as "Our Lord of Bonfim" is associated with Oxalá, the king of the gods and creator of humankind. On the feast day celebrating Bonfim, the *Mae dos Santos*, the female adherents of Candomblé, clean the steps of the church of "Our lord of Bonfim" The Catholic Saint George represents *Ogun*, god of iron and fighting. A depiction of John the Baptist represents *Xangô*, the god of thunder, and so on. During years of slavery and oppression these religions fused into a common tradition, with mutual respect. Official statistics say that these Afro-Brazilian religions are small but the impact on Brazilian culture indicates that many Brazilians celebrate both their Catholic saints and *orixás*, at least to some degree, as if they are the same. No Brazilian touches an offering to an African god if they come upon one on the street or in the park, and even the richest white girls in Rio de Janeiro will dip their toes in the water at Midnight on New Year's, or more likely jump seven waves at the beach.

Likewise, during the saint's day of Our Lord of Bonfim, the female practitioners of Candomblé, dressed in wide white traditional dresses, join with Catholics in the procession of the feast day. After walking eight kilometers to the steps of the Bonfim church with the rest of the congregation, the women wash the steps with scented water singing chants in the Yoruba language in worship of Oxala, the god from Africa. The Catholic Church tried to ban this practice for a few years in the last century but today celebration is a large religious and tourist attraction. This is an example of how the culture of the oppressed had largely overturned the culture of the oppressor. There is a certain duality to the essence of being Brazilian that is part of their spirituality. They are strong in their faith and convictions, but perhaps this makes them respect the spirituality of others.

A Lavagem do Bonfim é um ritual católico ou do candomblé?
Source: *Jornal Grande Bahia* (JGB), 2012

A Lavagem do Bonfim é um ritual católico ou do candomblé?
Source: *Jornal Grande Bahia* (JGB), 2012

Becoming Brazilian

Capoeira
Source: *Toda Matéria*

If you go the Our Lord of Bonfim church, you will find colored ribbons for sale. Tradition holds that you should make a wish for each of the three knots you tie in this ribbon which you wear on your wrist. When the ribbon finally falls off on its own, your three wishes will come true. I do not remember this as part of my Catholic catechism!

Capoeira is another example of oppressed cultural resistance overcoming its oppressors. *Capoeira* is a martial art and a dance brought to Brazil by slaves, most likely from Angola. *Capoeira* is known for its acrobatic and complex maneuvers, often involving hands on the ground and inverted kicks. This martial art emphasizes flowing movements rather than fixed stances. The *ginga*, a rocking step, is the foundation of the technique which keeps rhythm with the music but also provides the core of both defensive blocking and offensive attacks. During the time of slavery, *capoeira* was used as self-defense as well as for settling disputes without the slave masters knowing what was going on. The *capoeira* practitioners would stand in a circle. One person plays the *berimbau*, which is a one string instrument which is used to keep time. In the circle members sing songs and keep rhythm by clapping their hands as the two fighters enter the circle (*roda de capoeira*). The fighters circle to the rhythm moving with kicks, punches, and blocking maneuvers to the rhythm of the music, often missing making contact with other fighter by inches. It does not take much imagination to see how the slaves would use the same ceremony to settle disputes or to see how this dance is also an effective martial art. Some of the Brazilian fighters in the UFC incorporate some aspects of *capoeira* in their technique.

In 1888, Brazil finally freed the slaves, but *capoeira* was so effective as a fighting technique that by 1890, the federal government banned its practice.[15] For many years *capoeira* was practiced in secret or under other names. However, in 1930, President Getulio Vargas, looking for symbols of Brazil, rehabilitated *capoeira* by having it performed at the presidential palace. Today capoeira is practiced around the world as well as being an interesting tourist site in Bahia. Visitors can find capoeira schools performing in the parks and open spaces in Salvador.

Fortunately for all of us, the same has happened with the food of Bahia and Victoria. The bland food of the Portuguese oppressors has been vanquished or at least greatly improved by the influence of African and native Brazilian influences.

Moqueca Baiana versus Moqueca Capixaba

There is a rivalry between the states of Espírito Santo and Bahia over which has the original and/or better version Moqueca, a famous Brazilian seafood stew. Both versions are delicious, and Bahia has so many great dishes that there are restaurants all over Brazil dedicated to this cuisine. The people of Espírito Santo state are known as *"Capixaba"* and the people from Bahia are *Baiana*. In Guarani *Capixaba* to weed their tidy plots of corn and mandioca. Capixaba became a term for all people of the state of Espírito Santo.[16] They are extremely proud of their version of this local fish stew. If you are visiting Victoria and you want to impress your hosts, tell them you understand that *moqueca* was first invented in Victoria and *moqueca Capixaba* is the true *moqueca*. I have no idea if this is true, it seems that both Bahia and Victoria have been making *moqueca* for hundreds of years. Even though *moqueca* is a fish or seafood stew in both states, the people of Victoria are especially proud of their stews. It is an ongoing controversy over which version is best.

If we look at the ingredients, *moqueca Capixaba* is a bit lighter with Portuguese influence seen using olive oil. The Guarani influence is evident

---

[15] Available in: https://en.wikipedia.org/wiki/Capoeira. Access in: 3/10/2021.

[16] Dicionario Illistrado Tupi Guarani seen at Capixaba - Dicionário Ilustrado Tupi GuaraniDicionário Ilustrado Tupi Guarani. Available in: dicionariotupiguarani.com.br. Access in: 12 ago. 2020.

from the use of *urucum* seed, a seasoning which gives the red color to the dish. This seed was used by the original Guarani Indians for many purposes due to its color red. *Moqueca Baiana* on the other hand is heavier and slightly more caloric with peppers, coconut milk, and traditional palm oil (*azeite de dendê*) which gives their stew a yellowish color. *Azeite de dendê* is typical in several dishes in Bahia.

Both versions of *moqueca* must be cooked and served in a mud baked pot, (*panela de barro*) or the dish will be a disaster. The pot speaks to the slave influence. However, two different versions are used: the Bahia *panela* is round on the bottom and the Capixaba *panela* is flat on the bottom and should be served on iron supports. See picture below. Both dishes are served with rice and *pirão* (mandioca flour with fish broth) and the rest of the ingredients are much the same.

Moqueca
Source: author's collection

Other dishes from the Bahia

Acarajé
Source: author's collection

Acarajé is a delicious street food usually sold by traditionally attired Baiana women, dressed in white. This dish is culturally and historically significant as *acarajé* is also an offering to the deity Iansã in the Afro-Brazilian religion Candomblé. *Acarajé* is made from a ball of mashed black-eyed peas that is deep-fried in *dendê* oil. It's served with *vatapá*, a paste made from coconut milk, as well as ginger, nuts, and *dendê* oil. Normally, small shrimp are stuffed with *vatapá* inside the fried mashed ball.

Vatapá

Vatapá is a stew-like mash of breadcrumbs, dried shrimp, spices, coconut milk, nuts, and *dendê* oil that is typically served with rice. Add fish or meat to make a filling meal. It's a common component of the ever-popular *acarajé*.

Bobó de Camarão

Bobó de camarão is a West African influenced shrimp stew or chowder. *Bobó de camarão* is made with a base of pureed *mandioca* (cassava flour). Shrimp, coconut milk, *dendê* oil, and cilantro are added to the stew, giving it a creamy texture. It's served with the usual sides of rice and *farofa,* cooked mandioca starch.

Tapioca

The tapioca comes from the same starch used in the desert Tapioca, but the Brazilian version is prepared much differently than the pudding commonly made outside of Brazil. In Bahia, and throughout Brazil, tapioca flour is used as a staple thickener and even as a base to make a wrap or tortilla. Think of a French crepe that can be stuffed with meat or sweet dessert. Tapioca is the same idea; it can be stuffed for a meal or a dessert. In Salvador it is best to try tapioca with savory foods like shrimp and garlic. Or try a sweeter version with bananas and condensed milk. Tapioca is versatile and can be prepared with a huge variety of foods, and it can be found all over Brazil.

Food of Minas Gerais: Comida Mineira

The people of Minas Gerais are called *Mineiros*. They have a unique accent and vocabulary that sets them apart from other Brazilians. The Brazilian state of Minas Gerais was the first area in the interior of Brazil to be settled, and it is dotted with several colonial cities, which are great to visit. Minas is also the state known for the best *cachaça*, another reason to visit the area. The people from Minas are known for being very prudent. Brazilians have a stereotype of the people of Minas Gerais that is a common source of humor. Mineiros supposedly love cheese, and in fact there is a large variety of cheese made in this region. They also love their cheese bread. This is one of the topics of Brazilian jokes made about *Mineiros:* that they will do anything for either cheese or cheese bread. The jokes also suggest that the women of Minas Gerais are known to be good in the kitchen, good with money, and good in the bedroom. The men of the region are known to be quiet about any such conquest, not bragging but being ever discreet.

In 1693, veins of gold were discovered in Minas Gerais followed up by later discoveries of gems and diamonds. Until then most of the Portuguese activity had been growing sugar cane in the northeast Brazil. But the discovery of gold impacted both Minas Gerais and Rio de Janeiro. The state of Minas Gerais obviously was affected because the subsequent gold rush brought Portuguese and slaves into the area to work the mines. The discovery of gold also put Rio on the map because the Estrada Real, or royal road, that was built by the Portuguese to transport the gold mined in Minas Gerais to port cities where it was shipped back to Portugal. The Estrada Real connected the Ports of Rio de Janeiro and Paraty to Ouro Preto in Minas Gerais. Today, Paraty and Ouro Preto are wonderful colonial cities with Brazilian baroque architecture. Both are well worth the visit. By 1789, the mines were running out of gold and the Portuguese Crown continued to take one fifth of the gold for themselves. Believing, perhaps correctly, that the Brazilians were shortchanging them, the Portuguese Crown became ever more oppressive. Influenced by the American revolution, and due to increasing demands of the Crown for more gold, a group of intellectuals planned to overthrow the Royal Government and start a republic.[17]

The attempted overthrow, known as the *Inconfidência Mineira* or Mineira Conspiracy, was a complete failure. This failure gives insight into some unfortunate Brazilian issues which I will further address later in the book. The entire conspiracy was poorly planned. There was no leader, but a group of associated idealists. There really was no ideology other than to begin a guerrilla war to wear down the Portuguese until Minas Gerais could become an independent republic. Some of the leaders wanted slavery abolished; most did not.[18] Although there were intellectuals and military participants it was not well organized, and with everyone so enthusiastic, it was obvious that the plan would leak as the group lacked discipline. Eventually one of the conspirators betrayed the movement to Portuguese

---

[17] Available in:: https://brasilescola.uol.com.br/historiab/inconfidencia-mineira.htm. Access in: 8/03/2021
[18] *Ibidem.*

authorities for forgiveness of his debts. All the original conspirators were arrested. All were condemned to death. However, many of the leaders of *Inconfidência Mineira* were sons of wealthy Brazilians, and in typical Brazilian fashion, the wealthy conspirators got "Brazilian *jeitinho*", or a way out of punishment. Queen Maria commuted the sentence of all the wealthy or intellectual conspirators, instead banishing them to Africa. That left only Joaquim Jose da Silva, or *"Tiradentes"* (tooth puller) who worked as a dentist, a soldier, and a mine worker, to pay for the collective crime with his life. He was taken to Rio and hanged. He died heroically, his body was cut into pieces and brought back to Ouro Preto as a warning against future revolts.[19] Even though the conspiracy failed his death is a national holiday. Today the flag of Minas Gerais has the Latin phrase Liberta Quae Sera Tomen inscribed in its flag, which is a wonderful wish for all Brazilians perhaps for all mankind. "Liberta Quae Sera Tomen" means "Liberty, even if it come late!"

    The best way to describe the food of Minas Gerais is big! The food from Bahia has African influence, São Paulo may be the most internationally sophisticated city, and Rio may be the most beautiful city, but a good number of Brazilians would call Minas Gerais the culinary capital of Brazil. *Comida Mineira* cuisine is a mixture of Portuguese, Indian, and African influences just like the people who live there. My wife, who is from Minas, always asks, "When are we going to eat real food?" When she says that I know she wants food from Minas Gerais. All over Brazil there are restaurants dedicated to *"Comida Mineira."* The food from Minas Gerais is solid, big-hearted, home cooked food with healthy portions. It is the type of food you want after a day of hard physical work. Dishes tend to be slow cooked, with heaping portions of rice, sausage, chicken, collard greens, bean paste, and pork ribs. If the restaurant says the plate is for two people, four people will be more than satisfied! Ask for a half portion for two people unless you are very hungry. Normally the food is not prepared spicy, but pepper sauces, usually homemade, are served as a side to the dish and you can make the food as hot as you like. By the way, Minas Gerais is also famous for the best artisanal *cachaça* in the country, so order a local *cachaça* with that *caipirinha*. There are also a wide variety of cheeses made in the state that are like European cheeses. The most famous cheese from this region is *queijo de Minas*, unique to Brazil, which is a light cheese used to make the famous cheese bread.

---

[19] *Ibidem.*

Pão de Queijo

Many a foreigner has commented that if they could find a way to sell these tasty biscuits in their home country, they would be rich. This cheese bread is a trademark dish of the region. The cheese is Minas cheese but there is no wheat in this bread. Instead of wheat, a mandioca-derived flour is used to make this cheese bread. This is commonly eaten for breakfast but should be served hot and is great any time of the day.

Pão de queijo
Source: *Globo*, 2020

Frango com Quiabo (Chicken with Okra.)

To start with, commercially raised chickens are not amongst the ingredients in this type of cooking. The chickens in Minas Gerais are raised free and are called *frango caipira*, (redneck or hick chickens) the meat is more flavorful, hormone free, and the eggs are dark brown not white. Brazilians pay a premium for both chickens and eggs compared to the commercial counterparts. *Frango com Quiabo* has both African and Portuguese influences which should surprise no one. It is a light chicken stew that is slow-cooked and served in a mud pot, usually with cornmeal, rice, and fried collard greens on the side.

Frango com quiabo
Source: *Menu com arte*

Tutu Mineiro

This is a bean paste, similar in consistency to refried beans but without the fat. Instead, the thickness comes from adding either *mandioca* or corn flour and maybe a little bacon.

Feijão Tropeiro

There are many varieties of this side dish made with cooked bean, collard greens, dried meat or bacon and fried mandioca flour. The most famous version of this dish is the one served at the football matches in Belo Horizonte, at the Minerão Stadium. At the stadium during halftime large portions of *feijão tropeiro* are served, with optional pork rinds and egg. Minas' version adds so many ingredients that sometimes it can be a whole meal by itself.

Feijão tropeiro
Source: *Tudo Receitas*, 2015

Other dishes from Minas Gerais

Angu: This is a cornmeal dish strongly influenced by Africa. It is simply boiled cornmeal with a little salt added. Angu is served as a side dish especially with chicken dishes.

Carne-de-sol com mandioca: Carne-de-sol is heavily salted beef, which is exposed to the sun for one or two days to cure. *Mandioca* is known by other names, some of which include yucca and cassava. This potato-like legume is quite delicious boiled or fried and smothered in butter.

Leitão a pururuca: *Pururuca* is crispy pork skin; *leitão a pururuca* is pork from a young pig, roasted with the skin. The words *pururuca* and the word *pipoca,* the Brazilian word for popcorn, come from the same word in Guarani, *poro'roka,* which means to make pop. Once cooked, it is usual to rub ice over the skin and then sprinkle hot oil over the top to make the popped skin extra crispy. Some chefs may use a cooking torch to get the same effect.

Torresmo: This is fried pig skin with or without pork meat. *Torresmo* without meat is just like pork rinds in America. *Torresmo* without meat is used as a side for soups and *feijoada*. *Torresmo* with meat is a snack. Both versions are served with limes.

Foods of Boteco and Bars – Not a region but rather a destination

Botecos de São Paulo
Source: *Bares SP*

In Brazil there are two special social and eating institutions, bars and *boteco*. They perform the same specific social function. Bars in Brazil are not just for drinking but are also social places for food and music. Brazilians will tell you that *botecos* are simpler, less upscale bars, but in practice both are informal. Both may have music, both have food and drinks, and both commonly have tables outside on the street. Bars and *botecos* are central social institutions in Brazil, and I have spent much time in both. If you Google "bars near me" or "*botecos* near me" you will get results for both. There are famous *botecos* as big as bars, and small places that call themselves bars. Brazilians will be able to tell you all about the food that you eat at a *boteco* because it is the food is always fresh and informal and is meant to be shared, whereas a Bar will typically have a bigger menu and complete dishes in addition to the "*boteco* food." It is true that most *botecos* are found in the states of São Paulo, Rio, and Minas Gerais, while bars can be found *all* over Brazil. Over many a beer and with many heated discussions with Brazilians, I have concluded, that the concept of bars and *botecos* overlap to such an extent that even though I use the word *boteco* for this chapter, you can find most of this food in a bar as well. The social function and the experience for Brazilians and *gringos* is similar.

A restaurant in Brazil is quite easy to identify and like restaurants all over the world. A restaurant or *restaurante* is a place primarily to eat well-prepared food with individual portions. Brazil has some of the best restaurants, with the most diverse varieties of dishes in the world. Restaurants are usually more elegant than both bars and *botecos*, and provide individual meals, not snacks. Within the most elegant restaurants in Brazil, there is a movement to create a Brazilian "nuovo cuisine" but this competes with French cuisine, Italian cuisine, Peruvian-Japanese fusion, and more. For the gourmet or gourmand, the restaurants in the major cities of Brazil will not disappoint. Eating in restaurants in Brazil is much the same as eating in a restaurant anywhere in the world. What is different is the experience of being in a Brazilian bar or *boteca* and eating what is commonly called *boteco* food.

Chopp

One of the best drinks in Brazil is *chopp*, and *chopp* is not beer! *Cerveja* is the word for beer. What is the difference? The Brazilian word *Chopp* comes from the German word "Schoppen" which is simply a unit of measure like a half pint. This difference between beer and *chopp* is a matter of Brazilian legislation. *Chopp* or (sometimes spelled *Chope*) is always an unpasteurized, usually a lightly colored beverage that is served out cold from draft barrel, but unlike draft beer the carbonation is natural. The bubbles from *Chopp* come naturally from the fermentation process, and not from injected carbon dioxide, so the bubbles are smaller, and the foam is lighter than a beer. As *chopp* is not pasteurized, so it tastes fresher. Pasteurization raises the temperature of beer to 70 degrees Celsius to kill any microorganisms and this changes the flavor of a beer. As *chopp* is unpasteurized it must be consumed quickly, or it will spoil. People go to the botecos because the *chopp* is fresh and the *chopp* stays fresh because lots of people go to the botecos.

There are a lot of famous boteco and *chopp* stories and certain botecos have a history in their hometown. One boteco is famous because supposedly the *chopp* came from a copper pipe, underground, directly from a beer factory besides the bar. *Chopp* is normally served at a temperature slightly below freezing. When you are in a boteco, the waiters will give you a tab where they will mark each *chopp* that you were served. In a boteco, the waiters are always walking around all the tables with trays of *chopp* to be served. When you are ready to leave you pay for all the *chopps* on your tab with your bill.

Chopp
Source: Bar do Jota, 2012

Coxinha de Frango

This is a typical snack in all types of places. It is made with cooked chicken sometime with cheese on the inside, surrounded by mandioca flour, deep fried and served. This is a finger food, but Brazilian will eat it with napkins or paper so that their fingers do not touch the food.

Bolinho de bacalhau and Bolinho de carne seca

Same sort of deep-fried finger food that you eat with a napkin. Bolinho de bacalhau is made with cod fish and flour served with lime juice. This dish comes from the Portuguese who traditionally eat cod fish. Bolinho de carne seca comes from Northern Eastern Brazil and is filled with jerked beef and both versions are surrounded with mandioca flour.

Pastel

Pastel are deep fried pies stuffed with a wide variety of meats or cheese.

Torresmo

Torresmo is similar to pork rinds however in Brazil it is common for the rind to come with fried pork attached. These are typically eaten with lime juice on top.

Kibe Frito

In the past century thousands of Arabs settled in Brazil, though there is a large number of Arabic restaurants, this traditional Arab dish made it on to the menus of Brazilian Botecos. It is made of ground meat, cracked wheat, cooked with mint and herbs.

Picanha na Jaca or Brasa

This plate that you and your friends cook collectively at the table by placing meat on a hot iron plate. Picanha is a uniquely Brazilian cut of beef that goes from the inside round to the sirloin. The Picanha is already sliced, and you and your friends cook it on the hot iron plate, sometime with grilled onions. It is served with farofa and vinaigrette of tomato and onions.

Costela no Bafo

Bafo in Portuguese means breath. Costela no Bafo are beef ribs cooked in their own steam or juices. Basically, the whole ribs with all the meat, fat and bones are wraps with spices, in aluminum foils. Costela no Bafo requires a special type of grill, where water is placed in a metal square. The ribs are wrapped in aluminum foil and placed above the steaming water to lock in all the juices. The steam cooks the ribs in its own *bafo* or breath. The meat should be so tender, that it falls of the bones. These types of ribs are shared at the table bones and all in a Boteco with Chopp, vinaigrette farofa.

History and Food from the North East

Endless beaches vibrant culture and the music and dancing of Frevo, Forró, and Maracatu, the people of the north east are recognized for their warmth and humility but also for their sense of justice and sense of honor. This is the land of famous bandits that fought the law and of a rebellion against the king of Portugal after he arrived in Brazil. The food of the region reflects its climate as well as the local produce. The area has lots of sun and beaches, but as you move from the beach to the interior, you find an area which is famously dry, and life is hard due to the drought and poverty. This area is called the *sertão*, and there really is not a good English word to describe it. The Australian word outback may be the closest. It is a vast area including northern Minas Gerais, inland Bahia and the states of the north east as you drive in from the coast. Despite its droughts and arid landscape, the *sertão* provides yet another cultural side of Brazil. The sertão gave origin to *sertanejo* music which is Brazil's form of country music. Sertanejo music is widely popular in the cities as well and the interior and have all the great themes typical of country music. Just like country music the usual themes are broken hearts, drinking too much, and true love.

For the purposes of this book, the north east includes the states of Alagoas, Ceará, Piaui, Maranhão Paraiba, Rio Grande do Norte, and Pernambuco. Bahia is excluded from this group. First is that the State of Bahia is larger than the other states. Second, from a culinary perspective, restaurants tend to be either *Baiana* or *Nordestino* style, but not both.

The food of the rest of the states of the north east are generally grouped together. Most importantly, I want the reader to know a little history of the different regions of Brazil. The North East played a special role in the history of Brazil separate from Bahia.

One of the major themes of this book is in relation to how Brazil was impacted negatively not only by colonialism and slavery but also by the flight of the Portuguese monarchy and aristocracy to Brazil to flee from the armies of Napoleon as they invaded Portugal in 1808. Whereas the elites of Salvador welcomed the Portuguese and begged King John to stay in Salvador, the people of the Northeast like the people of Minas Gerais before them, understood that their interests and the interest of the monarchy were not the same and revolted against the monarchy.

Today as Brazil struggles to stop corruption and impunity, which we will see are legacies of the Portuguese Monarchy, I wanted to highlight those Brazilians that stood up to the monarchy in the past, even though the revolt failed. I also want to point out the history of the *Cangaceiros*, which were groups of bandits that were both criminal and yet have the mythology like Robin Hood or Pancho Villa. Today unfortunately, this region remains a center of family dynasties of political corruption and inequality. On one hand the Cangaceiros predated the criminal violence of today and yet they are folk heroes for the people of northeastern Brazil. The source of the criminal violence then and now is the inequality in Brazil that has yet to be addressed.

The Revolt of Pernambuco 1817

While the elites of Rio and Salvador were generally obsequious, if not a little confused by the presence of the Portuguese monarch and aristocrats, the elites and people of the Brazilian State of Pernambuco and other cities in the north were starting to question the concept of monarchy. Free masons and the ideas of the enlightenment had vaguely entered the minds of the educated classes. The people of Recife had also had notions of democracy from their previous colonization by the Dutch during the 17th century.[20] However, the conflict was also economic. The local landowners of the region already had problems making money with cotton and sugar, but with the monarchy now in Brazil there were demands for more taxes.

---

[20] GOMES, Laurentino. *1808:* Como uma rainha louca, um príncipes medroso, e um corte corrupta enganaram Napoleão e mudaram a Historia de Portugal e do Brasil. São Paulo: Globo, 2014, p.274.

While the benefits of this royal spending were being received in Rio de Janeiro, the people of the northern states needed to pay for the expenses of the monarchy in the south. The arrival of the monarch and aristocracy placed a new burden of new taxes on the local Brazilians. An Englishman living in Pernambuco captured the feeling at the time, writing, "We pay in Pernambuco the taxes to pay for the lighting in Rio de Janeiro"[21] There was already great animosity to anything Portuguese felt by the military officers of Brazilian birth who were treated as second class by newly arrived Portuguese officers. Considering the disgraceful performance of the Portuguese military fleeing from Napoleon, this must have been quite irritating. Finally, the revolutionaries in Pernambuco did have some ideas from the enlightenment. We need to remember that at this time Brazil was made up of states separately administered under one king who had fled his home. The people of Pernambuco knew that other countries were replacing kings with republics. With the idea of setting up a republic, Pernambuco sent the first "Brazilian" ambassador to the United States, Antonio Goncalves da Cruz, or better known by his nick name Cruz Cabuga.[22]

Cruz Cabuga was a wealthy bi-racial landowner with an interest in French philosophy, who had returned to Brazil from France during the revolution in 1797. As the revolution in Pernambuco was being planned, he was sent as an ambassador from the new republic to the United States with money to try to get support and buy arms for a separate republic in the northeast of Brazil. [23] The United States after its own revolution, at first supported in the French revolution. However, after defeating the English in the war of 1812, the Americans had lost interest in promoting revolution and were interested instead in promoting trade. The English, who were the supporters of the Portuguese monarchy and had gained access to all the ports in Brazil, would be upset if the United States supported the revolution in the Pernambuco. Cruz Cabuga did meet with the Secretary of State of the United States, but he did not receive the support of the United States, who did not want to upset its trading partners in England. He did, however, get an agreement to allow ships from the new republic to trade in the United States during the revolution.[24]

---

[21] *Ibidem*, p.273.

[22] *Ibidem*, p. 271.

[23] *Ibidem*, p.272.

[24] GOMES, Laurentino. *1808:* Como uma rainha louca, um príncipes medroso, e um corte corrupta enganaram Napoleão e mudaram a Historia de Portugal e do Brasil. São Paulo: Globo, 2014, p. 275.

Cruz Cabugá
Source: *Diário de Pernambuco*

Cruz Cabuga: Brazil's first ambassador

Like the previous uprising of the Inconfidência Mineira, the Portuguese Governor of Pernambuco, Caetano Pinto, received rumors of the upcoming rebellion and sent soldiers to arrest the ring leaders in Recife. Only this time one of the ring leaders was a Brazilian military officer, Jose de Barros Lima who promptly killed the Portuguese commanding officer, Barbosa de Castro, sent to arrest him. When the Governor heard of the failed arrest, he sought refuges in Fort Brum in Pernambuco. The fort was surrounded by rebel forces and to governor surrendered.[25]

Recife easily fell into the rebel hands on March 6 1817, and the rebellion spread to Ceará, Paraiba and Rio Grande do Norte. On March 29, the elected representatives met to form a new government. This assembly created three powers of government, the Judiciary, Legislative and Executive. Finally, the assembly gave freedom of speech and press to the new republic. While the assembly kept the catholic church as the state religion, it also allowed freedom to other churches to practice as they wished. Slavery was maintained to keep the interest of the landowners, with the revolutionaries. Finally, a flag was created which is still the flag of Pernambuco.[26]

---

[25] *Ibidem*, p. 275.
[26] *Ibidem*, p.276.

Revolução Pernambucana
Source: *Wikiwand*

The reaction of the monarchy we immediate and violent. Outside of the rebelling states, all appeals to other states in Brazil for support were ignored or in the case of Bahia, the envoy from the republic of Pernambuco was immediately arrested and shot.[27] The Portuguese navy imposed a naval blockade on the Port of Recife while a government army arrived from Bahia to the South. The rebellion was defeated on May 20, 1817 with the four of rebels' leaders bodies drawn and quartered.[28]

Though unsuccessful the rebellion created panic with the monarchy in Rio, who up until this time expected submission from Brazil, now found that there was a limit on how much they could tax the Brazilians. Though Portugal mad queen had died, the Prince regent would delay his coronation to be king for a year for fear of another rebellion. Cruz Cabuga the republics envoy to the United States was among those pardoned by the Prince regent.[29]

There were two other attempts to overthrow the monarch and create a liberal society for the North East of Brazil. After Dom Pedro I famously decided to stay in Brazil, and as a reaction to the new Emperor Dom Pedro I dissolution of the Constituent Assembly, the Confederation

---

[27] *Ibidem*, p.276.
[28] GOMES, Laurentino. *1808*: Como uma rainha louca, um príncipes medroso, e um corte corrupta enganaram Napoleão e mudaram a Historia de Portugal e do Brasil. São Paulo: Globo, 2014, p. 277.
[29] *Ibidem*, p.279.

of the Equator was set up on 2 July 1824. The Confederation was another separatist movement which encompassed the provinces of Pernambuco, Paraíba, Rio Grande do Norte, and Ceará. On 29 November 1824, the Confederation's forces capitulated to the Imperial army with the help of the English naval mercenary Admiral Cochrane.[30] From his ships the Admiral bombarded Recife's churches and houses, while imperial army attacked from lands. Sixteen rebels including a catholic priest were executed.

Bandeira de Pernanbuco
Source: *Canal Blitz*

Finally, Pernambuco was the also site of the brief liberal republican Praieira revolt in 1848, which was Brazil's response to the European year of liberal revolutions. Deodoro da Fonseca, an army marshal of the Brazilian Empire, crushed this revolt. Much later, Fonseca would lead the overthrow of Emperor Pedro II, and serve as the first president of the Brazilian republic.[31]

---

[30] GOMES, Laurentino. *1822*: Como um homem sábio, uma princesa triste, e um escocês louco por dinheiro ajudaram dom Pedro a criar Brasil – um pais que tinha todo para dar errado. São Paulo: Globo, 2015, p.179.
[31] UOL Educacao Viewed at Marechal Deodoro da Fonseca - Biografia - UOL Educação viewed: 9/03/2021

Os Cangaceiros, Maria Bonita, and Lampião

Maria Bonita e Lampião
Source: *Uol*, 2020

It is impossible to go to the North Eastern part of Brazil and not see references to the *Cangaceiros*. They are almost mythical figures to the downtrodden of the region. In the 1920s, the Sertão was host to many large landholders who would higher bandits intimidate the people in the region for pay. These bandits would also work for themselves by robbing and kidnapping people for ransom. Historically these bandits seemed quite violent, but a myth has grown up around them like Robin Hood. The bandits that steal from the rich and give to the poor. There were many groups of *Cangaceiros* who would steal cattle rob and kidnap, but they also needed support of the local communities of the Sertão. The most famous of these bandits were Lampião, and his lover Maria Bonita.

Lampião became a bandit after his father was killed by police. He was intelligent and charismatic, he taught himself to read and was always seen with his spectacles. He was also extremely violent, and he and his gang would take over towns, kill the police without pity, demand ransoms from the rich and use that money to pay for all the provisions he and his gang needed. This and his reputation for being religious and honoring his word gave some level of support within the outback. Maria Bonita was his wife and joined the gang wearing the same leather clothes as the men, joining them on raids as well. With this history of violence, a code of honor along with a romantic relationship made Lampião and Maria Bonita soon become like the Bonnie and Clyde of the Brazilian Sertão. Even today you cannot travel the region without seeing photos and statues of Maria Bonito and Lampião.

Like Bonnie and Clyde, Lampião and his gang were betrayed by a fellow gang member. In July 1938, the police armed with machine guns ambushed Lampião gang killing 9 members including Maria Bonita at one of his hide outs in Sergipe. Supposedly the rest of the gang escaped. The police decapitated the nine *Cangaceiros* and the heads were displayed including Maria Bonita and Lampião, in Salvador. Only in 1969 were the heads buried, but the legend lives on.

Forró: Music and Dancing from the Northeast

Forró
Source: https://www.estudopratico.com.br/quais-os-tipos-e-as-caracteristicas-do-forro-e-quem-criou-esse-ritmo/. Access in: 03/25/2021

Forró originated in the northeast of Brazil but played in many parts of Brazil. The dance and the event of the dance is also called *Forró* and it is perhaps the most popular dance for couples in Brazil. There are two legends where the term comes from. One theory holds that it comes from the term *"Forrobodó",* which means a great party or a big commotion in Portuguese, the other theory is the term comes from the word "for all" in English. This later story holds that parties organized by the English managing the railway in the great western railway in Recife in the turn of the century or that US troops based in Natal during World War II would have parties that were open "For all." According to this legend, the Brazilians would hear the troops say, "for all" and *forró* was born!

Forró music and dance are popular in all the regions of Brazil today. Played with a minimum of a drum accordion and bell or triangle. The dance and the rhythm of the music is like the Texas twostep, but without the cowboy boots.

Food from the North East Region

Carne de sol com mandioca
Source: *Receita da Vovó*

Carne de Sol com Macaxeira: As you would expect from a hot region, the Brazilians would have needed some way to preserve meat. For the people of the region that answer was to salt the meat and drying it historically under the hot sun. Carne de sol literally means "meat from the sun", which differs from the dried beef (*carne seca* or *charque*) from Rio Grande do Sul, in that there is less salt, but a finer grain of salt used so that it does not require to be soaked in water before cooking. Macaxeira is the name in the region for Mandioca or Cassava.

Moqueca Cearense: This fish stew is not as well-known as the variations in Bahia and Victoria, but the major difference is that unlike the more famous version of Bahia the Moqueca from Ceará uses Olive Oil instead of palm oil, and unique to this version of this fish stew, caju (cashew fruit) juice that provides a special flavor.

Baião de dois
Source: *Terra*

Baião de Dois: This region combines carne de sol with a rice dish called which is a mixture of rice, beans, cheese onion and meat. Sometime the rice dish is served on the side of the meat other times it is all served together. It is a simple and filling meal but flavorful. The beans in this dish are specific to the region of the North East, called *feijão de corda*.

Cuzcuz Nordestino: This plate is not to be confused with Moroccan Cousous. This is a much simpler dish usually served on the side and the main ingredient is ground corn, instead of the fine wheat germ grains of Morocco. It usually is served as a side dish.

Rapadura: The north east is the biggest maker of rapadura, which is a hard candy made from boiling sugar cane juice. It can be found in other parts of Brazil and can be a good addition to a caipirinha!

Tapioca: Most of us know of tapioca as a sweet dessert. If fact the main ingredient of tapioca pudding comes from the cassava plant that is used to make the starch of Tapioca from the North east of Brazil. Tapioca in the Northeast is a traditional street food something like a French creape or and Mexican tortilla. It is filled with a variety of meats and cheese or is also stuffed with sweets filling as well. Carne de sol is a typical filling but there are so many others.

Escondidinho de carne seca: It is no secret that Brazilians eat plenty of beef, and escondidinho de carne seca is another must-try while in the Northeast of Brazil but can be found on the menus of bars all over the country. The name of this dish is from the word to hide in Portuguese (*Esconder*). The meat is salted beef like shredded beef that is seasoned and then "hidden" under mashed mandioca, butter, and cheese.

São Paulo and Rio de Janeiro

Brazilian readers will be surprised that I group these two states together in the same section, because while the two cities are both international and geographically close to each other, there is a tension and rivalry between *Cariocas* (those born in the city of Rio de Janeiro) and the *Paulistanos* (those born in São Paulo city.) If you live in the state of São Paulo you are a *Paulista*, if you live in the city of São Paulo you are a *Paulistano*. The term *Carioca* come from the Guarani meaning home of the white man and refers to people from Rio de Janeiro. From a cuisine perspective, both regions are far more inspired by outside influences than by the local food creations. As a Brazilian friend of mine said, these cities take the food from all over the world and make it better!

Arguing which city is best between *Cariocas* and *Paulistanos* is a long tradition. The people of both states are great rivals in football teams, lifestyles, and arguing which city is the best to live in. Over the last few decades many comparisons have been made, from traffic conditions, to employment opportunities, to cultural events. This rivalry is old, likely from the time that Rio was the capital of the monarchy, but it continues to this day through football rivalries and perhaps also mutual jealousy.

The typical Brazilian stereotypes hold that *Cariocas* are friendly, easy-going, and always late (probably because they just got off beach!) while *Paulistanos* are colder, fast-paced workaholics, and perpetually stressed. A quick look at the size and location of each city certainly explains the stereotype. São Paulo is high up in the hills, about an hour's drive from the beach. Rio is considered the most beautiful city in the world and is surrounded by high hills and beautiful beaches. You could make a comparison with São Paulo as the New York of Brazil and Rio the Los Angeles of Brazil, except that rather than being separated by a continent, the two Brazilian cities are only one day's drive from each other. *Cariocas* may be jealous of São Paulo's economic success and functioning government, and *Paulistanos* are jealous because *Cariocas* get to live in Rio.

If you are coming here to visit or coming here to work in Brazil, these two cities have the largest expatriate communities so this may be where you will live. Time for us to explore some of these cities' culture and food.

Food

São Paulo is simply one of the best cities in the world for food. This is not an exaggeration, nor should it be surprising. One of the things that makes São Paulo so interesting and culturally rich is its large immigrant populations, from Italian, Peruvian, French, Middle Eastern to Japanese. This has had a big impact on the gastronomic scene. The heavy Italian influence in São Paulo means great Italian restaurants. Every neighborhood has wood burning ovens that make the best pizza. Each neighborhood pizzeria claims to make the best pizza in São Paulo and many *Paulistanos* reserve Sunday as pizza night. Besides Pizza there is a large variety of Italian restaurants representing the different regions of Italy. The large Japanese population (São Paulo hosts the biggest Japanese diaspora in a city anywhere in the world) equals phenomenal sushi and other Japanese cuisine. Liberdade is an entire neighborhood in São Paulo dedicated to all things Japanese. Japanese cuisine, like all the other foreign influences, can be both traditional or prepared with a Brazilian flair. There is a large range of international restaurants and some are expensive. While you can still eat cheaply, or head to a trendy food truck, there is also the option of high-end (and high-priced) gourmet spots. Recently, Peruvian food and Peruvian fusion have become quite popular. Currently there is a movement of the most important Brazilian chefs, to take elements of traditional Brazilian dishes and create a Brazilian New Cuisine.

The food scene in Rio is also international, but due to its proximity to the beach it is more laidback. You can happily grab some fried bar snacks and a *caipirinha* to enjoy at the beach, or head straight from the beach to a *rodízio* (all-you-can-eat). The tropical influence is also evident in the much larger choice of fruit juice stands (on every corner in Rio), and the abundance of açai. Rio and São Paulo both have *botecos*. Once again, the geography changes the feel of these places. Bars and *botecos* always have access to the outside, so spilling out to the city street or a bar with a view of the ocean can make a difference.

City life and culture

Rio is known as "the beautiful city," and it is undeniably a major influence on Brazilian culture. Samba, bossa nova, and Brazilian Funk music comes from Rio. As the former capital of the country and home to many buildings and institutions from the Brazilian Empire, Rio has had a great influence on the culture of Brazil. Rio invented Brazilian beach culture. Surfing, volleyball, football, and footvolley are a constant presence on the beach. *Cariocas* want to live a life where they are having fun. Rio is a tourist city with lots of activities during the day and night.

São Paulo is the economic center of South America. It is the major center for finance and a hub for multinational corporations. No matter how you look at it, although there exist some great areas and neighborhoods, São Paulo is still a huge concrete jungle, and people are there for business. One positive is that it tends to have a more sophisticated nightlife. Along with bars and nightclubs, it has a big theater district, and the municipal theater has all the arts you would expect from a European capital. You really cannot feel too sorry for São Paulo. Even if it does work too hard, it also has great beaches an hour or two from the city.

Things to do, places to see

Campos do Jordão, The Switzerland of Brazil

Campos do Jordão
Source: *Amanda Viaja*, 2020

Brazilians have a strange relationship with anything cold. They generally do not like it, but some Brazilians are fascinated with it. When there is snow or ice, it is literally national news, and gives Brazilians the chance to dress warmly and complain how cold it is. For the Gringo, this behavior seems strange because we are used to much more colder climates. Brazil a tropical country, so there few areas that are cold. Some of these areas become tourist attractions for Brazilians who can get wear a lot of clothes and be cold for a change.

From this strange attraction of Brazilians to the cold, that the tourist resort of Campos de Jordão was created when it was settled by Swiss and European immigrants. Even though there is no snow or skiing, Brazilian love to come to be cold, which relatively cool but the temperature rarely gets to freezing. The city has the look of a Swiss or German mountain town and the idea is to come, ride the chair lift and explore the hills, dress for the cold of winter and enjoy hot wine, swiss fondue and the arts.

Barretos

Barretos is the capital of the Brazilian Cowboy and the center of the largest rodeo in South America. If you know anything about Rodeo you will already know that Brazilians are some of the best bull riders in the world. It is more likely that you will be surprised to see cowboys in Brazil. The cowboys in Brazil are like the cowboys in the USA but with Brazilian country music instead of the Texas two-step.

Barretos
Source: *Jornal Opção*, 2020

Paraty, Ouro Preto, and the Royal Highway

Outside of Rio is the Port of Paraty that during colonial times was used to ship gold to Portugal. What is amazing and fortunate is that when the port lost its importance the town seemed to have been stuck in time. Now this tourist resort still has all the colonial buildings. You can still travel the first road linking the colonial town of Ouro Preto where the gold was mined in Minas Gerais to the port in Paraty. Both cities are filled with charming colonial buildings. If you become a fan of Brazilian history taking a drive to both cities on the royal highway is a fun trip.

Paraty
Source: *Viaje na Viagem*, 2018

Ouro Preto
Source: *InfoEscola*

Food from the Amazon

Pirarucu fish
Source: *Live Science*, 2014

The Amazon has taken on significant importance to the world due to climate change. To foreigners this is perhaps the biggest problem facing Brazil, unfortunately Brazilians have many more pressing problems and although the vast majority of Brazilians support conserving the Amazon, they live extremely far away from the Amazon, and the Brazilians that do live in the Amazon are without many opportunities. If you are going to the Amazon it is likely you are going as a tourist. The Amazon is huge and unless you are trying to find deforestation, you will not see any deforestation. The Brazilians that you will interact with in Rio de Janeiro, São Paulo, or even in Manaus, will likely not have any interactions with Brazilians that are deforesting the Amazon. There is no point in trying to engage in arguments with the normal Brazilian about the Amazon. They likely share your ecological viewpoint and they, like you, live thousands of miles away.

The major states in the Amazon are Para and Amazonas. The Capital of Para is Belem and the Capital of Amazona is Manaus. The Amazon is huge and sparsely populated outside of these cities save for a few other small towns.

Fish is the king of Amazonian cuisine. There are dozens of exceptionally tasty species of fish: *peixe nobre* (noble fish), the *pirarucu* (the largest world freshwater fish which can grow to ten feet and weigh 450 lbs.) and the *tambaqui* are all good examples. They are big fish, almost boneless, and delicious when grilled over charcoal.

Also exceptional are smaller fish as *surubim, curimatā, jaraqui, acari,* and *tucunaré*. The freshness and the special flavor of all these Amazonian fish make the dishes based on them truly glorious. They are usually served grilled, but they can also be fried, or presented in tomato sauce (*escabeche*), or in coconut milk, or stewed in *tucupi* (a sauce made of fermented manioc juices).

Pato no tucupi (duck in tucupi sauce) is a traditional Brazilian dish found mostly in the area around the city of Belém in the state of Pará. The dish consists of a boiled duck (*pato* in Portuguese) in *tucupi*. (A sauce made from fermented cassava juice.)

Pato no tucupi
Source: *Receitas.net,* 2020

Açaí: Açaí is a berry that grows on palm trees in the middle of the Amazon. It is immensely popular, and in most of Brazil you can find açaí stands.

Eating açaí gives you a feeling of energy and happiness. The Açai fruit is very perishable so in most of Brazil this food is served as a cold dessert like a sorbet but served with fruit and granola. It is said to be a great antioxidant and have other health benefits. In Para however where the fruit is fresh and grows locally, açaí is served as a fresh thick juice, and eaten with tapioca. Where açaí is grown it is not used in desserts but instead as a staple part of a meal. In the region, if you are poor eating açaí with tapioca is a delicious and cheap way to get energy and get rid of hunger.

Açaí
Source: *Blog Eldo Gomes,* 2020

Places to see, things to do

Parintins Folklore Festival: This festival is not well known outside of Brazil but could be one of the largest productions outside of Carnival. The festival is a competition between two schools producing the folk theater presentation of "Bumba meu Boi". "Bumba meu Boi" is a folk theater about the reincarnation of an Ox and the suffering and exploitation of the people around him which is presented as a rowdy comedy. This play is performed all over the north of Brazil but only in Parintins as a contest between to schools. These presentations normally take place during the month of June. Refer to the chapter on Brazilian celebrations for more background on this play.

Bumba meu Boi
Source: *Raízes do Mundo,* 2013

The Brazilian Breadbasket: Mato Grosso, Mato Grosso do Sul, Goiás, and Tocantins

This region represents an area with the most amazing growth of agricultural production in recent decades. Settled by farmers from the southern Brazil, these regions make up a history of agricultural progress that makes Brazil one of the most important producers of agriculture in the world. Agriculture represents 25% of Brazilian GDP. This area was transformed into the breadbasket of the world only within the last 50 years. Because this region was recently colonized for farming largely by Southern Brazilians it does not have regionally specific foods. Most of the large cattle and farming operations are in this region. This is the fastest growing region in Brazil.

There are parts of these states that are wonderful to visit. Lovely waterfalls, clear streams, caves, and nature preserves all are parts of this region. However, this area is so large that you should look to a travel guide to find the wonderful areas near you. There are two nature preserves that are well known in Brazil. The Pantanal on the border between Mato Grosso and Mato Grosso do Sul, and the city of Bonito which has many natural wonders around it.

The Pantanal is the world largest wetlands hosting unique wildlife and fauna. Eighty percent of the flood plans are underwater during the rainy season. This provides a habitat for unique wildlife. There are several lodges and guides to provide help on your visits. The wetlands take up large parts of both the state of Mato Grosso and northern Mato Grosso do Sul.

Onça-pintada
Source: *All Accord Live Limitless*, 2019

Bonito, which means pretty, is a small town on the southern side of Matto Grosso do Sul. The area is known for the extraordinary nature excursions you can take around this town. When you get to Bonito you can take various day trips to caves, rivers, and waterfalls. The natural wonders are all accessible with just a short drive from the town, where you sleep and eat at night.

Bonito, Mato Grosso do Sul
Source: *Segredos de Viagem*

Every day is a different adventure. Sort of like a safari. You can take one- or two-day trips to visit the local sights and come back to the town to eat and sleep.

Chapter Five

Brazilian Relationships

Brazilians are a social and happy people, and central to this happiness is the importance of relationships in their lives. While work is important, success is important, and education in important, but strong interpersonal relationships is a cornerstone to a happy life for Brazilians. All friend, family, work, and dating relationships have a greater intensity and importance than in most other cultures. Being successful but friendless is not a goal that most Brazilians would accept. Rather, Brazilians prefer to establish strong relationships in all aspects of their lives. Brazilian life is at times precarious and strong relationships help get you through the hard times.

Family Relationships

Brazilians tend to have large extended family structures that maintain close relations with extended family on both sides of a couple's family. The husband is expected to get along with his wife's family and vice versa. It is not uncommon for multiple generations to live under the same roof. It is common that the extended family will get together for a large meal once a week. Social and economic factors can and do influence the ability for extended families to interact, but it is fair to say that although Brazilians are hardworking, if there is a question between career and family, family normally comes first. It is unusual to abandon elderly parents, who normally end up living with one of their children. Placing elderly parents in a nursing home is uncommon. The concept of a retirement community or a retirement community that restricts children would be considered peculiar or strange. Both children and the elderly are considered part of normal life and no effort is made to exclude either. The idea that a retired person would not want to interact with the rest of society or choose to live in a retirement community is like wanting to be alone. For a Brazilian these concepts are simply bizarre.

Brazilians are very fond of children. They care for and spend time with parents and other extended relations -- aunts, uncles, and cousins. In the past these relationships even extended to godparents and godchildren as well, but this relationship is losing its historical importance due to daily living in the hustle of a modern country. It is not uncommon for a married couple to live near their family. In some cultures, adult children are encouraged to leave the home and live alone; in Brazil it is common for adult children to live with their parents until they are married.

Brazilians have a reputation of being a patriarchal society where the man is head of the household, but this has not been my experience or perception. If you ask a Brazilian man who oversees his house, he will more likely than not and perhaps sheepishly admit it is his wife, especially if they have children. Now it is true that the wife does more domestic work in the house, and it is expected that the man works outside of the house, but the person who runs the household is usually the woman.

Brazilian love children and include them in all sorts of activities that they would not be included in ordinarily in other cultures. Children and families are welcome in the finest restaurants, and it would not be uncommon for the waiter to play with the child if he was not busy. Children are included in adult parties but not business dinners. Children are brought up as an integral part of the family and are expected to study and contribute to the overall welfare of the family. It is common for Brazilians to help families with small children. Families with small children can board airplanes in advance along with elderly or disabled parents. Brazilians are typically happy to rearrange seats so that families can sit together. It is also not uncommon for a stranger offer to hold a baby if the mother is with some difficulty. Brazilians tend not be authoritarian in their upbringing of children and encourage them to try multiple activities outside of school. Because many Brazilian children go to half-day classes, they usually participate in a wide variety of afterschool programs.

Brazilian children play in groups that mix a wider range of ages. As children are accepted in the adult world, they too are more accepting of children of different ages. You can see this when watching children play soccer on the beach or hanging out in shopping malls.

Children's Birthdays

Children's birthdays are huge events in comparison to other countries' standards. The entire extended family and friends, as well as classmates

Becoming Brazilian

and parents are invited. A child's birthday could have more than a hundred guests. There are buffets that specialize in these parties, and alcohol may be served, but not to the children of course!

Normally children's birthday parties, like other social events in Brazil, do not have a set time to leave. However, in the city of São Paulo this has changed. People normally leave shortly after the final birthday acknowledgement. The finale of the party comes after singing the Portuguese version of Happy Birthday, *"Para Bem para você"*. After the singing there is a customary cheer that involves shouting and clapping which is uniquely Brazilian. This cheer goes like this: the birthday boy is named Bobby for this example, replace as required.

Brazilian Portuguese	English Translation
Para Bobby Nada!	For Bobby nothing!
Tudo!	Everything!
Como que é?	How is it?
É!	It is!
É Pique E Pique, é Hora Hora Hora	It is animated, it is Time Time Time!
Ha Chim Boom!	Ha Chim Boom!
Bobby! Bobby! Bobby!	Bobby! Bobby! Bobby!

Source: the author

The most extravagant children's birthday party takes place when Brazilian girls come out to society at the age of fifteen. The fifteenth birthday, as in other Latin American countries is the age that these girls symbolically have left childhood behind. There is usually a large party and the girl is expected to waltz with her father, her date, and grandfathers. Family members typically travel to these parties if required. The parties tend to be enormous affairs with live music or DJ's, food, drinks, and of course a huge birthday cake. Mostly these parties are formal events with men in black tie and the women and girls in evening gowns. The birthday girl dresses in white. Parents of the children invited, and close family friends also attend. Drinks are served. These parties tend to last all night, and sometimes breakfast is served! The first waltz is with the father, then other male relatives and ends with the birthday girl's date. After the waltzes are done modern music comes on and the party goes till dawn. When I say that the children grow up quickly in Brazil, this give you an idea of what I mean. Brazilian boys and girls seem to avoid the awkward teenage years. Brazilian young people are given more freedom to enjoy themselves at a younger age, so they tend to grow up faster.

One of the traditions that goes in and out of fashion is a waltz which is the called the *Bolo Vivo* or live cake. There are many variations of this tradition, but all require 15 couples. In one version the friends of the birthday girl, each hold a candle and form a circle. As the birthday girl waltzes with her boyfriend or father, around the circle as the birthday girls lights the candle of each couple. As each couple's candle is lit, they join the waltz. In the end you see fifteen couples with fifteen candles waltzing together to symbolize the candles on the cake.

Figure Retratos da vida
Source: *Portal Anna Ramalho*

Working relationships

Brazilians look at work as an extension of their social life. Having a good work environment socially means Brazilian's work well naturally in teams. No one needs to teach Brazilians how to work as a team. If anyone needs extra help the coworkers automatically pitch in. In most western countries work is still organized for the most part as if it were done on an assembly line. Joe does task A, and hands off to Bill who does task B, who gives it to Mary who does task C. Rodger the supervisor reviews and signs off and gives the work to George the manager. In most western countries, if Bill is having a problem getting his work done on a Friday afternoon, Mary complains to Rodger and asks for overtime or just leaves the office at 5:00pm to see everyone on Monday. In Brazil, if Bill were having trouble getting his task done, Joe and Mary would pitch in and if there was really a problem ask Rodger for help. Rodger, knowing that vacations are coming up, uses this as a training session and everyone learns a little bit more of each other's jobs. Unless there is an emergency everyone, including Rodger and George, will work a little later so that everyone can go home together. This happens in the factories as well as in the offices. If a machine goes down, the engineers and the mechanics roll up their sleeves and solve the issue as a team.

Brazilians also tend to be particularly good with changes in technology and processes. Brazilians are used to change, and if you are introducing a new technology or process that will save time or effort and you can get the input and understanding of Brazilian workers, they will be champions of implementing and perhaps even improving your processes. If, however, they do not believe in the proposed changes or technology, it is doubtful the change will succeed. Brazilians have a saying, *para o Ingles ver*, or "for the Englishman to see!" There is an interesting story about how Brazilians came to use this phrase. This phrase came from the time of slavery when the British were trying to get the Portuguese emperor to free the slaves. Great Britain was an especially important trading partner and had gotten rid of Napoleon for the Portuguese King, but the Portuguese had no intention of freeing the slaves. So, the Portuguese enacted lots of regulations that they did not actually enforce to trick the English into thinking they were serious about liberating slaves. If Brazilians are not engaged and believe in a change, they will likely go through the motions of implementing the process, hoping the *gringo* will leave. They will do just enough for the Englishman to see!

For your project to succeed in Brazil you will need local Brazilian input. If the legal and business environment is complex, or the logistics are limited, or if there exists any other type of constraint, your Brazilian employees are a creative and ready resource to use for whatever project you may intend.

Create a Strong Personal Relationship First.

If your intention is to sell a product or introduce a product in Brazil, you will need to invest in your relationships to make progress in your business. If you are not prepared to make friends while working with, selling to, or buying from Brazilians, you are likely to fail. The basis of all friendships is trust, and trust is a necessary commodity to do business in Brazil.

It is essential to understand from the Brazilian point of view, why personal relationships in Brazil are critical in business. The Brazilian legal framework is weak, and judicial judgements and contracts can take years to enforce. Brazilians will want to size you up as a person before engaging in any business. Brazilians will spend a lot of time checking you out. It is important to show that you are educated and from a good family. You need to show interest in the Brazilians you are working with as people, not as an objective of a deal. The best protection you have in business in Brazil is your integrity and the integrity of your Brazilian counterpart. As they say in Brazil, it is better to make a bad agreement than a good fight!

Family-Owned Businesses

Most Brazilian private businesses are family run and many of them are hierarchical. This power of decision is not usually delegated outside family members or perhaps a few trusted high-level outside management employees. Some exceptionally large businesses in Brazil are run in this manner where there is little in the way of outside professional management or governance. JBS and Odebrecht were family run companies at the center of some of Brazil's largest corruption scandals. Odebrecht was the largest construction company in Brazil, and its founder was imprisoned for 18 years due to 30 million dollars in bribes in a corruption scandal called *Lava Jato* (Car Wash) which had significant political implications in Brazil. In another of JBS, a large meat processing company, two brothers who turned their father's slaughterhouse into a billion-dollar company by gaining access to government subsidized loans while allegedly making bribes to a series of individuals including the former president of Brazil. In both cases, company leadership considered these practices normal and no one on the management team could challenge them in their corporate governance.

Even in the Brazilian branches of multinational companies, employees will defer to senior Brazilian managers and may need to consult higher managers before they can decide. You as the outsider need to bring engagement to get all the voices heard prior to making a critical decision.

Nepotism: These close family ties commonly run over into business relationships. One of the drawbacks of these tightly knit family networks is nepotism. Many businesses are family owned or started, and you can understand wanting family members to be in an area of trust. Many famous large Brazilian companies, however, are family owned and a number of these large companies ended up in famous cases of corruption with the government. Family businesses in Brazil with a strong founder or close family relations in the top managements tends to curtail discussion on ethical or legal practices for the company. The patriarch of the firm assumes that business always works with overbilling and bribes and would not prosper if they did otherwise. Professional outsiders are rarely consulted or dare to speak up.

The problem of nepotism is even more common and inappropriate in government. Sadly, it is common to find family members, frequently unqualified, working in government jobs where it is never necessary to show up to work. The problem of phantom workers with ties to political family members is common and enduring in Brazilian government. The most recent well-known example is when the current president proposed his son to be ambassador to the United States. This certainly set a limit, and fortunately that name was withdrawn! Perhaps even worse is when family members show up to work to continue political dynasties. The Sarney Family in Maranhão, the ACM family in Minas Gerais, and the Collar family in Pernambuco are all examples of entrenched political oligarchs. We will address political corruption in a later chapter, but it is significant to note that nepotism played a significant role in the political scandals that have rocked Brazil this decade, both from private industry as well as the government and political parties, and in all levels of the government.

Romantic Relationships

Visitors frequently make the mistake of assuming that there are lots of casual sexual relationships in Brazil, but you will find that even short physical relationships need to have a romantic component in Brazil. All relationships are taken seriously in Brazil, so why would romantic relationships be any different? On the contrary, romantic relationships in Brazil quickly become not only the central point of existence between the two partners but quickly evolve to include the other relationships in the two partners lives. Non-Brazilians will be surprised at the extent to which a romantic relationship impacts the friends, family, and coworkers of the couple. Brazilians have developed a social contract that formalizes these stages. It is important for a foreigner to understand these stages as the relationship progresses. Before you notice it, you will know your partner's friends and your partner will know your friends. Then your partner's friends will know your friends. If the relationship continues these connections will expand to family. Sooner than you could imagine it will seem that everyone in your live knows or participates in your romantic relationship, and this is quite intense for someone not used to it. So, far from casual relationships, Brazilian romantic relationships tend to become the focal point of a person's existence.

This is a notably different Brazilian paradigm from most other societies in the world. In most societies, people try to get a good job and hope that this allows them to attract and find a good mate. Brazilian focus is on all relationships in general, and especially romantic relationships, to have a good life. Brazilians have specific stages and definitions to describe the level of commitment in a romantic relationship. The interaction with friends and family is so important to the development of the relationship because this helps develop and define the how the group defines the relationship level. If you get into a Brazilian romantic relationship, the definition of the level of intensity of the romance, should be a guide for your commitment to that relationship.

All Brazilian romantic relationships, even short ones, have a passionate component to it. Brazilian romantic relationships tend to progress at a very rapid pace. Brazil has a tropical climate, it is a beach culture, and people try to stay in good shape. Brazilians tend to dress revealingly, so you have all the ingredient to spark a romantic relationship. Brazilians take all their relationships seriously so even if you have a short-term relationship it will still be meaningful. Even a one-night stand will need to have a romantic component. All the modern dating apps are used in Brazil, and there are single bars, so it is easy for a foreigner to enter a relationship in Brazil. Brazil simply does not have, however, a hook-up culture. The idea of just having sex for sex is not a Brazilian concept. Other cultures have friends with benefits or booty calls and the closest Brazilian equivalent is *ficar*, or literally "to stay". But *ficar* does not imply a level of physical intimacy but a level of emotional intimacy. A booty call is explicitly sexual without emotional attachment. *Ficar* denotes an undeclared emotional attachment with an undefined physical intimacy. You may have only kissed or slept with a Brazilian partner but the kiss or the sex denotes the status *"ficar"* only because something physical happened to signal the beginning of a relationship. The concept of *ficar* is itself more romantic because a kiss if viewed in this way is a symbol of a promised intimacy in the future. The simple act of kissing puts you in the status of *ficante* but having sex in with a new person also gives the status of *ficante*. Brazilian men and women like the social engagement of flirting and do not like the idea of a purely sexual relationship. Do not misunderstand me, Brazilians love sex and there is a great deal of physical intimacy in a Brazilian relationship. However, from the perspective of both the man and the woman there needs to be meaning and romance in a relationship, even if it is for a short time. For the man, he needs to feel that he is seductive in his pursuit. The woman wants to be pursued and flattered and be the center of his attention. The idea of a hook-up is unappealing, especially to a woman. However once in a relationship, the speed of development and level of intensity will sometimes surprise the you if you are not from Brazil. The best thing to do is to know certain ground rules and enjoy the adventure.

Romantics Stages

Brazilians have a universal language for romantic relationships. There are strong social conventions, expected social behavior, and obligations at each stage. How you are referred to and what stage you are in in any given relationship provide important clues on how serious the relationship is and what your obligations are. Brazilians take all their relationships seriously, and your romantic relationships are no different. Here are the standard words and descriptions of the levels and status of a relationship:

Levels of commitment and other useful words for Brazilian romantic relationships

- *Paquera*. *Paquerar* means to flirt. So, someone you like or are flirting with is a *'paquera'*.

- *Cantar*. This literally means to sing, and in romantic slang it is a stronger word than flirt, usually meaning trying to seduce.

- *Ficante*. From the verb *Ficar* or to stay. As in someone you are staying with. This is as close as you are going to get with a non-committed relationship, but the term implies an intermediate stage between flirting and making a commitment. The relationship either moves forward or it stops. We are just *ficando* (Staying together for now).

- *Estar de rolo* or *enrolado*. This is an intermediate stage between *Ficar* and *Namorar*. If you are being with the same person but are not ready to admit it, you are *"estar de rolo"* The next stage requires you knowing each other's friends and hanging out together, so in this way it is more an intermediate stage between having a relationship and having a commitment. At this stage if you break up there will be a fight but no drama.

- *Namorar* or *Namorado*. This stage is a big deal in Brazil. It means her friends and yours like both of you. You have likely met parents. You go on dates. This relationship may be announced, and you introduce each other with the term, *Namorado/a*. You are seeing this person exclusively. At this stage breaking up is going to have lots of drama.

- *Noivo /Noiva*. You are engaged. Brazilians do not normally make surprise engagements. Usually, couples and their families discuss this decision and if they are going to get engaged the couple usually buy matching rings. Typically, rings are exchanged and worn on the right hand. Brazil is too dangerous to use diamond rings in public, so they use gold bands. While you are engaged you use the right hand for the ring, when you are married you use the left hand for the ring.

- *Marido/Mulher*. Husband and wife. Used for religious, civil, or common law marriages.

- *Amante*. This is the term given to an extramarital partner. Even though the word means lover literally, it is a pejorative term in Brazil.

- *Cornudo/a*. This word translates to "horns," and used to describe the person being cheated on.

- *Saudades.* Use this word to get an immediate result and impact from your Brazilian partner. It is a powerful word and a word that Brazilians prize because there is no word like it in other languages. The word conveys the feeling you have when you miss someone or something or some time or event in the past. It is not a verb, so *saudades* does not mean "I miss you." It is a noun, it is the state of being or longing for someone, or the feeling of nostalgia or the blues. *Eu tenho saudades de você.* If I had to translate it would be, "I have the longing of your absence and the nostalgia of when we were together!"

- *Apaixonar.* It is a verb that means the act of falling in love.

- *Magoar.* This term means to hurt someone's feelings. Brazilian relationships are so intense that they have a verb specifically for hurting feelings. *Magoar* is to hurt someone emotionally, not physically.

Brazilians tend to be possessive and can be jealous. As a foreigner, especially accompanied by a Brazilian, you will be a center of attention and many more eyes will be on you than you are used too. Your partner will, except for an exclusively same-sex outing, not want to leave your side. There are benefits to this. One is that Brazilians are very affectionate and kiss and hug in public. Not just pecks on the cheeks but big sloppy kisses too. If you have aversion to public displays of affection you are going to need to get over it. This will make your partner more comfortable, and you get to enjoy the benefits. It is common for couples to sit side by side in restaurants, married couples usually sit together in a group. Also, say nice things to your partner. Call him or her *querido/a* (Dear,) or *Meu bem* (my treasure) because pet names are good.

Jealousy and Cheating in Brazilian relationships

When you are in a relationship with a Brazilian it will be wonderful but perhaps a little overwhelming. Brazilians tend to pay a lot of attention to their romantic relationships. Because you are the foreigner, all eyes will be on you. Romantic relationships are important to Brazilian identity so Brazilians can be jealous and with you as a foreigner you will be the center of attention, not just for your partner but for others. There will be many an opportunity for cheating for both sexes while you are in a Brazilian relationship. It is natural for your Brazilian partner to be jealous. The Portuguese used to say there was no sin south of the equator, and the stereotype of macho Brazilian men and attractive Brazilian women seems to support this. Brazilians, however, simply value their romantic relationships more than others, and as a result are more jealous. Breakups are more dramatic. That there is more fun, romance, and drama in a Brazilian romantic relationship is undeniable!

Meme
Source: Antonio Guillem, *iStockphoto/Getty Images*

Cheating is not OK in Brazil, so my advice is to use the level of commitment that is listed above as a guide to your behavior. You can go to a club and kiss five people and not cheat, however if you kiss someone and you are in a relationship where you refer to your partner as *namorado*, or *namorada*, you will cause great drama and pain. Cheating with another person's partner is also dangerous in Brazil. Traditionally Brazilian law allowed the defense of honor to be used as a legal defense in crimes of passion. Defending one's honor in Brazil can literally get you killed.

Motels

Motels are a uniquely Brazilian institution, not be confused with Motor Hotels in other countries. It is not uncommon for adult children to live with their parents until marriage. Motels in Brazil are designed specifically for romantic encounters. Motels in Brazil are not motor hotels as in the U.S. but instead are establishments dedicated to enhancing the sexual experience, and this is part of mainstream Brazilian culture and practice. Married couples will occasionally use motels to spice up their love life and take a break from the kids. Extraordinary rooms are rented for short periods of time. Rooms can include pools, steam saunas, hot tubs, as well as a full-service bar and a restaurant that will send food and drink to your room through a dumbwaiter. If you want to try this adventure, make sure to go to a top-rated motel and you will not be disappointed.

Ending a romantic relationship.

So long as human history has existed, no one has come up with a good way to end a relationship. This goes for Brazilian society as well. The best that can be done is offer some advice on how to end a relationship less badly. All relationships end with someone who being abandoned and someone ending the relationship. If you are ending the relationship you may suffer feelings of guilt. If you are the person being left, you will suffer the misery of rejection and perhaps blame yourself for the failed relationship. However, being a foreigner in either circumstance provides both benefits and responsibilities in Brazil. You as a foreigner in a Brazilian relationship are in a unique position. You, as a foreigner, are away from your home, and with this status should come certain challenges, opportunities, and ethical responsibilities. Here is some advice for those who have their hearts broken and break hearts in Brazil.

If you as the foreigner are being left, then there is no difference in how you should behave in your home country, you are the one with the broken heart and suffering is universal. However, being in Brazil can make the pain easier to deal with. You will feel the misery of rejection and you may feel isolated and blame yourself, but Brazilian society provides a safety net for broken hearts. Try to go out with your friends and share your feelings. Romantic relationships are central to Brazilians and they will always give you helpful advice and sympathy. You do not have to go through your break-up alone. Avoid speaking badly about your ex-partner even though sometimes this is impossible and even though it might make you feel better to get it off your chest, do not dwell on your ex-partner. Try to avoid contact with your ex. This is more difficult in Brazil especially if your relationship was at an advanced stage of development, because you and your ex now share a network of friends. You need to move on and avoiding contact with your ex-partner is the only way to shorten your period of misery. On the bright side you are a foreigner in Brazil, and this implies a certain social value and that can help you get back on your feet. I fully agree that reflecting on and learning from failed relationships are important to your personal development and improve your ability to have more meaningful relationships in the future. Feel free to feel bad for as long as you need. It will eventually dawn on you that you are in Brazil, and there are many more wonderful people for you to meet. Brazil gives you the ability to have fun relationships without being serious. Remember you can just *ficar* with somebody, and that may be the best cure for a broken heart.

If you are a foreigner who is leaving a Brazilian, you have an ethical duty to analyze the level of relationship that you have established and act accordingly to avoid unnecessary heartbreak and drama. Perhaps the best advice is to not let the relationship progress to stages that you are not prepared to support. Brazilian relationships progress in stages in Brazilian culture. Stopping a relationship at the *rolo* or *ficante* stage is not very traumatic and your partner likely will have gone through this before. The problem is that Brazilians are incredibly attractive and romantic, and it is easy for a relationship to progress to the *namorado* stage without you realizing it or understanding what it signifies. For this reason, you should use the Portuguese words for the stages of your relationship to describe your situation. Do not use the word *namorado* or *namorada* unless you mean it. The word *ficante* can used for a less serious relationship than what is implied by *namorado* and *namorada* in Brazil.

Do not let other people call your relationship using the words *namorado* unless you have agreed to this with your partner. *Namorando* means that you are in an exclusive relationship with the intention that this relationship develops into something even more serious. It is not a relationship to be entered into lightly if you are a foreigner. You need to have a serious conversation with your partner prior to using this term. Remember, if you still think you are going back to your home country unaccompanied, you should likely avoid this sort of relationship. It is at this stage of *namoro* in Brazil where you and your partner start to develop the social network of friends and family that does not necessarily happen when you have a girlfriend/boyfriend relationship in other countries. Being engaged or *noivo* is a profoundly serious relationship in all cultures and breaking these relationships have profoundly serious and similar consequences in most cultures.

As a foreigner leaving a Brazilian partner, communication is the key to a good and ethical breakup. Good communication is the key to an ethical breakup. It reduces stress, misery, and despair. As a foreigner you have an elevated social status in Brazil, and with that comes responsibilities. You need to communicate in advance if you plan to end a relationship and this communication should be in person. You owe it to your partner to take some responsibility for the breakup and help ease them through their disappointment. Do not just disappear or break up with a text message, it is unethical. You need to protect your partner's dignity and not complain about them to others. It is important to establish boundaries at this stage to reduce contact and drama. Remember, in Brazil your relationship status is known not only to you and your partner but also to most of your friends and her friends. How you act not only eases the misery and damage to self-esteem of your partner, but it also reflects on you. If you can remain friends after a breakup, you have done a great job.

Chapter Six

Brazilian Faith and Spirituality

With the overthrow of the Brazilian Monarchy, the Brazilian constitution eliminated state religion in Brazil. However, most people continued following the Catholic faith. Sometimes this faith is mixed with other minority beliefs which makes Brazil such a dynamic place. Three quarters of Brazilians are Catholic and even though there is no longer an official state religion, many Brazilian holidays are also Catholic holidays. Brazil is also home to many different religions due to the incredibly rich influence in its culture. This is a brief overview of uniquely Brazilian spirituality.

Catholicism

When the Portuguese arrived in Brazil in the 16th century, Catholicism was the only religion they practiced. They declared Catholicism the official religion of Brazil, and that mandate remained until the monarchy was overthrown in 1888. In 1589 the King of Portugal sent Jesuits to Brazil. What happened next depends on your point of view. Seen positively, the Jesuits created large communal societies, educated, and converted the Guarani Indians, and protected them from the Portuguese and Spanish colonists. Seen another way, the Jesuits forced Christianity on the indigenous populations and used their labor for large agricultural operations. Anyone who saw the movie "The Mission" starring Robert De Niro recalls it depicted the expulsion of the Jesuits and their missions by the Spanish and Portuguese in 1759. However, during the period 1589 to 1759 one of the most ambitious experiments in human interaction took place. The Jesuit missionaries decided to create communally governed agricultural societies with the Guarani Indians. This was in sharp contrast to prevailing Portuguese colonial policy at the time who aim was to use the Indians as slave labor.

Many missions were created in an area that overlaps the borders of what is today Argentina, Paraguay, and Brazil. From the ruins here you can see that the native Guarani language had been translated into a written language. Bibles were translated and printed to this indigenous language, so it is safe to assume that the Jesuits were actively educating the Guaranis. The churches were decorated by local artisans; that, plus the fact that these churches are still intact and well-preserved after hundreds of years gives one hope that a peaceful, communal society was created then. When visiting the falls of Iguaçu, it is worth a side trip to see one of these missions.

Today most Brazilians are still Catholic, however in recent years evangelical and fundamentalist Christian churches have gained many adherents. Perhaps because of this competition, many Catholic masses have adopted characteristics of evangelical services, incorporating live bands and much singing. Some Catholic priests have mega church services which are televised on Sundays.

Another characteristic of Brazilian religion is the blending of the Catholic faith with other religions and practices. Catholicism is predominant but there are also people who practice mixtures of Afro-Brazilian religions in the country which influence a mixture of celebrations. As the images of many Saints are adored in both Catholic and Afro-Brazilian religions, it is hard to tell where one religion ends and the other begins. Today most Brazilians Catholics tend not to be dogmatic about their beliefs. Brazilians tend to emphasize faith and celebration over rules and dogma. For example, at a celebration of a saint's day you will see traditional Catholic and Afro-Brazilian celebrations at the same time. For example, New Year's celebrations see a mix the celebrations of the Virgin Mary and the African goddess *Iemanjá,* and Brazilian traditions for this holiday are a blend of both religions.

Protestantism

Brazilians tend to call all Protestants *Evangélicos.* The traditional protestant churches arrived with the European immigrants of the last century. Just like the European protestant churches, they more recently have been losing members. You can still find traditional protestant churches in the bigger cities. These Churches are easily identifiable due their traditional appearance.

What has made big progress are a series of new churches that are better described as evangelical or fundamentalist churches. These churches are located everywhere; you will find them in office blocks or store fronts, in the *favelas,* and in the country. These new churches are rapidly growing and becoming a political force. More than 20% of Brazilians now are protestant and this number is growing. Many of these new protestant churches originated in Brazil. Unlike the stereotypical image of Brazilians as partying free spirits, some of these churches are very conservative and require conservative dress for its congregation. The churches provide Brazilians a social platform to help promote each of its members to better themselves. These churches are always looking to increase their congregation size.

The strict conduct demanded by the conservative churches combined with a competition for new members has led to growing popularity of a newer style of protestant churches in Brazil. New churches with more relaxed codes of conduct have started to pop up everywhere in Brazil. It is not uncommon to see on one city block several different Brazilian protestant churches.

Afro-Brazilian Religions: Learn the difference between Candomblé, Umbanda and Macumba

For the most part there is religious tolerance in Brazil. Even though there is a certain prejudice against some religions (for example Afro-Brazilian religions, and Spiritualism, not to mention atheism,) hate crimes related to religion in Brazil are rare. Many Brazilians categorize these beliefs together, but they are different. Even though the number of adherents that openly admit to practicing these religions is small, they have had a large impact on Brazilian culture. If you stay in Brazil, you will eventually come across a shop that sells trinkets for these religions; and you inevitably will happen upon an offering made to the deities of these religions, who are called *Orisha* or *Orixás,*[32] perhaps while walking on the beach or near a park.

Because there remains a great deal of discrimination, many Brazilian who follow these religions identify as Catholic in public. There unfortunately is good reason for this; followers of Afro-Brazilian religions historically have been persecuted. This has led to the adoption and incorporation of images of Catholic saints into the Afro-Brazilian religions to represent its various African gods and spirits. Even though there relatively few openly declared practitioners of the Afro-Brazilian religions, there remains a strong cultural impact from these religions in Brazilian celebrations.

---

[32] Wikipedia, "Orisha". Available in: https://en.wikipedia.org/wiki/Orisha. Access in: 24 oct. 2020.

Candomblé

During the years of slavery in Brazil, Candomblé was introduced by Nigerian and Benin slaves coming into the country. Many times, you will see this religion and the Catholic religion co-exist in an odd manner. Slave owners were almost always Catholic. They wanted their slaves to convert, but of course the slaves wanted to keep their own religion.

Although having multiple spirits and deities, Candomblé claims to be a monotheistic religion. Practitioners of Candomblé believe in one all-powerful deity called Oludumaré who is served by lesser deities.[33] These deities are honored with "gifts" such as songs, dances, special clothes, vegetables, and the sacrifice of hens, pigeons, sheep, and goats.

As an attempt to escape from religious persecution, African slaves used elements from Catholicism as a disguise when worshiping their own god and deities. To appease their owners and keep from getting in trouble, slaves likened their religious practices to Catholic ones and identified their deities called *Orixas* with saints of the Catholic faith. Their goddess of the sea, Iemanja, is depicted with an image like the Virgin Mary and their god named *Oxala* was given the image of Jesus Christ.

The usage of Catholic images and symbols ended up being incorporated into Candomblé but was not enough to avoid persecutions from Christians and government members who saw the religion as pagan and witchcraft.[34] Government persecution continued until as recently as the 1970's. Candomblé and Catholicism are still intertwined to this very day in Brazilian religion.

Umbanda

Umbanda is a totally Brazilian religion founded in the early 1900's, based on Catholicism, Spiritualism, as well as Indigenous and African religions.[35] Umbanda followers believe in the existence of a supreme god named *Zumbi*. It preaches fraternity, charity, and respect to others.[36] Umbanda incorporates the practice of mediumship as a means of contact between

---

[33] BBC,"Beliefs,"February2,2007.Available: https://www.bbc.co.uk/religion/religions/candomble/beliefs/beliefs.shtml. Access on: 3/10/2021

[34] Wikipedia, "Candomblé". Available in: https://en.wikipedia.org/wiki/Candomblé#Reception_and_influence. Access in: 22 oct. 2020.

[35] ReligionFacts.org, "Umbanda". Available in: http://www.religionfacts.com/umbanda. Access in: 28 oct. 2016.

[36] *Ibidem.*

Becoming Brazilian

the physical and the spiritual world. The mediums are called *Mae do Santos*, Mother of Saints, or *Pai do Santos*, Father of Saints. These same terms are also used for the leaders of Candomblé. Some of the sprits of Umbanda are quite influential in Brazilian culture. Two Umbanda spirits are well known to all Brazilians. Though she goes by many names, the spirit *Pomba Gira* is famous for expressing female sexuality.[37] The *Malandro* is a also an Umbanda spirit as well as Brazilian cultural male icon. A Brazilian *malandro* is man who celebrates a life of fast living and uses all sorts of ways to get ahead in life. This archetype is celebrated in Samba, Brazilian Literature, and Carnival. In Umbanda, the spirit named *Ze Pelintra* personifies what Brazilian call *Malandro*.[38] Walt Disney created during a visit to the Copacabana Palace a comic character call Ze Carioca based on the Malandro, perhaps best thought of as a Brazilian "Bad Boy"

Umbanda is based on the pursuit of a peaceful life and respect to humankind and nature. Animal sacrifice is not practiced in Umbanda. Umbanda followers endeavor to respect all different beliefs, regardless of religion. However, its followers still suffer a great prejudice in Brazil, especially because many Brazilians believe that all African religions are directly connected to witchcraft.

Macumba is a Brazilian catch-all phrase, not a religion

Macumba is not a religion per se, but you might be led to believe it is. Brazilians use the term as if it were a religion like *Umbanda* or *Candomblé*. *Macumba* is a general term used by Brazilians who do not practice an African religion. The term *Macumba* is used to describe all Afro-Brazilian religions or anything that seems to have a magical element. *Macumba* is sometimes used as a derogatory term, but it really is just a phrase created in the last century cover all the different practices.[39]

While most Brazilians do not practice an Afro-Brazilian religion, most respect them. Practitioners of *Candomblé* and *Umbanda* leave offerings on streets and in parks. If you happen upon an offering like what is shown below, do not touch it. Brazilians for the most part are tolerant of each other's beliefs. Part of becoming Brazilian is being tolerant of these beliefs and the beliefs of others. Many Brazilian customs such as jumping seven

---

[37] Available in: https://en.wikipedia.org/wiki/Pomba_Gira viewed. Access in: 26 oct. 2020.
[38] Available in: https://pt.wikipedia.org/wiki/Z%C3%A9_Pelintra. Access in: 26 oct. 2020.
[39] Verdades sobre o candomblé | Jornal Carlos Lima - Jornal da Povo (cljornal.com.br) viewed 3/10/2021

waves on New Year's and wearing good luck bracelets are rooted in Afro Brazilian culture. So, when you find yourself in the ocean at midnight on New Year's Eve, feel free to thank *Iemanjá!*

Figure Verdades sobre o candomblé
Jornal Carlos Lima - Jornal da Povo (cljornal.com.br)
Macumba
Source: *Carlos Lima Jonal On-line*, 2016

Brazilian Spiritualism- Espiritismo

Have you ever heard of Allan Kardec or Chico Xavier? If you are not from Brazil it is unlikely. Largely forgotten in his home country, Allan Kardec was a Frenchman who created a theory that spirits could communicate and interact with the physical world. He developed these theories in the second half of the 19th century when seances were quite popular. Kardec claimed that during these seances spirits conveyed to him how the spiritual world and the physical world coexisted. He professed that God had created a universe composed of spirit and matter, and therefore, of two worlds: the visible human sphere and the realm of invisible souls. People pass back and forth from both worlds though death and reincarnation. Since these spirits were imperfect when created, Kardec believed in the need for their moral and intellectual evolution through time toward their inevitable union with God.[40]

These ideas caught on in Brazil, where they were further developed by several Brazilian mediums, the most famous of which was Chico Xavier. Chico Xavier was born in Minas Gerais, and reportedly and famously had the ability to communicate with spirits from the time he was a child to his death in 2002. This ability to communicate with spirits made him famous, and many Brazilians, both celebrities as well as common people, would seek his aid to communicate with those who had passed. Xavier published more than 400 books which he claimed he never wrote. Rather these books were written by several spirits who used him as a medium for writing these books. Chico Xavier's abilities dovetailed with the theoretical beliefs of Alan Kardec. Spiritualism in Brazil grew and today there are about 5 million believers. It is hard to be sure about this number because spiritualist beliefs overlap Christianity, or at least they are not mutually exclusive. Brazilians who are spiritualist will also claim to be Christian. Xavier appeared on Brazilian national TV and became famous. He was awarded many honors including being recognized as being the most important Brazilian by SBT television network in 2012.[41] Despite his fame he always led a simple life.

Spiritists, the practitioners of spiritualism believe that spiritual and physical health can be achieved through the practice of charity, the study of Spiritist books, by receiving and giving spiritual energy, or by interacting with the spirits. Spiritist meetings usually take place at centers where believers congregate to teach the doctrine to the spirits that manifest themselves, conduct physical and spiritual treatment of members, and hear lectures. These centers are called *casa de espirito*, where the adherents conduct these spiritual healings. The centers practices vary depending upon the medium running the service.

Santo Daime

Perhaps the most exotic native Brazilian religion is Santo Daime. Santo Daime is a purely Brazilian religion. The practice is based upon eating *ayahuasca*. *Ayahuasca* is a tea that comes from combining a mixture of roots and plants to create a psychoactive tea. This natural version of *Ayahuasca*

---

[40] Wikipedia, "Allan Kardec," October 13, 2020. Available at https://en.wikipedia.org/wiki/Allan_Kardec
[41] Wikipedia, "Chico Xavier," October 28, 2020. Available at https://pt.wikipedia.org/wiki/Chico_Xavier

is made from plants that can only be found in the Amazon.[42] *Ayahuasca* can also be found in other countries of South America. Santo Daime combines Christian beliefs with Spiritual and Indian religious elements. *Ayahuasca*, referred to as *Daime* within the practice, and containing several psychoactive compounds, is drunk as part of the ceremony. The drinking of *Daime* can induce a strong emetic effect which is embraced as both an emotional and physical purging. By physically purging, let me be clear, you likely will throw up after taking *Ayahuasca*!

The founder of this religion, an Afro-Brazilian named Mestre Irineu, took *Ayahuasca* and experienced a spiritual event, which inspired him to use it as a central practice in his ceremonies.[43] Just as some North Americans natives use peyote, the South American natives likely used Ayahuasca for centuries. Like Peyote, you will likely become physically sick and throw up prior to feeling any effect. Also, there are many rules regarding this ceremony which merge several religious practices about diet and abstinence prior to participating. Experimenting with the practices of Santo Daime is not to be taken lightly. Normally you must be invited to take part in this ceremony.

---

[42] The Brazilian Report, "Ayahuasca puts Brazil on the shamanic tourism map," May 9, 2019. Available in https://brazilian.report/tourism/2019/05/05/ayahuasca-brazil-shamanic-tourism/. Access in: March 14, 2021
[43] *Ibidem*.

Chapter Seven

Knowing Brazil though its Celebrations

Brazilians love to celebrate and celebrations are great way to learn about this diverse country. Celebrations are ways for Brazilians to step outside their day-to-day lives and become part of something bigger. By now you should know that Brazilians are very social people and when they come to party, they do it to enjoy themselves. A simple celebration or Saturday night out may end up as one of the best nights you have ever had. If you get a chance to participate in one of these celebrations it will be memorable.

Brazilian Exceptionalism: Music and Celebrations

Music is a cornerstone of Brazilian culture and celebration. The fusion of African and European cultures created many musical genres that are unique to Brazil. Music is part of celebrations in Brazil, but Brazilians also are brought together by music in their daily life. Brazilians make a habit of singing together familiar songs from various Brazilian artists. To become Brazilian, you need at least an overview of the major musical styles of Brazil. To start with, the most famous rhythms are associated with these musical styles.

Samba and related music: The most famous music from Brazil is samba. Samba needs to be divided into smaller categories because although the rhythm is the same, the sound is quite different. Originating with African rhythms, samba is the genre of music most associated with Brazil, yet it was not always this way.

- *Carnaval* **samba:** The rhythms of samba are part of the history of *Carnaval*, and one type of samba played with brass instruments is called *Carnaval* samba. During *Carnaval* you will see brass bands playing samba songs from a century ago. The samba schools play samba rhythms during the *Carnaval* parades. In the case of Samba schools, the song is new each year and usually represents a theme for that individual samba school's parade. Samba schools play a variety of percussion instruments. Both types of samba are very loud, and you hear this type of samba only during *Carnaval*.

- *Modern samba:* This is the type of samba you have heard listening to Brazilian music today. It started in the 1950s. It is jazzy and melodic and is still commonly played in bars. Some of the most famous artists include Cartola, Zeca Pagodinho, and Martinho da Vila.

- *Choro: Choro* in Portuguese means to cry but the music is happy. The music started in the 19th century in Rio, so some say that the music predates samba, but *choro* has a rhythm like samba, and merges musical styles using European classical instruments such as guitars, and flutes, with Brazilian instruments such as *cavaquinho* and *pandeiro e reco-reco*, adding in a samba beat. This music shows the mixture of European and African cultures.

- *Pagode:* Musically it is hard to find a difference between samba and *pagode*, but for many Brazilians there is a difference. These differences seem more social and cultural than musical. When samba started it was looked down upon by the upper classes. Over time, however, samba became more sophisticated and was admired internationally. As samba gained international acceptance, upper-class Brazilians began to accept samba in the 1970s. Though samba was at last widely accepted it soon became popular to play for Europeans in nightclubs. *Pagode* then took the place of samba as a music to be played while eating and drinking in bars, with simple lyrics and heartfelt singing by common Brazilians. Brazilians will insist that these musical genres are different, but if you ask them for a good explanation why there are different, you will not get a good answer. Perhaps the lyrics are simpler, but the instruments and the rhythm are mostly the same.

- *Bossa Nova: Bossa nova* started out as a new way to play and sing samba. *Bossa nova* is a Brazilian musical movement from the late 1950's made popular by João Gilberto, Tom Jobim, Vinícius de Moraes, and countless other middle-class young singers and/or songwriters from the south area of Rio de Janeiro. *Bossa Nova* has very sophisticated chords and rhythms. Foreigners like to compare *Bossa Nova* to Jazz, but the roots of *Bossa Nova* are *Samba* without any outside influence of Jazz.

These other forms a Brazilian music have different beats and traditions:

- *Axé:* This music comes from Bahia. It dominates the radio in Bahia. *Axé* mixes the fast rhythms of the northeast such as *frevo*, *forró* and *maracatu*. There is also a strong bass line like in reggae or ska music. The word *Axé* was a greeting in west African languages that slaves used. It means good vibrations. It is all good. Bahia does not have samba parades but has large street parties where the bands ride on top of converted buses and play *axe*. In Bahia they dance carnival to *axé* not *samba*.

- *Frevo:* In the state of Pernambuco, *Carnival* is about *frevo*. *Frevo* is rapid dance and music. The word *frevo* is like the word meaning "boiling" in Portuguese and that is what the music and dance are like. Think about if you had to jump up and down to keep your feet from burning, or the speed of the bubble of rapidly boiling water. That is a rather good description of *frevo*.

- *Forró: Forró* is music that originated in northeastern Brazil. The word forró refers also to a couple's dance as well as the event where this dancing happens. As for the origin of the name, there is a story that while this music was becoming popular in the 1940's in northeastern Brazil, American soldiers were stationed in the same area for World War II. According to this story forró came from the English words "for all." Another version of this story was that English engineers working on the railroad at the turn of the century would throw dance parties "for all" and that term became adopted for the music and the dance. The musical form and dance quickly became popular all over Brazil. The dancing is enjoyable, and the music reminds you of folk or country music, but the time is kept by beating a metal triangle and the melody is played from an accordion.

- *Sertanejo: Sertanejo* is Brazilian country music. Once again, there are no direct influences from American country music or bluegrass.

Sertanejo developed in the back country of Brazil independent of foreign influences. Many of the most popular groups are duos. Like country music in the United States, *sertanejo* popularity is widespread throughout Brazil but particularly in the countryside. The themes of the music are comparable to American country music: heavy on broken hearts, romance, drinking too much, and life in the countryside.

- **Funk:** Brazilian Funk grew out of the *favelas* of Rio de Janeiro. Despite its name it does not sounds anything like American funk of the 1970's, but its lyrics are analogous to American rap or hip hop. Like rap and hip hop, this music has many sexual and violent themes. The music is performed at parties called *baile funk* which are popular in the inner city.

Carnaval

Carnaval is easily the biggest celebration in the world and the biggest *Carnaval* is in Brazil. *Carnaval* is one celebration, but each city has developed its own unique character. Many cities in Brazil have *Carnaval*, but the main cities for *Carnaval* are Rio de Janeiro, Salvador Recife, Ouro Preto and most recently São Paulo.

In Brazil, a county of great inequality, during *Carnaval* the poor dress as kings. The rich come to the street to party with the poor. Women are celebrated as queens, the men dress as women, and women dress to be seen and noticed. It is a celebration where poor are rich, weak are strong, and women are exalted and praised. It is a world turned upside down and provides an escape for a few days from the very real social injustices that exist the rest of the year. If there is a sociological explanation for this paradox it may be found in the history of *Carnaval*.

Some holidays can be traced to Roman and pagan festivals. For example, the timing of Christmas was clearly designed to coincide with the Roman festival of Saturnalia as well as the pagan festivals for the solstice. We see evidence of this in one of the best-known symbols of Christmas: the famous decorating of a Christmas tree. Although a tourist could be forgiven for thinking the origins of *Carnival* are pagan, they would be mistaken. Attempts to link *Carnival* to an ancient Pagan or Roman festival do not have a good historical basis. But the origins of *Carnival* are found in the Catholic religion and the Catholic liturgical calendar. *Carnival* ends on the day of Ash Wednesday before the forty days of Lent. These are the forty days when Christ resisted temptation prior to being crucified on Good Friday. The word *Carnival* comes from the folk saying, *carne vale*, which translates to "say goodbye to beef." Either way, this implies a period of fasting. But *carne* also means flesh. After *Carnaval,* we take away flesh in the sexual sense, as a of a period of abstinence. *Carnaval* is not only a party of eating and drinking, but also a party celebrating sex. Participants during *Carnaval* can be pardoned for sexual transgressions in the same way they can be for drinking too much. It can all be blamed on *Carnaval*!

Venetian Carnival, 1879
Source: Vincent G. Stiepevich

Carnaval ends on midnight the Tuesday before Ash Wednesday, which starts 40 days of fasting for lent. The term Mardi Gras in French means Fat Tuesday and is the name of the celebration in the Creole population of the United States. One big difference between Mardi Gras and *Carnaval* simply comes down to geography; while they are celebrated at the same time, Mardi Gras takes place in winter in New Orleans, Venice, the Caribbean islands, while in Brazil *Carnaval* takes place in Summer.

Not all Brazilians love or go crazy for *Carnaval*. Some people think it is too much to handle, others are deeply religious and seek sanctuary before Lent. There are Brazilians that take advantage of *Carnaval* to leave the country or rent their house to tourists during the festival. Some cities in Brazil do not even celebrate *Carnaval*. *Carnaval* unofficially goes for a few weeks or longer, but despite the months of partying, the official state holiday of *Carnaval* is just one day.

There is something inherently irreverent or non-conformist about *Carnaval*. From its origins *Carnaval* seems to have questioned authority. Sometimes the authorities win, most of the time the authorities give up and submit to the mostly harmless revelry that mocks the established order. *Carnaval* itself is not a religious holiday. It is a folk holiday which purposely reverses the intention of the official church holiday. Just as Halloween celebrates the Eve of All Saints Day with witches, devils, ghosts, and tricks, *Carnaval* acknowledges the spiritual need to sacrifice during Lent paradoxically with indulgent food, drink, and pleasure, to prepare for the inevitable lack of earthly fun for the next forty days. There is something subversive in *Carnaval*, as the common people thumb their noses at authority. At the time of *Carnaval's* inception, religious authority and civil authority were not truly separate; as a result, many *Carnaval* traditions subvert all authority. Normally, the state permitted this tradition, and the elites joined the fun with the plebeians.

The first true Carnival took place in Venice, Italy. It is still the home of the best Carnival in Europe and inspired many of the characteristics of Brazilian *Carnaval*. The Venetian Carnival was popular. Its origin stems from a celebration that occurred after the liberation of the Venetian Republic in 1163. Upon hearing of the victory, gathering and dancing took place in St. Marcos Square also.[44] The wearing of masks at *Carnaval* also comes from Venice. Venice as a republic had a merchant class as well as nobility. It became fashionable to use masks to hide your identity and class rank. The nobility objected to this practice and tried to restrict the use of masks. The first known restricted use of masks was in the 13th century when authorities outlawed their use for young men who had a habit of throwing scented eggs filled with perfume at their young friends or ladies that they admired.

Lançar-perfume is a Portuguese phrase which translates literally meaning "to throw perfume." *Lança-perfume* is very famously associated

---

[44] Wikipedia, "Carnival of Venice", October 31, 2020. Available at https://en.wikipedia.org/wiki/Carnival_of_Venice

with Brazilian *Carnaval*. Early in the history of Brazilian *Carnival*, an ether-based gas called *lança-perfume* was extremely popular in Brazil before it became illegal in 1961.[45] *Lança-perfume* is made with chloroform and ether; its use provides a pleasant high. No one can prove that the tradition of young men in Medieval Venice throwing perfumed-filled eggs inspired *Lança-perfume* in Brazil, but it is a fun idea. Instead of perfumed eggs, the Brazilians squirted *lança-perfume* at others, intoxicating the victims. It was thrown at party participants of all social classes in the early years of *Carnival*.

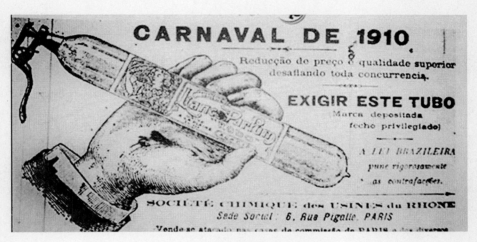

Lança-perfume
Source: *Hypeness*

During the eighteenth century the Carnival of Venice was famous for its pleasure and its activities. The use of masks and costumes became widespread. As in Brazilian *Carnival*, certain costumes were used to depict specific characters, such as a maidservant, popular in Italian opera, to the doctor of the plague, which would be a very scary costume indeed. Eventually the decadence of the Venetian Carnival became its downfall. After the Austrians overthrew the Republic, Carnival was outlawed in Venice in 1797 and the use of masks was strictly forbidden.[46] Carnival finally was revived by the Italian government in Venice in 1979 to bring back the historical

---

[45] Wikipédia, "Lança-perfume," August 13, 2020. Available at https://pt.wikipedia.org/wiki/Lança-perfume
[46] Wikipedia, "Carnival of Venice". Available at https://en.wikipedia.org/wiki/Carnival_of_Venice. Access in: 31 oct. 2020.

culture of the city and promote tourism. A unique feature of Venice is that the costumes for Carnival remain like those worn in the eighteenth century.

Influence of Portuguese Entrudo

Carnaval
Source: *Resus Review*, 2012

Carnaval in Brazil, like everything in Brazil, is a mixture of cultures and influences. As *Carnaval* spread throughout Europe and came to Brazil by way of the Portuguese, the Portuguese from the Azores celebrated a pre-Lenten festival called *Entrudo* during the time of their discovery and colonization of Brazil.[47] *Entrudo* was a celebration that included eating and drinking. It also included parading giant dolls and throwing water, vinegar, or flour on unsuspecting people. The nobility were special targets of this joke.[48] *Entrudo* also featured giant puppets or dolls that people followed behind in the parades during the three nights of this party. This parade of giant dolls continues in the *Carnival* of Ouro Preto, Recife and Olinda, which are some of the oldest colonial cities.

---

[47] "History of Carnival in Brazil." *Study.com*, June 24, 2016. Available in: https://study.com/academy/lesson/history-of-carnival-in-brazil.html. Access in: 3/10/2020
[48] *Ibidem*.

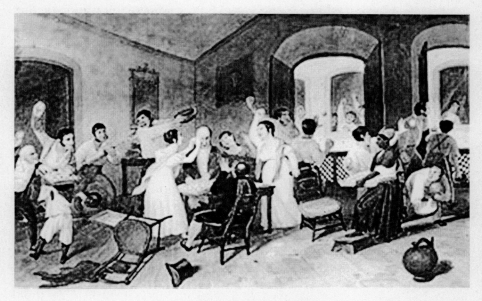

History of Carnival in Brazil
Source: *Study.com*

The throwing of water, flour and other substances got out of hand, and *Entrudo* was banned in Rio de Janeiro in 1904 by its mayor Pereira Passos.[49] In its place the Portuguese Brazilian upper classes began holding masked balls while Afro-Brazilians began their own street parties, often dressing in ways that mocked the upper class.

During the late 19th century to the early 20th century, *Carnival* incorporated many Portuguese traditions such as wearing costumes and masks, as playing music, and dancing in the streets. Brazilian *Carnaval* created an event that best could be described as a disorganized water balloon and food fight like Portuguese *Entrudo*, with dancing and music.[50] The music of *Carnaval* varies from city to city: *Samba* is played in Rio and São Paulo; *frevo* and *forró* in Recife and Pernambuco; and *axé* in Bahia. All *Carnaval* music has African roots. The *Carnaval* music in the city of Rio is samba! Samba at first was the name of a percussion rhythm, later it came to denote a style of music. All *Carnaval* music is heavily influenced by the Brazilian African community and samba is no exception. Samba rhythms

---

[49] *Ibidem.*
[50] *Ibidem.*

comes from the rhythms of the drums of Candomblé religion and *capoeira*, an Afro-Brazilian martial art, the roots of which came from West Africa with the slaves brought to Brazil. When the slaves were freed, many came to Rio since it was the capital in search of opportunity. Around the turn of the 19th century the freed slaves, mulattos, and poor whites started parading and dancing with percussion instruments. By 1928 a group of these musicians decided to practice together and organized the first samba school, or *escola de samba* and they called themselves *"Deixa Falar."* This group became very influential shortly followed by *Mangueira*, a rival samba school, and soon other shanty towns organized their own groups and took up the term *escola de samba* to describe each group. Many of today's samba schools can trace their beginnings to this era. During the 1920's these samba schools performed for fun without rules or structure. The point was to have fun and not to compete. The competition and judging of Samba schools began with the sponsorship of the media company "O Globo" which set up the rules and judging of samba schools that evolved to the competition we have today.[51] The competition between the samba schools as it exists today could only have started with organization and money.

History of Carnival in Rio de Janeiro
Source:*Ipanema.com*

---

[51] Rio Carnival Org A Step inside Samba School's History. Find the Origin and Details of your Samba School's History Right Here. Accessible at https://www.riocarnival.org/rio-samba-school/samba-history#:~:text=Samba%20School%27s%20history%20started%20with,banner%20of%20Estacio%20de%20Sa. Viewed 3/10/2021

Becoming Brazilian

The organization and money for this party, which transformed the fun-loving samba schools into the huge organizations that attract tourists to Brazil, originally came from underground bookies who ran illegal gambling lotteries called *"Jogo do Bicho". Carnaval* as we know it today would not exist without samba and *Jogo do Bicho*. Both began in the periphery of society around the turn of the 20th century, where the poor blacks and mulattos would interact with the rich in Rio.

Jogo do Bicho started as a simple marketing idea for the Rio Zoo by Baron Joao Baptista Drummond, a Brazilian-born Englishman. Emperor Dom Pedro II awarded Drummond the title and the concession to the Rio de Janeiro Zoo, in the late 19th century. As a publicity stunt, Drummond encouraged visitors to guess the identity of an animal concealed behind a curtain, and paid prizes to winners. In time, the guessing game became a tremendously popular numbers game, with different numbers assigned to 25 animals.[1][52]

Jogo do Bicho
Source: *Yuri Eiras*, 2016

---

[52] Wikipedia, "Jogo do Bicho". Available at https://en.wikipedia.org/wiki/Jogo_do_Bicho#cite_note-time-1. Access: 10/16/ 2020.

1 - *Avestruz* (Ostrich)	6 - *Cabra* (Goat)	11 - *Cavalo* (Horse)	16 - *Leão* (Lion)	21 - *Touro* (Bull)
2 - *Águia* (Eagle)	7 - *Carneiro* (Ram)	12 - *Elefante* (Elephant)	17 - *Macaco* (Monkey)	22 - *Tigre* (Tiger)
3 - *Burro* (Donkey)	8 - *Camelo* (Camel)	13 - *Galo* (Rooster)	18 - *Porco* (Pig)	23 - *Urso* (Bear)
4 - *Borboleta* (Butterfly)	9 - *Cobra* (Snake)	14 - *Gato* (Cat)	19 - *Pavão* (Peacock)	24 - *Veado* (Deer)
5 - *Cachorro* (Dog)	10 - *Coelho* (Rabbit)	15 - *Jacaré* (Alligator)	20 - *Peru* (Turkey)	25 - *Vaca* (Cow)

Soon *Jogo do bicho* became a betting game outside of the zoo as well, and people made bets with bookies. Anyone could play for any amount of money and soon it was being played in cities outside of Rio. According to Time Magazine's March 25, 1966 issue, at that time 1% of the total workforce of Brazil earned its living promoting *Jogo do Bicho*. The government would crack down on the game but as is today, the judicial system was inadequate to close the illegal betting. To buy favor in the communities and shanty towns, or *favelas,* the organizers of *Jogo do Bicho,* or *bicheiros,* began financing and organizing the Samba schools.

If it seems strange that an essentially illegal and criminal activity could at the same time have fostered the organization of *Carnival* in Rio, one needs to recognize that the *favelas,* or shanty towns, where the members of the samba schools lived and worked, are also outside the official state. Entire communities of hundreds of thousands of residents live in communities that both sponsor and promote the Carnival Schools and are outside the legal framework of the Brazilian state. There are no deeds to the property in these communities, yet these communities have history, Some traditional communities date back a hundred years. Electricity and cable TV in the *favelas* are often provided using illegal connections to the grid. Even though today celebrities and tourists participate in these samba schools, the samba schools identify with these communities as they did in the beginning.

Jogo do Bicho culturally impacted Brazil in several ways besides Carnival. For example, when an unexpected upset occurs in sports it is called a "zebra". This is because the zebra is not an animal that appears in *Jogo do Bicho*, so the chance of winning with a zebra is impossible. The number 24 deer, or *veado,* is also a slang term for homosexual. In Brazil, no professional athlete uses this number on his jersey. This may seem homophobic and politically incorrect, but just recently, an Argentine player who used the number 24 outside Brazil, was advised by the Corinthian football director that 24 is not a number used on his team. The player, after learning this aspect of Brazilian culture instead wore the number eight.[53]

"The animal game is a deeply embedded cultural phenomenon with a certain romantic aura, and thus hard to eradicate," according to Denise Frossard, a former judge who became famous for sending 14 *bicheiros* (bookies who take bets in the Jogo do Bicho) to jail in 1993. She continued, "But it is also a quintessentially Brazilian way of laundering money and contributes greatly to the problem of impunity in this country."[54]

With the monetary support of the *bicheiros* the samba schools began to organize and compete. The samba schools grew bigger and evolved into sections and classes or *alas*. By 1932, the first organized competition was sponsored by Mario Filho who owned a sports magazine. He needed something to write about after football season. He organized the first parade of samba schools, and set the first requirements for competition, the basic rules, and judging. Although samba schools existed in São Paulo, the first competition was not held there until 1950. Now, both Rio and São Paulo have large stadiums for these samba school contests. The judging is independent and Brazilians cheer for their samba school as they do for their football team. Sometimes their samba school is related to where the live, sometimes their football team determines what samba school they support.

Some football teams have close associations with samba schools. In both cities multiple samba schools present the parades in specially built facilities called *"Sambódromos"* each night, all night long. In São Paulo, the Corinthians football team, and the samba school *Fiéis da Gavião* share the same fan clubs; likewise, *Mancha Verde* shares with the football team *Palmeiras*. This same relationship between football and samba schools is found in Rio as well. Football, samba schools, and *jogo de bicho* are all interconnected in Brazilian Culture with *Carnival*.

---

[53] "Cantillo deixa de usar número 24 no Corinthians; clube cita Rincón, e diretor faz piada: "24 aqui não". *GloboEsporte.com*, October 1, 2020. Available in https://globoesporte.globo.com/futebol/times/corinthians/noticia/cantillo-deixa-de-usar-numero-24-no-corinthians-clube-cita-rincon-e-diretor-faz-piada-24-aqui-nao.ghtml. Access in 3/10/2021.

[54] Wikipedia, "Jogo do Bicho". Available in: https://en.wikipedia.org/wiki/Jogo_do_Bicho#cite_note-time-1. Access in: 10/16/2020

At first the monetary support for samba schools first came from *Jogo do Bicho*. Later, funding came from the government to promote the tourist trade. These funds created an infrastructure that provides work for some of the poorest people in these communities. Each major city now has its own organization for the governance of these samba schools and their competitions. The Sambódromos of Rio and São Paulo

Samba Schools Organization and Judging

The first organized competition of samba schools and the rules for judging were created by Mario Filho in 1932, who needed something to fill the pages of his sports magazine after football season ended. In 1933 the biggest new organization in Brazil, "Globo" joined the judging and created four criteria for judging the first samba schools. The first competitions were held in Praça de Onze in Rio de Janeiro and included 19 samba schools.[55] Rio was already the center of samba. Competitions started for the samba schools in São Paulo only in 1950.

Rio Carnival Tour
Source: *gocarnivalrio.com*

---

[55] Available in: https://en.wikipedia.org/wiki/Samba_school. Access in: 3/10/2021.

Just as a school is broken up into classes, so too are samba schools broken up into sections called *aulas*, which translates to classroom or class. A samba school presentation has a theme and a song which inspire the floats and costumes. The theme elements are judged along with the required classes or *aulas* that provide the common structure for each Samba school for that year. The following are *aulas* within each samba school. They are listed below in the order they normally appear in a samba school presentation.

The Aulas or sub sections for a Carnival School

The Front Commission: This is the first of several *aulas* in a samba school. The function of the front commission has changed over time. In early days of samba schools this group was led by men who were prominent in the school and whose job it was to clear a path, when the Carnival schools paraded in the streets. In modern times this *aula* also became responsible for welcoming the audience and introducing the theme of the Samba School in the "Sambódromos." The Front Commission continues to be small aula. It is now composed of the best individuals who can introduce the theme of the samba school.

Allegorical Floats and Props: The floats and props created by the samba schools are famous for their size and splendor. They can be interspersed though out the parade, incorporating the theme of the presentation. Usually, the samba school's own theme, colors and symbols serve as the inspiration for the floats and props. On top of these floats local celebrities will sometimes dance on specially designed platforms.

Mestre-sala and Porta-Bandeira

The next *aula* consists of two people. The *mestre-sala*, or room master, is a male role. His counterpart, a woman, is the *porta-bandeira*, or flag holder, who carries the samba school flag. This couple's dance is evaluated and judged according to several rules and requirements. Some schools may have several of these pairs in any given *ala,* but only the first couple is judged. The role of *mestre-sala* and *porta-bandeira,* must perform exceedingly difficult dances; these roles are too important to hand over to celebrities, so these positions are reserved for the best dancers in the samba school. It is not unusual for adolescents to begin training for these roles years before they perform as principals for the school.

Figure Mestre-sala e porta-bandeira
Source: *SRde*, 2019

Drumming Section: The drumming section is the percussion band that starts the parade in the middle of the samba schools, then moves off to a special section of the *Sambódromos* to provide music for the rest of the Samba school to parade. As the last *"Aulas"* passes, at the end of the parade, the drumming section goes back on to the main street to follow the rest of the *aulas* to end the presentation. This is a large band of 100 to 300 people. It also includes the following characters:

Director of the drum section: Mestre de Matéria

This is the conductor of the drumming section of the samba school.

Queen of the Drum Section, and Other Related Characters: Traditionally the queen of the drum section was given to a woman in recognition of her special importance in the community. Some schools created additional roles of grandmother or godmothers to honor more women for their service to the samba school. There are also kings of *Carnival*. Over time, many schools have begun introducing celebrities in these roles. But unlike the celebrities on the floats, these really need to know how to samba.

The Singer and Backup Singers: These are men with strong voices that accompany the drum section. They sing the same samba school song, over and over and over again.

***Aula das Baianas* or Class of the Bahian women:** This *aula* is required in all samba schools. The *aula das baianas* is made up of women, usually older, dressed in wonderful costumes based on the traditional dress of Bahia.

***Velha Guarda* or Old Guard:** This *aula* provides a similar function for older men in the community. Costumes tend to include panama hats.

Classes for Tourists: To raise money most samba schools have a class or Aula where you can parade with a Samba school. For a fee you can get a costume and an area where you and your friends can dance down the *Sambódromos* with the rest of the school. These tourist *aulas* are not judged. Participating in one of these is a really good way to get a unique and unforgettable experience not just of *Carnival* but of the communities that promote them. It requires some time and connections to participate but the cost is nominal. To make this experience worth it, you need to participate in rehearsal and other events of the Samba school. You will be rewarded with an amazing experience before, during, and after the parade.

Many of the themes of samba schools are used to promote social change. What is common to all *Carnaval* celebrations is that they seek to upset the status quo. *Carnaval* has always been a social movement for the poor and underprivileged. Some view it as an escape from their daily lives. During Brazil's periods of dictatorships, *Carnaval* was used to protest, albeit in an indirect and irreverent way. Because it is carnival the authorities permit this thinly disguised criticism. The use of samba school themes to promote social change continues to this day.

Basics of Samba; Step on the bug, Smash the bug

Brazilians dance samba with such ease and grace, yet the dance is so difficult to pick up for visitors because the rhythm is not clearly the 4/4 or ¾ time that Europeans and American are accustomed to. However, it you are going to be in Brazil for *Carnaval*, you will want to dance, and Brazilians would love to help you if you just ask.

The best thing to do at this moment is to put on some samba music and try to listen to the rhythm. The rhythm is 1 and pause 2 and pause. The problem is not the 1 and the 2, but what do you do in the pause? A Brazilian gave me the following advice: for your feet think about stepping on bugs. You step on the bug, and you turn on the ball of your feet and smash the bug. Step on the bug on the one and smash the bug on the pause and change feet. Left foot forward on the 1, smash the bug on the pause, left foot back, right foot forward on the 2, smash the bug on the pause! So essentially you are going back and forth on your right and left feet smashing bugs, turning the balls of your feet, and stepping back. If you able to do this to the rhythm of samba, then you are doing great. If you are a woman and want to add a little flourish, kick up your heels after you smash the bug; then you will be a star!

Now what to do with your arms? I know you are tempted to point them up in the air and march around like the head of a military band. Resist this temptation! Why do *gringos* want to dance Samba pointing fingers up and down in the air? Fewer things will identify you faster at *Carnival* as a tourist! Leave your arms at your sides when you dance.

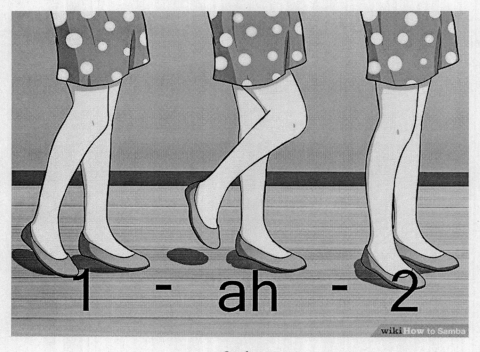

Samba
Source: *Howto Techno*, 2019

Carnaval in other regions of Brazil

Many Brazilians prefer the *Carnavais* held outside of the centers of São Paulo and Rio. These smaller *Carnavais* have different styles and do not have the organized samba schools like Rio and São Paulo. Each region has its own traditions and music.

Carnaval of Bahia

There are so many festivals in Bahia preceding *Carnaval* that it seems like it could be one continuous party from New Year's Eve to the post-*Carnaval* parties of Bahia. The first thing you will notice is that the music is different. Instead of samba, *axé* is the music of *Carnaval* in Bahia.

Axé comes from Yoruba, a west African language. The original Yoruban word, "*ase*," means soul, or light, good vibrations.[56] The music is a played with a large band playing a rhythm that seems like a blend of ska, calypso and reggae mixed with Brazilian music such as *frevo* and *forró*. It is just impossible to listen to *axé* without wanting to jump up and down. It is pure energy. Every summer there are new bands and songs; all the locals know the words, and sometimes popular songs are accompanied by local dances that also all the locals somehow know the dance steps. The dance moves interpret the meaning of the song.

Olodum
Source: *Agência Brasil*, 2017

---

[56] Wikipedia, "Axé (music)".. https://en.wikipedia.org/wiki/Axé_(music). Access in: 10/3/ 2020.

The percussion band Olodum deserves special mention as an institution of Bahia *Carnaval*, because it is an internationally renowned percussion band which promotes African culture and self-esteem in the poor sections of Bahia. Olodum is famous for is flamboyant drumming that has a signature sound which blends samba and reggae. They became internationally famous playing songs with Michael Jackson and Paul Simon.

The *Carnaval* in Bahia is based around street parties following a large specially built truck platform called a *trio elétrico*. In 1950, two Bahia men, Dodo and Osmar, created an open-air float out of an old truck for musical presentations, and the *trio elétrico* was born. Instead of featuring elaborate floats like São Paulo and Rio, Bahia has the *trio elétrico*, which are specially designed trucks designed so that a musical group with all its instruments and amplifiers can move through the streets the band plays and the people follow.

Carnaval of Salvador
Source: *Soul Brasil Magazine*, 2020

A *bloco* is the name for an organized group of people that promote a parade at a street *Carnival*. The *Carnival* in Bahia has many of these groups, and they parade similar to the way the early samba schools did. When the *trio elétrico* took off and *axé* music became popular many *blocos* supported *the trio elétrico* the bands that play on top of them. These organizations earn money by allowing tourists, for a fee, to parade with their *bloco*. The same thing happened with the samba schools in Rio and São Paulo who let tourists for a fee, parade with them. Over time these *blocos* have evolved into huge organizations supporting the biggest stars of Brazilian music.

Frevo and Dolls, The Carnaval of Olinda and Recife

Frevo is the music and the dance of the *Carnaval* of Olinda and Recife. *Frevo* is a mispronunciation of the Portuguese word *fervor*, which means to boil. The bands that created *frevo* were military brass bands that competed against one another to play the fastest and loudest. Both the dance and music have a fevered rhythm, reminiscent of jumping around boiling water; or perhaps the sound of popcorn popping comes to mind. *Frevo* sounds like a fast polka, but with the dance includes dramatic jumping and kicking not unlike a Russian Cossacks' dance. Just add hot weather and little parasols! The dancers wear skimpy costumes to show off their footwork. The steps or kicks are very elaborate, and the steps are called *passos*. *Frevo* features brass horns and drums beating a quick rhythm, but it is clearly a ¾ time, in stark contrast to the Afro-tropical rhythms that are heard at other places *Carnaval*.

Some Brazilians say that the Carnival of Recife and Olinda is the true Carnival. Certainly, the dolls that parade in the *Car* of Olinda and the dolls of "the rooster of the morning," or *Galo de Madrugada* that parade in Recife, harken back to the dolls used in the parades in during the Carnivals of the Middle Ages and the Renaissance. While the dolls of the Portuguese festival of *Entrudo* are scary and ugly, the dolls of Orlindo and Recife are colorful. Certain dolls have significance. The *Galo de Madrugada* and the Midnight man, or *O Homem da Meia-noite* officially start the *Carnivals* of Recife and Orlindo, respectively. As the two cities are close to each other you can enjoy both the same time. At the end of the carnival these two dolls meet during the last night, and dance on, and leave together until next year.

Frevo
Source: *Educa Mais Brasil*, 2019

Carnaval in Ouro Preto

Many smaller cities also have their own *Carnaval*. Especially in beach areas, the celebrations are promoted by the local government, but few have the history and architecture of Ouro Preto. Ouro Preto is a colonial city in Minas Gerais where gold was discovered in the 16th century. The first interstate road in Brazil connected Ouro Preto and other colonial cities to Parati, which is a small colonial port town near Rio de Janeiro. This ancient road is called the Estrada Real, or Royal Highway. Traveling along the Estrada Real is an interesting trip for the traveler, to get to know some wonderful colonial cities in Brazil. While Rio and Belo Horizonte have grown to huge metropolises, Ouro Petro and Parati remain much the same as when they were built, with most of the colonial architecture and churches still standing and little subsequent development. Ouro Preto is a tourist town and home to one of the oldest colleges in Brazil. The students are housed in building called *repúblicas*, each building having its own identity and history. To make money the *repúblicas* open for housing tourists. Guests who stay in the *repúblicas* can participate in certain *Carnival* groups. The *repúblicas*, in conjunction with the municipal government, organize the *blocos de Carnaval*. Students of both sexes live in *repúblicas* while they are going to university and if you are young enough, staying in a dorm situation could make Carnival seem like a frat party mixed with Brazilian colonial history.

Like the *Entrudos* of the old Portuguese, the *Carnaval* of Ouro Preto features dolls leading the parade. Its *Carnaval* starts with the crowning of the King and Queen. Like the old *Entrudo*, the people throw water at each other. Even the local fire department joins in, which is welcomed by the crowd to cool off.

Other Celebrations

Ano-Novo, or New Year's

Festa de Nossa Senhora dos Navegantes
Source: *Catholicus*, 2020

As in the rest of the world, Brazil celebrates New Year's Eve with parties, fireworks, champagne, and kissing at midnight. But the mixture of races and cultures in Brazil also provides a unique celebration of diversity. New Year's Day may be a secular celebration in much of the world. In Brazil, it is also a holy day of for Catholics, for the Virgin Mary and for the those who practice Afro-Brazilian religion Umbanda, it is a holy day for Iemanjá, the goddess of the sea. Umbanda and Catholicism mix within the Brazilian culture, and both Iemanjá and Our Lady of Navigators, are both the protectors of fishermen, are represented with similar images and ceremonies on the same day. January 1st in Brazil is the day honoring both the Virgin Mary and Iemanjá. Brazilians celebrate New Year's honoring them both.

Festa de Iemanjá
Source: Metropoles, 2020

On New Year's Day you will see processions and ceremonies for the Virgin Mary as well as works or offerings being dedicated to Iemanjá. Some people send wishes to Iemanjá by boat, others make offerings in the sand for her. The feast day of the Virgin Mary is also January 1 and on February 2 another feast day to her also celebrated with processions to the sea. These celebrations peacefully coexist. Both are protectors of fisherman.

At midnight however, all over Brazilian beaches, people will jump seven waves in honor of Iemanjá. The number seven is considered good luck in the Umbanda religion, so you jump seven waves or eat seven lentils to bring good luck. According to another Brazilian belief pomegranates brings wealth, but you must store the seven pomegranate seeds in your wallet and your wallet will never be empty! Even the most sophisticated Brazilians at penthouse parties will dip their feet in the pool, while eating seven pomegranate seeds, seven lentils, and champagne. The following day on January 1st, Brazilian Catholics will go to mass to celebrate the Virgin Mary.

What you wear for new years has meaning

Ano novo
Source: *Ceert*, 2016

The clothes you wear for New Year's also have meaning. People tend to dress in white to bring peace to the next year, but other colors can be used. Different colors will bring different luck: green is worn for health; yellow for money; red for love, passion, and romance; and purple for inspiration. The most popular color to wear for carnival is white. White is for peace.

Brazilians do not eat turkey or chicken for New Year's. Because chickens and turkeys walk backwards, they are considered unlucky for a new year. According to Brazilian beliefs, New Year's is a time to look forward, not backwards. Pigs, unlike chickens and turkeys, are always pushing forward so pork is considered good luck for New Year's. Due to Portuguese influences, cod fish, or *bacalhau*, is considered a great delicacy. It is made with many different recipes and is a common dish all year round, but especially on New Year's.

Several foods have special meaning. The Italians and Portuguese brought the tradition of eating lentils for good luck. Pomegranates are to bring money, but you must eat only the bit of fruit from seven seeds. Do not throw away the seeds! You must dry them and put them in your wallet so that your wallet will not be empty. Then you will have plenty of money. This tradition may have arrived in Brazil with the Arabs and the Turks.

Festa Junina

June is wintertime in Brazil. As a result, these festivals are not well known to tourists who tend to visit at other times of the year. *Festa Junina* is a festival that overlaps and includes St. Anthony's Day on June 12, Saint John's day on June 24, and ends after St. Peter's Day on June 29. The tradition comes from Europe and was brought to Brazil by the Portuguese. Big bonfires are typically held in the countryside for *Festa Junina*. Obviously, for safety reasons bonfires are not common in cities. Instead, big cities celebrate *Festa Junina* by decorating large halls with a country theme.

In Brazil, these holidays are a celebration of country living. Participants dress up as *caipiras*, which translates to "hicks" or "country bumkins." Dances are held called *quadrilhas* which are like square dances. This dance is like square dances in Europe or the United States but *quadrilhas* are accompanied by Brazilian *forró* music.[57]

Saint Anthony is the patron saint of weddings and lovers. Brazilians celebrate their version of Valentine's Day on this saint's day, June 12. In honor of Saint Anthony, these dances usually incorporate a theatrical enactment of a wedding, usually forcing a reluctant man to marry a bride. Sometimes parties are held during the day for children, then at night for adults. Children play traditional games and win prizes, while adults eat drink and dance.

The food and drink for *Festa Junina* vary from region to region in Brazil but all maintain the theme of country living. Corn is harvested at this time, so a wide variety of corn-based dishes are served. This includes popcorn, corn bread, and corn cake. *Pamonha,* which is similar to a tamale, is popular in Minas Gerais. *Polenta,* an Italian dish, is popular with Italians and Gauchos in the south of Brazil. Traditional sweets are also served. Candy Apples, or *Maçã de Amor*, and *pé de moleque,* which is like peanut brittle, are typical, as well as other traditional sweets.

---

[57] Wikipedia, "Festa Junina," November 9, 2020. Available in: https://en.wikipedia.org/wiki/Festa_Junina. Access in: 4/1/2021

Because it is cold during *Festa Junina*, drinks are served hot and with alcohol. *Quentão* is a *cachaça* laced version of hot spiced rum. Like spiced rum it contains sugar, cinnamon, ginger, and lime, but *cachaça* is used instead of rum. In the South of Brazil, they also drink *vinho quente* which is hot spiced wine. The wine is made from local Brazilian vineyards.

Bumba Meu Boi: Dance My Ox Folkloric Street Opera

One of the most fascinating plays and forms of social entertainment are presented during the time of *Festa Junina*. To the uninitiated visitor and even to Brazilians, *Bumba Meu Boi* looks like *Carnival* with a cow, but it is much more. *Bumba Meu Boi* is a uniquely Brazilian form of theater founded and created by poor downtrodden people. From its lowly beginnings *Bumba Meu Boi* is now widely popular. *Bumba Meu Boi* is an interactive form of folk theater with music, costumes, and audience participation. It is a unique form of performance art. *Bumba Meu Boi* is not as well-known as *Carnival* but perhaps has a deeper, more poignant social relevance. On one level it is a spectacle for tourists, but on another level, it is a story of social injustice, redemption, and resurrection. There are hundreds of versions of *Bumba Meu Boi* performed by hundreds of groups.[58] It is impossible to declare only one official storyline for *Bumba Meu Boi* because it is folklore that has been passed down through oral tradition and each telling, changes the tale somewhat. The most famous performances are presented in Maranhão, Amazon and Pernambuco, but there are hundreds of variations of the play.

Bumba Meu Boi is unlike any theater in the world. The themes are both simple and profound. The performances are varied and theatrical. Because this is truly folk art, there is no common author nor is there a set cast of characters. It is impossible define one consistent plot. The story shares certain similarities no matter the version because the people who have suffered the same great injustices share a common history and ceremonies. Like a good opera, *Bumba Meu Boi* plays to your emotions as well as your intellect. In ancient Greek theater, and in Shakespeare's time, or in early Italian opera, audiences would talk, jeer or cheer; that tradition has been lost as we have tried to be become too civilized. Today, audiences are expected to follow certain rules to go to the theater. In fact, many times the most important rule is not talking! This is not the case with *Bumba Meu Boi*.

---

[58] Wikipedia, "Bumba Meu Boi," November 11, 2020. Available in: https://en.wikipedia.org/wiki/Bumba_Meu_Boi. Acess in: 1/4/2021.

In performances of *Bumba Meu Boi*, the audience is part of the performance; audience members are expected to cry and cheer during the performance. In typical Brazilian fashion, like *Carnival*, the play expresses social injustice without being bitter. Like an ancient Greek play, it has a chorus that is not in the play or seen as a character but serves as a guide to the audience and introduces to the major characters. Unlike a Greek play, but like *Carnival*, there is a percussion band that plays the music for the performance, while also being part of the performance.

Bumba Meu Boi started in the 17th century as folk theater. It was created by slaves to mock the rich and entertain themselves. During the 18th century it spread through many communities and began to be performed to entertain others, not just for their own amusement. Today there are hundreds of groups that perform *Bumba Meu Boi*. The performances started in Maranhão but have migrated to other regions of Brazil, including the Amazon. Each region personalizes the performance by incorporating details specific to its community. The basics of the drama and the story remain the same, but each region and production can change details, not only on the characters, but the plot as well. As this play was passed down through oral history, there is no historical script to reference as the true original play and changes continue to be made.

The story of *Bumba Meu Boi* is set in the class-divided colonial period of Brazil. The Ox was a major source of power and wealth. The story is told from the point of view of the oppressed poor, who mock and exaggerate the wealthy characters. It is impossible to write about a single plot or list of characters, but below is a general outline of the theme and story. The overarching theme is always social injustice and redemption. Here are the major characters in the play:

The Band: This is a percussion group onstage playing drums.

The Chorus or Master of Ceremonies: Offstage, it provides the singing and introductions of the major characters.

Amo or Cavalo Marinho: Amo is the farmer and owner of the Ox. In other versions the character is called Cavalo Marinho who appears in military uniform. Both are white and represent property, prosperity, and authority. Many times, this character can be seen with a sword or riding a horse. He is from the privileged landed class.

Catarina: She is an unmarried pregnant black woman, sometimes depicted as a house slave. She is a comedic character and dances the samba

Becoming Brazilian

frenetically. She is critical to the story because she is seeking an ox tongue which she must eat to avoid losing her baby. She serves as the protagonist, giving a reason to kill the Ox, which is central to the play. She is sometimes played by a man.

Pai Francisco, Chico or Matheus: The main male character. He is a cowboy peasant who is Catarina's boyfriend or husband, and presumably the father of the baby.

Figure: Amo, Catarina and Pai Francisco. Bumba-meu-boi show
Source: *UFG*, 2011

The Doctor, the priest, the healer, witches and others: They try to heal or save the Ox.

The Ox: He is the main character of the play. The people cheer when he is on stage and cry when he is killed. He is killed to save the unborn baby, then he is resurrected. This is a metaphor, as it is almost Christ-like. People love the ox, because through him the play is redeemed. During all the singing and dancing it is the Ox's death and resurrection that is the central theme of the play.

Cowboys, Indians, and others: who may both mock the authority figures as well as follow the authority figures orders.

27º Festival de Bumba Meu Boi
Source: *Tribuna Hoje*, 2019

What follows is a general outline of the story: The chorus and band provide music and song for the event. The first character to appear is Amo or Cavalo Marinho, the owner of the Ox and symbols of authority. The chorus announces the entrance of other characters like the Indians and Cowboys and Pai Francisco, (or Chico or Matheus, depending on which version.) When the Ox arrives, he is greeted with cheers and great show because he is loved and the central character of the play. Eventually Catarina arrives and dances until she announces that she needs to eat the tongue of the Ox or she will lose the baby. Pai Francisco or Chico, the main male character, goes off in search of the Ox and here ensues a variety of adventures with different characters. Usually, Chico kills the Ox to take the tongue needed to save the baby, and everyone is sad and cries. Songs are sung to mourn the Ox. Pai Francisco or Chico cuts out the tongue for Catarina to eat and thus saves the baby. Amo/Cavalo Marino, (the owner of the Ox,) rejoins the play and demands justice for his dead Ox, and sends cowboys or Indians to capture Pai Francisco and Catarina, who flee to escape. Sometimes the couple hides with the Indians, sometimes there are chased. Meanwhile, the owner of the Ox searches for someone to try to resuscitate it. Most of these attempts fail and are designed to make the crowd laugh. A priest comes, and though he does not resurrect the Ox, he might, depending on the version, perform the marriage of Pai Francisco to a pregnant Catarina.

In some stories the traditional healers, witches, or doctors try and fail to cure the ox many times; eventually a healer of some sort succeeds in resurrecting the Ox, which makes everyone happy again. Dances and songs are sung to celebrate the renewed life of the Ox. Eventually police may come, but because the Ox is now alive, there is no crime. The police are then mocked by the crowd. The farewell begins as the chorus sings and the dancers leave the stage. The Ox is resurrected, and the husband and wife are forgiven.

PART II

Chapter Eight

The Problems of Brazil, Blame the Portuguese

Unless foreigners live in Brazil, they commonly assume the biggest problem in Brazil is the deforestation of the Amazon. While most Brazilians support the goal of saving the Amazon, they have other complaints that impact their daily lives and as soon as someone moves to Brazil these areas of concern become important as well. Of the great complaints of Brazilians, they mostly fall in these major areas:

1. Crime and Violence

2. Poverty, Social Injustice, and Inequality

3. Lack of Education, Lack of Jobs

4. Impunity in the Judicial System that favors the corrupt.

Except for deforestation of the Amazon, which is truly a global problem all the other major issues come directly from Brazil's history with Portugal as a colony and later as a Brazilian Empire. When all other countries in Europe and western hemisphere were trying to create republics, Brazil ended up importing a monarchy from Portugal. In trying to understand the roots of these problems of Brazil, they all seem to trace to this specific period of history and anomaly that is uniquely Brazilian. How would Brazil had been different if the native indigenous peoples and the French would have been able to resist the Portuguese in Sao Sebastian in the 15th century? What would have happened if the Dutch were successful is colonizing the northeast of Brazil? Would we have less social inequality if Zumbi and the escaped slaves defeated the Portuguese in the North East? Would Brazil have had stronger democracy and more honest government if the revolts of Minas Gerais and Pernambuco would have freed those states from the Portuguese crown? We will never know the answers of these questions because history of Brazil was shaped by three major events that retarded its social development. The first was the Portuguese legacy of slavery in Brazil. The second was the colonial policy of the Portuguese while Brazil was a colony. This policy was designed to keep the Brazilian regions separate and ignorant, while forcing all trade exclusively with Portugal. The third event was the arrival of the Portuguese Monarchy to Brazil in 1808, that delayed aspirations of independence and democracy at the same time importing as system of corruption and bad government that exists to this day. As we shall see, these three factors retarded Brazil social development by about 150 years. Seen in this context, Brazil may only now be addressing the social issues that could have been addressed if Brazil separated from Portugal earlier.

The history of Brazilian colonialization and empire are wonderful and heroic at times, and at other times, corrupt, cowardly, and humorous. Looked at from a comparative history of the rest of western civilization, Brazil has a unique colonial and post-colonial history. When the rest of the world was in a struggle between republican ideals born of the enlightenment, Portugal and Brazil remained an absolute monarchy, heavily dominated by the church and a society continued with the medieval ideals about the divine rights of kings.

Today, we take it for granted that all people should be treated equally before the law, but these ideas had not reached Brazil or Portugal when the monarchy arrived in Brazil in 1808. For the people of Brazil and Portugal the power of the monarch was absolute. Later in 1822, Brazil would find itself in the unusual position of fighting for a monarchy for an independent and united Brazil against Portuguese progressive efforts to form a constitutional monarchy. These events and later military governments would retard the development of Brazilian social institutions. It seems like only recently, after restoring democracy, impeaching two presidents, and suffering innumerable scandals of corruption that Brazilians have had enough and are ready to change their social institutions to govern the country.

We could be at the tipping point of change in Brazil. After a series of political scandals and massive corruption discovered in previous administrations leading to the impeachment of one president, the imprisonment of another and the resignation of a third president, almost two thirds of the federal legislature was replaced. All the major traditional political parties were tarnished with revelations of corruption, and yet the impunity continues. The forces of impunity still reside in all the major branches of government that try to weaken the efforts of the Federal Police and Prosecutors to stop the criminal and political corruption. The fight is far from over.

Brazil has 500 year of history of inequality, violence impunity and corruption and it will take time to reverse this history. Part 2 of this book will argue that social inequality, as a result criminal violence are inherited in the Portuguese widespread use of slave labor in Brazil to exploit the wealth of Brazil for the Portuguese Crown. Though inequality is part of the heritage of being a colony with slaves, the Brazilian colonies were too small and isolated to be corrupted prior to the arrival of the Portuguese monarchy. Brazilians may have diverted gold from the Portuguese or not paid duty and taxes to the Portuguese, but this was a normal practice in many colonies, in including the United States. From a republican point of view these actions are admirable and even patriotic. The history of the revolutions of the United States, France and Mexico are filled with stories of what could be considered illegal activities from the point of view of the colonial ruler, but these same acts are looked upon and acts of resistance to the republicans. Once the king no longer has divine right to govern, than on what basis are these taxes justified? If the king had no right to govern Brazil, how should the Brazilians govern themselves. The problem with Brazilian history is that these great ideas of French and American revolutions were never fully developed because instead of fighting for liberty against a common enemy, the Portuguese King, royal family, and court all arrived in Rio de Janeiro in 1808.

All western countries with stable and well-functioning democratic government have their own histories of the struggle to gain these freedoms. Each country has its own events of revolution, wars and crisis that helped mold the institutions that allowed democracy to take hold. To compare each of these to Brazil, at least a few common themes can be seen. The first theme is that while Europe was engaged in a period of intellectual change of the philosophers of the enlightenment. Economically in other European countries were being changed by the industrial revolution, both trends were either censured or did not exist in both Portugal and even less so in Brazil. The second theme is that when other countries and colonies in the western hemisphere entered a period of revolution against their monarchies or colonial rulers, the Portuguese monarchy fled to Brazil. The arrival of a European king moving and setting up the capital of its kingdom in one of its colonies is unique in the world. That and subsequent events related to the rise and fall of the Brazilian monarchy directly retarded the development of democratic institution that continue to plague Brazil to this day.

Though each country has a unique struggle to gain a successful democracy, there are two revolutions that influenced the entire world. The first is the American Revolution of 1776 which superficially seems comparable to the situation of Brazil. Both countries were governed by colonial policies that imposed exclusive trade arrangements with the home country, and both were divided into sperate states or regions that did not consider themselves one nation. However, as we shall see while comparing events with Brazil this comparison is not quite fair. Education, and industry were booming not only in the Britain but also in the American colonies. England, Scotland, and America were providing many of the great philosophers for what would later be called the enlightenment. While literacy and printing presses were widespread in the American colonies, this was not the case with Brazil. At the time of the American revolution, most Americans, including some slaves, were literate. The leadership in the American colonies participated in active correspondence with European intellectuals and some like Benjamin Franklin. were celebrities in Europe. In Brazil by comparison, printing presses were illegal and only a few free Brazilians could read and write. Slavery was practiced on a larger scale with close to a majority Brazilian enslaved. Books had to be reviewed by three censures in Portugal before publication.[59]

The major historical event that puts Brazilian history in motion, is the French revolution of 1793 and the subsequent rise of Napoleon Bonaparte. Napoleon not only had a direct impact on the history of Brazil, but also the history of all of Europe and most of Latin America as well. The United States after successfully completing it revolution, saw no need to export its revolution or ideas to other countries. Rather the young America wanted to focus on commerce and growth, so as a result it traded with everyone including its old foe Britain. This left the French revolution with the distinction of exporting revolutionary and republican ideas to the world. Whatever else you may think of him, Napoleon Bonaparte overthrew most of the royal houses of Europe and overturned the idea of the divine right of kings by force forever.

---

[59] GOMES, Laurentino. *1808:* Como uma rainha louca, um príncipes medroso, e um corte corrupta enganaram Napoleão e mudaram a Historia de Portugal e do Brasil. São Paulo: Globo, 2014, p.122.

The Royal Braganza family of Portugal which escaped to Brazil was the exception. As Napoleon would late say when he was imprisoned in isolation on the island of Saint Helena, the king of Portugal was the only man who fooled him.

Today to affirm that all people are created equal under the law and have human rights including life, liberty. and the pursuit of happiness, seem to be obvious, but these ideas were far from obvious in Brazil and Portugal in 1800. Considering how rare and unique the concepts of democracy and human rights are in the history of mankind is it a shame that this period is not studied closely today. Before the period of the enlightenment, it was commonly thought that kings had been given a divine right to rule by God. This remained the belief in Portugal until the French and Spanish soldiers arrived in Lisbon in 1808. But as for rest of Europe and the colonies of the United States a slow but methodic revolution of thought from philosophers, scientist, and economist, from many countries began challenging these beliefs and exchanging ideas through publication and correspondence. One of the first to start to chip away at the idea of the Divine Rights of King was the French Philosopher Jean-Jacques Rousseau, who made an ingenues argument that was both effective and safe enough to keep him out of jail. Instead of attacking the idea of the divine right of kings directly, he argued that at some time in distant history man lived without government whatsoever in a primitive state. Although he had no proof that this state of man existed, it seemed like a reasonable assumption at the time. If this state of primitive human freedom existed, then at some time in the distant past human beings had agreed to a social contract to be ruled. The benefits of living in a society was entered into voluntarily instead of living as individuals. This idea was later developed by the Scotsman David Hume, the Englishman David Locke, and French Philosophers Montesquieu and Voltaire. These ideas became immensely popular in Europe and became the foundation of the Declaration of Independence of the United States. The Declaration of Independence makes a direct address to the King of England for the abuses of the British Parliament. Jefferson using the idea of Rousseau's social contract, argued that all men are created equal and when the social contract that binds countries together is abused, it is the duty of men to break that social contract. Gone are references to divine rights of kings, and in its place is the idea of common human right for all. These ideals were won by force, in all countries in some way. In the United States these ideals need to be one by force twice. First against Britain to win its independence in 1782, and then again against slavery during the Civil War in 1865 to amend the incompatible practice of slavery in the United States with the ideals of human rights of the enlightenment which was the foundation of the republic.

The United States was not, however, interested in exporting its revolution. When Brazilians came from Pernambuco to look for assistance to revolt against the Portuguese king, they were largely ignored. The French revolution by contrast sought to export the revolutionary ideals Liberty, Equality and Fraternity to other countries overthrow the divine rights of kings by force. These ideals were embraced by many in Europe but largely censured in Portugal and Brazil. But though a series of events. the arrival of French and Spanish armies into Lisbon would change the history of Brazil forever.

Colonial Brazil

Prior to the arrival of the Royal family and court to Brazil, it is impossible to image Brazil as it is today with an integrated system of roads and communication and a population that identifies themselves as Brazilian. Brazil existed as 15 separated colonies under individual administration. The term, Brazilian, did not exist with the meaning it has today. Hipolito da Costa, who owned one of the few free printing presses printing news in Portuguese in London. There he could write freely about topics in Brazil. Hipolito considered the term Brazilian, *Brasileiro* to be used to describe Portuguese who moved to Brazil to live, whereas Brazilians born in Brazil should be called *Brasiliense* or *Brasiliano*.[60] Rather like the colonies of the United States, each region in Brazil was isolated and autonomous province had its own money, army, and administration. Like the colonies of the United States, Brazilians of the 18th century identified themselves by their state. Part of this was Portuguese colonial policy. In 1733 laws were passed to stop roads from being contracted between states.[61] The road to take gold from Minas Gerais from the mines and towns to the port in Paraty was the first road to cross state borders. This road is called the *Caminho Real*, or Royal road. This road can still be traveled to this day. The lack of ease in land transportation

---

[60] GOMES, Laurentino. *1808:* Como uma rainha louca, um príncipes medroso, e um corte corrupta enganaram Napoleão e mudaram a Historia de Portugal e do Brasil. São Paulo: Globo, 2014, p.112.
[61] *Ibidem*, p.115.

was by design. The Portuguese crown was suspicious that the Brazilians were smuggling gold and diamonds to avoid paying the king the 25% of all gold and diamonds mined. Having few roads made the surveillance of the smuggling easier. The Portuguese colonial policy to keep the Brazilian separated and making overland travel difficult resulted in less commerce between the states. The Portuguese wanted each province to trade with Portugal separately and not with each other within Brazil.

It was Portuguese colonial policy to keep Brazil isolated and ignorant. Prior to the arrival of the Portuguese monarchy in 1808, it was illegal to own a printing press in Brazil, which was why the only Brazilian newspaper was printed in London.[62] This and the lack of schools and education were also part of Portuguese colonial policy. During the previous hundred years there had been a great increase in population in Brazil. An estimated 800,000 Portuguese had migrated to Brazil between 1700 and 1800, while at the same time 2 million slaves had been sold and forced to Brazil to work in the sugar plantations, mines, and other forms of forced labor. By the 1800 Brazil had a population of around three million people, the majority slaves and mixed race. The overwhelming majority illiterate, poor and in need of everything. In 1818 only 2.5% of the population of São Paulo was literate. The legacy of poor education in Brazil was an intended result of Portuguese colonial policy. The Portuguese plan was to keep the Brazilians under control and ignorant.

The leaders of the American colonies, by contrast, were not only literate but engaged in discourses with the intellectuals of Europe. In the Colonies of the United States there were six major universities at the time of the revolution, in Brazil the Monarchy would establish some schools of higher learning but the first universities were chartered only in the beginning of the 20th century. During the age of enlightenment and revolution, apart from a few Brazilian free masons who inspired revolts in Minas Gerais and Pernambuco, there was no intellectual exchange of ideas with Europe. The free mason movement played an early part of both American and Brazilian history. Part of the lack of education in Brazil was Portuguese colonial policy and part of the lack of education was Portuguese conservatism to ideas outside of traditional catholic ideas protecting the divine right of kings for ideas of the enlightenment. As far as Portugal and Brazil, there were no ideas to be exchanged on either side of the Atlantic

---

[62] *Ibidem*, p.112.

or between Europe. This left the Portuguese Monarchy unprepared for the upheaval to come.

The equivalent of Portugal having Brazil as a colony would be something like discovering vast oil or mineral reserves. The country becomes instantly rich but if care is not taken, the development of the economy becomes distorted, and the country becomes lazy. This is what happened to Portugal. Portugal in the 1800 was no longer the adventurous nation that explored the world and discovered India and China while opening the world to trade. With the Portuguese monopoly on the control of the slave trade and commerce with Brazil and other colonies, Portugal entered a period of slow and decadent decline. With these easy riches from trade, Portugal never developed the manufacturing abilities that were quickly growing with the industrial revolution in England, France, the United States, and most of Northern Europe. All colonies had to sell there good to Portugal and could not trade with other nations. In the 1800, the principal products of the Portuguese colonies were gold, diamonds, tobacco sugar and slaves. This easy prosperity and wealth in Portugal did not promote industry or science. While most of Europeans intellectuals were pursuing science, medicine, economics and political ideals of the enlightenment, Portugal was a closed and religious society where critical thought was not valued. In most ways Portugal was more in the middle ages than modern, with the Portuguese Inquisition persecuting converted Jews, witches, and other heretics in the Portugal and the Portuguese colonies until 1821![63]

The Portuguese Court escapes to Brazil

How the Portuguese Monarchy and Aristocracy abandoned Portugal to arrive in Brazil is one of the oddest stories in European History. Portugal who was profiting greatly selling the products of its colonies to the rest of Europe found itself in the middle of the struggle between Napoleonic France and Britain. In the Battle of Trafalgar, the navy of Britain defeated the combined navies of Spain and France. Meanwhile Napoleon had conquered most of central Europe and what he had not conquered agreed to his economic blockade of England call the continental system which he decreed in 1806 and 1807. The idea was to weaken Great Britain economically by eliminating trade.

---

[63] Available in: https://en.wikipedia.org/wiki/Portuguese_Inquisition. Access in: 3/11/2021.

Brazil and the World Revolutions at the Beginning of the 19th Century
Source: *JHI Blog*, 2018

Portugal was the exception to this economic blockade. England was Portugal's oldest allies and largest trading partner. The alliance between England and Portugal dated to the time of the crusades when in 1147 English knights headed to the holy land helped the first Portuguese King Afono Henriques de Borgonha to expel the moors from what is now Portugal. Likewise, it was with the help of the Portuguese in 1704 that helped win the Rock of Gibraltar for England from Spain.[64] The Portuguese economy was largely sustained as being a middleman between goods made in Brazil and the other colonies and resold to the British. England was also the biggest market for Portuguese olive oil and wine. During this period of the industrial revolution, Portugal did not develop a manufacturing industry.

The French economic blockade against Britain forced the Portuguese to make decisions to align with either the British or capitulate to Napoleon. Under increasing stress from the French, Portuguese policy became

---

[64] GOMES, Laurentino. *1808:* Como uma rainha louca, um príncipes medroso, e um corte corrupta enganaram Napoleão e mudaram a Historia de Portugal e do Brasil. São Paulo: Globo, 2014, p. 59.

increasingly erratic. Pressure from Napoleon lead the Prince to flip flop without any defined policy. Napoleon was getting increasingly irritated with the Portuguese noncompliance to his decrees regarding trade with Britain. In July 1807 Napoleon ordered Portugal to close their ports to the British. The Portuguese passed laws to stop trade with the British, but no one enforced these rules. Brazil today has many rules that are not enforced, which may be a legacy of the Portuguese. Later the Spanish and French Ambassadors gave Portugal and ultimatum to either declare war on Britain or be invaded. All of this required skillful diplomacy and decision making but the Portuguese monarch was ill prepared to make any decision whatsoever. Amazingly, it is as if the incompetence and lack of policy made by a dysfunctional Braganza monarchy of Portugal was so sincere that they were able to fool Napoleon and keep their kingdom while many more competent monarchies were wiped out forever.

Technically the ruling monarch of Portugal was Queen Maria I who unfortunately was quite mad after the untimely death of her husband and first son. Her second son Prince John (Don Juan) had never been trained to be a king. Don Juan disliked making decisions of any kind. Though he formally became prince regent in 1799, he was lazy, he was terribly afraid of thunder and tried to avoid bathing at any costs. As his government could never establish a firm policy neither the French nor the British could truly trust him. His wife Carlota was a Spanish princess, always unhappy, and spiteful. She was infamous for her scheming and intrigue. She plotted to over though her own husband, which lead to an unhappy married life. Due to this lack of marital intimacy, the prince regent took up a form of uninterested homosexuality with his servant, who later was given a title of nobility for his efforts.[65] All three of these characters are popular figures in Brazilian folklore, which any Brazilian child can tell you. Queen Maria I, because she arrived in Brazil as queen and was completely and obviously mad. This made a big impact upon arrival in Brazil. Prince John because he was fat and loved to eat chicken all day. He was rumored to hide cooked parts of chickens in the sleeves of his coat.[66] Finally, Princess Carlota to be mean, petty, and unhappy who was rumored to have had many lovers in Brazil. All the above is historically true, except the infidelity of Princess Carlota which cannot be proven. While all the other royal houses are being overthrown

---

[65] *Ibidem*. Page 162
[66] Available in: https://aventurasnahistoria.uol.com.br/noticias/reportagem/do-insano-apetite-a-morte-misteriosa-5-fatos-bizarros-sobre-o-monarcadom-joao-vi.phtml. Acsess in: 3/10/2021.

by Napoleon, the house of Portugal perhaps because of its flaws was able to escape and finally return to Portugal with their heads and crowns intact.

Dom João VI e Dona Carlota
Source: *Uol*, 2020

From historical documents of the time, it appeared to the French and British the Prince regent had only two options. 1) Portugal could agree to Napoleons terms declare war on Britain and hope that Napoleon would let him keep his crown. 2) Follow the plan of the British where the British Navy would take the royal family and court to escape to Brazil and let the British fight Napoleon on their own. The British were so concerned that they would be double crossed by their wavering ally and undecided prince, that the British Admiral Sidney Smith who oversaw the Portuguese evacuation had two sets of orders. If the Prince and court should any sign of staying in Portugal the Admiral had orders to bombard Lisbon and destroy the Portuguese fleet in harbor.[67] The British had reason to be worried that the Portuguese would double cross them. Not because the Portuguese had a plan to double cross their ally, but Prince John and the Portuguese were totally panic stricken and made up their policy as they went.

At first Prince John (Dom Joao) did not believe that Napoleon would overthrow him, but as the intentions of Napoleon became clear he panicked

---

[67] Available in: https://en.wikipedia.org/wiki/Sidney_Smith_(Royal_Navy_officer). Access in: 3/10/2021.

and blocked the entry of all British ships. On October 1807, the Portuguese captured and jailed the few remaining British citizens in Portugal and confiscated their goods. Dom João closed his ports to British shipping, hoping to stave off the French invasion and negotiate a secret agreement at the same time with the British.[68] He planned to allow the British to trade directly with Brazil in exchange for the protection of the Royal Navy should the court be forced to leave Lisbon. As British fleet appeared off Lisbon, a French army under French General Jean Junot headed through Spain for the Portuguese border. Dom Joao simply could not decide who to support and who to double cross. Portugal's tightrope act was beginning to falter. Dom João, having ordered the British out of Lisbon, tried and failed to appease Napoleon with a present of Brazilian diamonds and the offer of his son, D Pedro, for marriage into Bonaparte's family. On 23 November, Admiral Sidney Smith arrived with his fleet in Lisbon with newspapers from France that Napoleon and already decreed the end of the Portuguese Royal family, which quickly caused Prince John to change course again and instead of war with Britain, he decides to evacuate the Royal family and court to Brazil under the guard of the British Navy. Dom João and Admiral Smith set the date of November 27, the last possible date, for the court's exodus to the New World. Tellingly, Admiral Smith had two sets of order at the time of the evacuation. If the Portuguese Prince and court were not to be evacuated, and had joined Napoleon, his orders were to destroy the Portuguese navy and bombard Lisbon.

What was extraordinary was that neither the French, British nor Portuguese considered a third option that would seem normal to any other country. No one considered an option to stay and fight along with the British to save Portugal from invasion! As it turned out, Napoleon was fooled by the by the Portuguese Prince who both declared war on Britain and escaped with British help to Brazil. But why wouldn't the British want the Portuguese to stand and fight as allies? Could the Portuguese government have been so corrupt that for the British it was better to simply remove them to Brazil?

Corruption is one of the major problems still impacting Brazil and it was during this time that the Portuguese arrival started corruption as we know it today in Brazil. It is almost as if the British and the Portuguese knew that Portugal so decadent and corrupt that they would not want the

---

[68] GOMES, Laurentino. *1808:* Como uma rainha louca, um príncipes medroso, e um corte corrupta enganaram Napoleão e mudaram a Historia de Portugal e do Brasil. São Paulo: Globo, 2014, p. 47.

Portuguese as an ally during the war. It is true that the Portuguese Army was ripe with corruption. Brazilians are aware of this type of fraud today. The practice of paying salaries to worker who do not exist only to have the funds pocketed by corrupt politicians is still common in Brazil and was common in the Portuguese Army at the time. Portuguese officer would pocket the salaries of non-existent soldiers and supplies for nonexistent horses in the cavalry. On paper at least the Portuguese army was equal in size as the French and Spanish invasion force. Yet no thought was given to resistance or orders issued to mobilize the militia or the army. It is almost as if the British had decided that the Portuguese would be more trouble as an ally and simply better to get the Portuguese out of the way. As history would later show, almost any resistance could have stopped the invasion due to poor weather and poor execution by the French and Spanish.

A major problem facing Brazil today that also comes from this period, was the introduction of is a large and ineffective government. We can get a feeling for how large, corrupt, and ineffective the Portuguese government was. when we compare it to the change of the seat of government to the United State. When the young United Sates moved its capital to Washington D.C. in 1800, only 1000 permanent federal government employees moved from New York. When the Royal Family fled to Brazil with the court and government the total number of Portuguese that fled was 15,000 aristocrats, judges, priests, clerks' officers, lawyers. and other government officials and family members. The first printing presses, which previously had been banned in Brazil, were transported along with thousands of government records. What is sobering is consider that not only was the entire population of the Portuguese empire at the time was nine million people including the 2.7 million in Portugal abandoned by their Prince. United States had only recently moved its seat of government to Washington D.C. in 1800 had a population of 5.3 Million including nine hundred thousand slaves. The population of Brazil by comparison was 3.2 Million in 1800 of which half were slaves. The United States was overwhelmingly literate when most Brazilians could not write. How could Portugal justify a government of this size and what were all these newly poor aristocrats going to do to earn a living in Brazil?

Finding a place for the newly arrived Portuguese was straight forward. The Brazilians we simply forced out of their houses, by the army, to make room for the newly arrived aristocrats. 10,000 houses were branded with the letter's 'PR' standing for *principe regente* or prince regent, which meant that the homeowners had to evacuate to allow for the nobility to move in. In an almost silent form of protest, Brazilians quickly gave another meaning to the letters. They started to read 'PR' as *"ponha-se na rua,"* a phrase that directly translates as "put yourselves out on the street".[69] It is hard for us today to understand, that there was no expectation of equality under the law. Rio de Janeiro had three centuries of slavery and close to half of the population were slaves. It was Portuguese colonial policy to keep Brazil illiterate and without means of communication with the rest of Europe that were undergoing a change in philosophy due to the ideas of the enlightenment. Brazilians in 1808 simply accepted that the monarchy had absolute rule. Aristocrats were privileged, and no one at the time imagined that there would be equality under the law. This leads us problems of social inequality and lack of justice that still plague Brazil to this day. Today the idea that 15,000 Portuguese would dislodge the Brazilians from their homes should cause an uproar, however many Brazilians today are still fighting for equal justice under the law, and social inequality in Brazil remains one of the worst in the world.

Besides lodging the Portuguese court needed to be fed, and few of them were expected to toil for their food. By 1820 the Portuguese court was consuming 513 birds, ninety dozen eggs, a day.[70] This comes to 200 thousand chicken and 33 thousand dozen eggs per year. The demand for chicken was so high that the king made an order to give priority to the court for chickens. This caused a revolt in Rio, where the Brazilians created a sperate market to keep some chickens for themselves. To keep this inefficient government fed, the government went further into debt. The legacy of inefficient government that takes care of itself, with taxes and debt is something that all Brazilians can identify to this day.

While the Portuguese seemed to have no policy other than escape, the British were clear about their objectives. Upon arrival in Brazil, the Prince regent Dom Joao was forced to open ports of Brazil to trade with all countries, which was to say the British. The port of Rio de Janeiro quickly became the most visited port in South America. Business boomed, but financing a royal court is expensive. Prior to the invasion exclusive trade, the colonies financed Portugal, but the gold and diamond mining was ending in Minas Gerais and part of the agreement with Britain reduced tariffs, so the Portuguese needed to find new ways of financing itself.

---

[69] Available in: https://en.wikipedia.org/wiki/Transfer_of_the_Portuguese_court_to_Brazil. Access in: 3/11/2021.
[70] GOMES, Laurentino. *1808:* Como uma rainha louca, um príncipes medroso, e um corte corrupta enganaram Napoleão e mudaram a Historia de Portugal e do Brasil. São Paulo: Globo, 2014, p. 176.

One way was creating titles of nobility and selling these titles to wealthy Brazilians. We once again need to remember that at this time social and legal inequality was normal and the creation of new nobility would achieve two objectives for the newly arrived monarchy. First would be to raise desperately needed money, and secondly it would make allies of the wealthy Brazilian elite and large landholders. As these wealthy Brazilians were largely slave owners or slave traders, Prince Joao, created new layers of social inequality onto that which had already existed. In the first eight years in Brazil Dom Joao created more titles of nobility than in the entire three hundred years previously in Portugal.[71] Prior to leaving Portugal the entire aristocracy of Portugal consisted of 16 marques, 26 counts, 8 viscounts, and 4 barons. Upon arrival in Brazil, Dom Joao created a new aristocracy. Within the first 8 years he created 28 marques, 8 counts, 16 viscounts, and 21 barons. In additions to these newly minted titles to raise money from the less wealthy Brazilians he awarded 4,048 knighthoods, and great crosses of the Order of Christ, 1,422 commendations of the Order of Saint Bento, and 590 commendations of the Saint James.[72] None of these newly created aristocrats in Brazil had much sophistication to accompany their now titles and medals. A visiting American navy officer, Henry Brackenridge, was curious to find on the streets of Rio de Janeiro the number of nobles, businessmen, public servants and even slaves who would display medals and ribbons of various colors on an everyday basis. The constitution of the newly created United States forbids the use of orders and titles of nobility to Americans, so he may have found it ironic to see these medals and noble orders displayed in such a banal way by the newly created elite of Brazil.

One way to become noble in Brazil was to become a shareholder in the new Bank of Brazil. Between 1000 to 1500 Brazilians became shareholders in this bank that helped finance the monarchy in Brazil.[73] These funds of which would be taken back to Portugal upon the return of King Joao in 1822 and with the struggle of independence put Brazil deeply in debt, which is still is as of today.

What set in motion Brazil's independence and monarchy was a revolt in 1820 against the de facto British rule in Portugal. Dom Joao was happy in Brazil. He stayed in Brazil many years after the French were defeated in 1814. His forces needed to conquer a republican rebellion in Pernambuco

---

[71] *Ibidem*, p. 184.
[72] *Ibidem*.
[73] *Ibidem*, p. 185.

in 1817 and this postponed his coronation to be Emperor for a year. The revolt was in response to higher taxation to fund the monarchy with all the benefits going to Rio de Janeiro. While Brazil was prospering as the new capital of the Empire, Lisbon and Portugal were abandoned to the French, until the British army arrived. From 1807 to 1814. Portugal lost half a million people. Even though Napoleon was defeated in 1814, Dom Joao was quite happy to allow the British in the person of Field Marshal of the Portuguese Army, William Beresford to rule in his place. Imagine how frustrating it would have been to be a Portuguese commoner at that time. First your monarch runs away to Brazil with all the nobility and government, then you suffer years of war first with the French and later under English Occupation. Then after the war is over in which your countrymen fought on the winning side, you find yourself at the end of six years, still under what is essentially and English military occupation. This foreign head of state was an English General, William Beresford.

William Beresford has originally arrived in Lisbon on April 22, 1809 with the Duke of Wellington to begin what is now called the Peninsular war against the French. He was placed in charge of the remaining Portuguese Army and reformed the army with discipline and organization. The Portuguese Army fought several battles with great distinction in the war against France.

After peace was made and he returned from leave in England to resume is role and commander of the Portuguese army in 1815, but he did not limit his activities to just military administration but soon was placing himself in charge of civil administration of Portugal as well. To make sure this was appropriate he traveled to the court of Dom Joao in 1815 and returned 1816 with his powers expanded to essentially rule Portugal in the name of Dom Joao. By 1817 the Portuguese had had enough of British rule and with the help of Portuguese officers that had served under Napoleon began revolts against British rule. The plot was discovered, and the Portuguese rebels were executed with the consent of Dom João, but this only increased the anger of Portuguese people. When Bedford traveled again to Brazil to get still further powers to deal with the rebellion, the revolutionaries took advantage of his absence to set up an independent government under the Liberal Revolution of 1820. By the time Bedford returned the independent government was already in place. Bedford was forced to return to England. The independent government called themselves the Cortes, which was the historical parliament of Portugal that had not been summoned of 160 years. The members were not the old aristocrats but republicans which included representative from Brazil. The Cortes demanded the return of the Dom Joao to Portugal and one of the major objectives was to return Brazil to its prior colonial status. Surprisingly, many of the Brazilian representatives from the North East of Brazil that had not shared the prosperity of the capital but suffered high taxation agreed. supported and were represented in the Cortes.

This rebellion once again forced Dom Joao to make a policy decision, which he detested. The Portuguese Army in Brazil upon hearing of the Revolution in Portugal mutinied in Rio de Janeiro on February 26, 1821. It was left to Dom Pedro to negotiate with the soldiers and agree to accept the Portuguese constitution. This forced his father Dom Joao to return to Portugal. If he did not go back, then Portugal would declare a republic. To try to retain both Portugal and Brazil he returned but left his son Dom Pedro I to be prince regent of Brazil. Dom Joao left for Portugal to submit to the Cortes in April 1821. Dom Joao took all the funds of the Bank of Brazil with him and left Brazil with his government debts.

Don Pedro was completely different from his father. He grew up in Brazil and was used to traveling in the outdoors on horseback. He chose to dress usually like a commoner and disliked using uniforms or court protocol. He is known for treating his wife the Austrian Princess Maria Leopoldina, particularly poorly due to his extramarital affairs. He was tall dark and strong, and determined to stay in Brazil. Pedro had read the works of Voltaire, Edmond Burke and other thinkers of the enlightenment so he was not really interested in being absolute ruler in Portugal. As his father had returned to Portugal with all the funds of the Bank for Brazil, the bank was left to fail which caused and economic crisis. This forced Dom Pedro to reduce extravagances and expenses of his government. The Cortes in Portugal wanted Dom Pedro to return to Brazil, which he refused. Many Brazilians were not eager to become a colony again of Portugal. The situation came to ahead, when Dom Pedro on a trip to São Paulo and Minas Gerais received news that the Cortes had dissolved his government in Brazil as well as the independence of Brazil. The Cortes of Portugal now demanded Don Pedro's return now too. Upon learning this, Don Pedro did famously, what Brazilians called the *"Grito"* or shout of "Independence or Death," which is celebrated to mark Brazilian independence and is a national holiday.

Most Brazilian do not realize today how bloody the civil war between the Brazilians who sided with the Portuguese Cortes and the Brazilians who sided with Dom Pedro for independence. Dom Pedro had the allegiance of Rio, São Paulo, and Minas Gerais but the rest of Brazil needed to be conquered. This war of independence went against the historical tide of history. Whereas most of the western world were fighting absolute monarchy to establish democratic republics, Brazil was fighting a revolutionary republic to set up an independent monarchy! Later the North Eastern states lead by the state of Pernambuco and Ceará would try to separate and create in 1824 the Confederation of Ecuador, which has nothing to do with the country of Ecuador, but the proximity of the separatist north states to the equator. This republic was based on the same democratic ideas of the French and American revolution and once more the rebel tried to get help from the United states and once again, they were ignored. This was the second time the North East tried to get independence from the monarchy and establish an independent republic, but this rebellion was defeated militarily by both naval and military invasion ending with all the republican leaders executed. The slaves of course, which was roughly half of the population were not liberated and seemed abandoned by both sides. These events and war did create a unified country, which would likely have split into separate republics if not unified into a Monarchy by Dom Pedro and his forces.

There were no physical barriers limiting the size of Brazil, unlike the United States which had recently the Louisiana Purchase from Napoleon and was just discovering its territory. Though Dom Pedro was responsible for unifying Brazil as we know it, he did this by crushing Republican movements that could have resulted in responsible democratic institutions. Many Brazilians at the time did not believe that Brazil would be ready for democracy. You can even find Brazilin that think this today. Dom Pedro unified the country but did not create the government institutions, for a functioning constitutional monarchy. When the Monarchy was finally overthrown in 1888, instead of a republican government the crown was replaced by a military dictatorship. Later military dictatorships also kept Brazil from developing the democratic institutions to govern well. There is one happy exception to the sad story. The one Brazilian Province that did successfully succeed from both Portugal and the Brazilian Monarchy went on to become perhaps the most successful democracy in South America.

The Brazil of the 1820s geographically looks much as it does today. The major rivers and the Amazon had been explored and mapped. The war of independence had united sperate provinces into one country. In addition to the Brazil that we know today there was an additional southernmost territory which was called *Província Cisplatina*. This territory was invaded by Brazil in 1816, due to fears of the Brazilian empire that republican ideas of the people in this region would spread in Southern Brazil. The territory was placed under the administration of Rio Grande do Sul. To this day the state of Rio Grande do Sul and Uruguay share a common culture and even a dialect as Portuguese and the Spanish of these two regions are comingled. The Gaucho culture has always valued independence.

By 1822 Dom Pedro had reconquered the north of Brazil and Brazil had declared its independence. In southern Brazil, however, what started as a minor rebellion in a former Brazilian region called *"Cisplatina"* soon became a war when this province was joined by what had been the rouge northern most provinces of Argentina called the Untied Provinces of the Rio Plata. In 1825 the United Provinces declared independence from the Kingdom of Brazil and Brazil declared war on the United Provinces. Dom Pedro had largely bankrupted the country by this time, though his wars of unification. The Brazilian army was soundly defeated by the Argentine and Uruguay forces in 1828 at *Itzuaingo*. In total more than 8,000 Brazilian died the campaign.[74] Though there was intermittent warfare by 1828 the Brazilian Monarchy had largely given up due to war fatigue and lack of volunteers to continue the war. A peace treaty brokered by the British was signed on August 27, 1828 which recognized a new country. This new country would go on to be the strongest democracy in South America. This country became present day Uruguay.

Uruguay has the functioning democratic institution that Brazil still lacks. The country has a well-educated population and functioning judiciary. It ranks high in social equality, safety, health, and lack of corruption. These institutions had to be fought for to create a society that values a stable democracy. The historical experience of the people of Uruguay successfully fighting and defeating a monarchy unified the country around the ideals of the enlightenment to produce the required institutions of a functioning democracy. Like the American and French revolutions before it, war against a monarch and later invasions tempered the Uruguay people to be prepared for liberty. The distortion of the unification of Brazil with a monarchy distorted and delayed Brazilian society for the development of the ideals of the enlightenment, and for these reasons Brazil has yet to develop a functioning democracy. The simple concept that are people are treated fairly

---

[74] GOMES, Laurentino. *1822*: Como um homem sábio, uma princesa triste, e um escocês louco por dinheiro ajudaram dom Pedro a criar Brasil – um pais que tinha todo para dar errado. São Paulo: Globo, 2015, p.226.

and equally under the law remains and aspiration that Brazilians know they need to achieve but are still looking for the way to reach this goal.

In the end Dom Pedro abdication on April 7, 1831 left one final legacy of Portuguese domination of Brazil, that of unstable and ineffective government. Dom Pedro was widely admired and the hero of the unification of Brazil had lost the support of the people for four major reasons. One was the campaign in Uruguay that drained blood and treasure for which Dom Pedro was given much of the blame. By 1828 the monarchy which had always used mercenaries, had employed many European mercenaries to help in the war in Uruguay. These French, German, Irish and others were disciplined with the same brutality that Brazil treated its slaves. These European soldiers refused not be whipped and rose in rebellion in 1828 in the streets the capital. The rebellion was contained with a high cost of forty Brazilians and 120 mercenaries dead. The second reason was Dom Pedro's open sexual adventures, which humiliated his much-loved queen, a princess of Austria.[75] The third reason was his dissolving of the constitution of 1823 which could have prepared Brazil for a constitutional monarchy. Within Brazil there was an important struggle between the King and Parliament as to who should appoint the government minsters. Instead, Dom Pedro censured the press, persecuted his political enemies, and crushed the Confederation of Ecuador, yet another rebellion in the North East of Brazil looking to create a democratic republic. The final reason was the political instability resulting from his impetuous nature.[76] In the end not only the people, but his army and even imperial guard turned against Dom Pedro and on April 12, 1822 he abdicated to leave Brazil in the hands of advisors to his 11-year-old son, Dom Pedro II.

There is a touching exchange of letters between the abandoned son and new monarch and his father who had already left the palace in secret which gives a human side to the two Brazilian Emperors. Dom Pedro kissed all his children before leaving while they slept. When the 11-year-old Pedro and heir to the Brazilian empire, upon not finding his father in the palace wrote.

> *My dear father and sir,*
>
> *When I awoke, I could not find your imperial majesty, and mommy to kiss your hand, I am so upset my dear father. I ask*

---

[75] Ibidem, p. 226.
[76] Ibidem, p. 226.

your imperial majesty to never forget this son who has always had obedience, respect, and love, for his parents who he has lost so early. I kiss respectfully the hands of your Imperial Majesty. This of Your Imperial Majesty's longing and obedient son, Pedro.[77]

Five days later upon an English ship, Dom Pedro I responded to his sons' letter.

My dear son and my emperor,

I thank you so, for the letter you wrote me. I could barely read it for the tears in my eyes would hardly allow me to see... I leave children, my country and friends, there could be no greater sacrifice.... Remember always that your father loved you and yours and my country, follow the advice of those I have left to see to your education, and conduct yourself so that the whole world will admire you. Receive this blessing from your father with great longing and without hope of seeing you again.

Dom Pedro de Alcantara.

To his credit under the reign of Dom Pedro II, was particularly good for Brazil. While a child, Brazil was governed by regents which created much political infighting. By 1840 the politicians and country were tired of the intrigues and in the hopes of creating a more stable government reduced the age for Pedro II to have power become Emperor from 18 to 16. In general, Brazil prospered under his rule, and to his great credit, Pedro II finally began to dismantle slavery. Since 1826, Brazil had promised to stop the slave trade, and though this had been agreed to with the British nothing was implemented. So, when a Brazilian says "Para Ingles ver" it means this is a rule that a Gringo wants us to do something, but we are just going to act like we will do it but do what we want.

Slavery took years to be dismantled and was extremely popular with most free and powerful Brazilians. There was no popular abolitionist movement in Brazil. If there was one policy that united all the different factions in Brazil it was that slavery needed to be maintained. After the civil war in the United States a group of Southerner came to find a city in São Paulo called Americana. Under continuous British pressure slavery

---

[77] *Ibidem*, p. 222. (Translation my own).

was on its way out despite the wishes of the slaveholders. In 1871, there passed a free womb law so that newborns of salves would be free. In 1885, all slaves over 60 would be freed, and finally in 1888 the golden law was passed by Dom Pedro's daughter Princess Isabela, who finally freed all the slaves. This policy of abolition would gain no favor for the imperial family. The large local landowners who were slave owners, shifted in favor of a republic. This oligarchy would support the overthrow of the imperial family the following year.

The Brazilian Monarchy when it was overthrown in 1889, was not replaced by a republic, as we understand that word, but by a military government. Dom Pedro II had been hard working monarch and was overwhelmingly popular with common Brazilians at that time. Military officer and the landed establishment however, plotted the overthrow of what was becoming a constitutional monarchy. The military coup happened so peacefully that the Brazilian people had no time to react. The abolition of slavery was likely one contributing factor to the overthrow Dom Pedro II, but most people did not even know a coup had happened and Dom Pedro was not interested in raising a resistance. He was tired and he accepted his retirement and returned to Europe. Power then transferred back and forth between various oligarch supported republics and back to a military government which only created a democratic government in 1980. However, without the history and institutions of a democracy the core problems of Brazil were never addressed. Inequality, corruption, and a large and ineffective government continue to this day in Brazil. The Brazilians have been disappointed and deceived by both the politicians of the right and left. They are disappointed with a judiciary that seems to protect the well-connected and grants them impunity. Only in this decade after countless deceptions, is there a glimmer of hope that Brazil can start to create the institution needed to address its historical problems. The second part of Being Brazilian is written to give hope for a better future.

Chapter Nine

Jeitinho and Malandragem: Underclass Survival Skills

Jeitinho Brasileiro

In the Simpson episode "Blame it on Lisa," in which Homer gets kidnapped as the family tires to find the Brazilian orphan that Lisa is sponsoring, we get a look at Brazilian *Jeitinho*. The following dialogue happens in the Brazilian version of this show. Bart and Homer are walking on the beach with cloths and shoes like typical Americans. This is the following dialogue:

> *Bart: Hey, look! There's Copacabana beach! The heart and soul of Rio!*
>
> *Lifeguard: Excuse me, Americans!*
>
> *Homer: How did you know?*
>
> *Lifeguard: There is a dress code on this beach. But don't worry, we have Brazilian Jeitinho!*
>
> *Bart and Homer then instantly appear in Brazilian bathing shorts and sandals in proper Brazilian style.*
>
> *Bart: I feel so European.*

In the version in the United States the phrase "we have *Jeitinho Brasileiro* is changed to "we can help you with that". This is what *Jeitinho* is, it is a way Brazilians help each other out, at time by bending the rules! Brazilian life is so full of rules that the average Brazilian cannot comply. Rather than look at *jeitinho* as some form of petty corruption as some Brazilians do, it is more realistic to look at *jeitinho* as a way Brazilians help each other out in the problems of daily life. Brazilians use *jeitinho* every day, yet they are uncomfortable discussing the topic to non-Brazilians because they think they will be looked down upon. Many Brazilians think that *jeitinho* is the beginning of the slippery slope to of corruption and bribery. Some Brazilian intellectuals point to *jeitinho* as an intrinsic moral failing, that dooms Brazilians to endless cycles of immunity and corruption. *Jeitinho* is one thing and corruption is something entirely. *Jeitinho* is a survival tactic creatively invented by Brazilians to survive in a society with too many rules and regulations and an unjust power structure. Corruption and Impunity favor the elite and must be stopped.

"*Jeito*" means way, and *jeitinho* means little way. To be Brazilian you should look at *jeitinho* the same way the producers of the Simpson do. Look at jeitinho as a way to help someone out, or to help another. "*Jeitinho*" can also mean finding a creative solution a problem with your own resources and personal connections. It is a wonderful Brazilian characteristic, and nothing to be ashamed of in most cases. *Jeitihno* is not corruption. *Jeitinho* is a survival skill.

Think of looking at two walls in your house. On one wall you have your real life, and on the other wall you have all the rules regulation, and social convention that exist in an oversized and ineffective state. In the middle where the wall of real life intersect the wall of rules, in the corner is "*Jeitinho Brasileiro*". It is the place where the reality meets the rules. It is a mechanism for self-survival, and though it may make someone's life easier, there is no underlying corrupt purpose or intention other than just helping someone out of asking for a favor. You can use the term as follows:

> "How did you get these tickets to the football game? I thought they were sold out!"

> "I know the owner of a travel agency, and he gave me a *Jeito*."

Brazilian life is full of rules and laws many of which are contradictory. For the common Brazilian to start a business, or get a place in school, get documents, or do any number for simple things requires help from somebody. There are whole industries of people who are intermediaries that facilitate daily life. These are called *despachantes*. Some despachantes execute function like a custom broker or freight forwarder. Other functions are not so clear but can help you get your driver's license back when it has been suspended or help you speed up your passport process if you cannot drive across the city to present the documents in person.

An excellent example of *"Jeitinho Brasileiro"* happened to an American friend of mine. He was starting a high-tech business venture in Brazil and he had venture capital funding to hire lawyers to start this company legally with all the proper tax requirements. However, what he had not anticipated was how long this was going to take and as a result he overstayed his visa. He was petrified that he was going to go to jail. In his home country this would have been a dangerous problem with potential jail time or deportation. He arrived at the airport extremely agitated because not only did he have to go back to his home country, but he had just finished creating the legal entities and requirement for his new business in Brazil and he was afraid he would lose all that work and not be able to return!

When he arrived at customs in the airport and he presented his passport with his expired visa, he was worried that this would lead to something dreadful. The customs agent asked my friend why his visa was expired. My friend told the truth that he was trying to set up a business and that he hoped to come back to Brazil in the future. The Brazilian costumes agent just waived him though and told him to get a new visa to enter Brazil the next time.

If my friend were a visitor to his own home country it is likely he would have been detained, perhaps even jailed, and eventually deported, without a chance for a second visa. But what was the thinking of the Brazilian customs agent?

1. This American is not a criminal he is trying to set up a business.

2. If I stop him and arrest him, he will be deported to his home country anyhow, and I will have a lot of reports to fill out and this will ruin his life.

3. He wants to come back to Brazil. I will give him *Jeitinho Brasileiro*.

Just like the lifeguard wanted to help the Simpson, the customs agent helped my friend. Some would say he was not doing his job correctly, and I would respond that he did his job excellently. Instead of hassling my friend he helped him and in return Brazil would soon get new jobs in the high-tech sector. Thinking independently and not applying all the rules all the time is not by itself wrong.

Jeitinho can be **implicit** in the sense that it is common practice to ignore the rules. *Jeitinho* can be **explicit** in that you must ask or do something to get your way around the rules. There are many instances in life when *Jeitinho* is assumed and therefor **implicit**. For example, the police in Brazil have dangerous jobs, they usually drive with their flashing lights on in traffic and it is generally assumed that not all this time is for a real emergency. However normally people give them the **implicitly** the right of way to help the police through traffic. You will also notice Brazilians immediately tailgating the police to get that benefit for traffic for themselves, which is an example of **explicit** Jeitinho even though there is a law that prohibits this, the police do not stop to enforce it! On the other hand, Brazil after dark is dangerous, so normal driving practice is not to stop and wait for the stoplight to turn green after 10 PM. The police know that this is not the law, but they know the parts of town that are dangerous, so the let this go. They will not stop you or ticket you for stopping and then going through a red light at night. This is **implicit** *Jeitinho Brasileiro*.

However, for explicit Jeitinho you need to ask for it or do something. For example, it has been raining terribly and you arrive at the opera late. Normally you would not be allowed in until the after the first act ends, but as the doorman and staff of the theater know it is raining and you can explain the situation with the traffic, and you say, *"por favor dá um jeitinho."* (Please give me a jeitinho!) Even though it is against the rules of the theater they will let you in. The theater doorman gave you and explicit *Jeitinho*.

Jeitinho can get you the extra orange juice or milkshake that the attendant makes for you at the diner, this is also called *"chorinho"* or "little crying" to get the extra. There is no need to cry, you just ask for the *chorinho* just like you ask for the jeitinho. It you paid money for this benefit this would be bribery and that is a topic for another chapter in this book. *Jeitinho* is innocent exactly because there is nothing linked to this favor. There is no money involved and there is no quid pro quo expected. It is just doing a favor.

Perhaps one reason I am so in favor of *"Jeitinho Brasileiro,"* is because the opposite practice of small-minded bureaucrats, blindly in forcing petty rules are so common in other countries. I am sure the reader can think of instances of their lives were small, minded people try to apply rules that caused you inconvenience at the least or even personal loss. I remember when police in Miami told my six-year-old daughter that she had to close her lemonade stand because she did not have a license! She came home crying. A Brazilian once joked with me that you are free in the United States if you obey all the rules! I prefer *Jeitinho Brasileiro* any day.

The rules of the formal economy create the need for Jeitinho

Millions of Brazilian make a living in the informal economy though *jeitinho*. The farmer selling fruits and vegetables from his truck in the middle of the city. Peddlers selling food and items on the highways in bad traffic or at stop lights. Domestic servants, lumberjacks, sugarcane cutters, cotton pickers, and others all are part of the informal economy. Government statistics of the IBGE in October 2019 pointed out that the informal economy represents around 41% of all the jobs in Brazil. The official unemployment rate was 11.8 % or 12.5 million officially unemployed but that include the 38.9 million Brazils that work in the informal economy. Working in the informal economy means that you are working without having your labor registered or your salary or profits taxed. Someone self-employed selling homemade meals to construction workers is in the informal economy, those construction workers, if not on a formal payroll and receiving, cash are also in the informal economy. The uber driver is the informal economy, but this is not a "Gig" economy that people choose as a lifestyle. The informal economy is a means of survival. This however also means that there are 38.9 million employees paying no retirement contributes, or payroll tax. The overwhelming majority of these people would be happy to have a job in the formal economy. The owners of informal businesses, in contrast to criminal enterprises, would prefer a registered business if it was not so difficult and costly. Business in the informal economy provide goods and services without coercion but do not follow the regulations and tax rules to operate.

How can you tell if a business is formal or informal? An informal business will never give you an invoice, however even formal businesses may ask you if you want an invoice, so perhaps even formal businesses are not completely formal.

The informal economy is one huge *"Jeitinho Brasileiro."* By some estimates the informal economy produces 16-17% of the GDP in Brazil and employees millions and creates thousands of unofficial businesses.[78] There are

---

[78] Available in: http://www.xinhuanet.com//english/2017-08/16/c_136529083.htm. Access in: 3/11/2021

two ways of looking at this. The informal economy is "bad." It deprives the government of taxes on payroll, goods, and services. The other way to look at the informal economy is good, and necessary. These businesses and workers provide goods a service to Brazil out of a necessity to feed themselves and their families.

Because the costs of hiring an employee legally or for that matter the complexity of creating a legal enterprise in Brazil is so costly, the informal economy tends to be sticky downward. An economic crisis as Brazil suffered in 2014-15 caused the official unemployment to jump. The cost of new hires and business make the unemployment rate to drop slowly. So out of necessity people work and join the informal economy.

The ugly version Jeitinho: "Você Sabe com quem está falando?" Do you know who you are talking to?

This is another strategy adopted by Brazilians for self-preservation, but not so friendly and plays to some of the darker weakness of Brazilian society. From the beginning of its history Brazil is a class conscience society. "Do you know who you are talking too" is a social mechanism to get you a favor by exerting your social satiation or presumed social station on top of the other Brazilian. This likely is an inheritance of colonial times in Brazil where the Portuguese aristocracy fleeing Napoleon and their country deemed themselves worthy of some undo advantage in the new world.

For example, you are on your lunch hour and there is a line at the bank, and you need to pay a bill. You do not want to stay in line. For whatever reason you think are superior, so you go to the front of the line and ask for service. If anyone behinds you questions, you say, "Você sabe com quem está falando?." Do you know who you are talking to! This is strangely a successful strategy. It works on me if the person making the statement is a well-dressed older woman or a man. This works with police too, if you have been out too late at night up to no good. That said, it is best to try Jeitinho strategy before you try the strategy of "Do you know who you are speaking to?" because it could backfire and get you in worse trouble.

Because you are a foreigner and most Brazilians will assume that foreigners are rich, this is a strategy that is open to you to use. I do not personally use it or recommend it because it perpetuates and reinforces the social stratification and implicit racism in Brazil that we should be trying to change. Let me repeat again, Brazil is not a racist county, on the contrary most Brazilians have African and mixed heritage. Some will argue that Brazil is a post racist society, but I will not go that far. What is am saying is that Brazil is a very socially segregated society were the poor live separate from the rich. Darker skinned Brazilian tend to be poorer than lighter skinned Brazilians. You as a gringo, independent of your skin color will be placed in the rich category so using this "Do you know who you are talking to?" strategy to get your way, simply perpetuates a social injustice in Brazil.

"Do you know who you are talking too" is an ugly strategy to get what you want as a foreigner, because you are exploiting a weakness in the Brazilian social hierarchy specific to foreigners. Mario Sergio Cortella, a Brazilian intellectual has argued that this strategy is of supreme ignorance because you are expecting a benefit above all the universe's creation. His argument is that the Universe is so big that any one individual is too insignificant to gain special importance.

I however I am against the use of "Do you know who you are talking to?" because it plays to a racist and class-based weakness in Brazilian ethos that needs to be overcome. Any strategy that the white, educated, and rich can use, but the colored poor and uneducated cannot use is immoral and against the categorical imperative ipso facto! As Emanuel Kant would argue, the strategy of "Do you know who you are talking to" may work for you as a visitor to Brazil and it can get you out of a jam, and even though you are hurting no one it is immoral.

Lei de Gerson or Gerson's Law

Everybody knows Murphy's law. "Everything that can go wrong will go wrong and the worst possible moment. Brazilians have another law called the Lei de Gerson. Gerson de Oliveira Nunes was a great midfielder who played on the national team with Pele. As a football player he was he played the beautiful game as it was played in the 1970's. He however did a cigarette commercial for a brand that was supposedly more smooth and cheaper than the other Brands. The key part of the slogan of this advertisement, that was taken out of context was.

"Gosto de levar vantagem em tudo, certo? Leve vantagem você também"

I like to take advantage of everything, right? You should too!

Gerson greatly lamented this distortion of the add and his participation in what soon became a popular saying. In any stereotype there is always a grain of truth, which introduces us to a Brazilian cultural icon, the Malandro.

O mistério da malandragem
Source: *Pinterest*

Malandro and Malandragem

The *Malandro* is a Brazilian cultural icon, a character seen in Carnival, Brazilian entertainment as well as a spirit in Brazilian Umbanda religion.

A *malandro* is an underdog, who gets what is wants through cunning and advantage. *Malandragem* is a lifestyle for someone who does not believe that hard work and honesty will get him, from the social positions that he comes from, a realistic good outcome. This perception is necessary to understand who the Malandro is and understand his behavior. Brazilians know that *malandragem* is not good, but they are not quite sure that it is bad. The *Malandro* looks as life as a game that you need to win, so he uses *jeitinho Brasileiro*, smooth talking, cunning and any other advantage he can use to bend people and institutions to his will to get a good outcome. The *Malandro* is sophisticated and subtle and uses his intelligence and cunning to win, but the use of violence is not out of the question either. *Malandragem* is all the strategies involved for the *Malandro* to get the best possible outcome with the least possible effort.

Brazilians cheer for the *Malandro* because though he is from the underclass, he is smart and can overcome obstacles in creative ways to win over his superiors. The word *mal* means bad or evil, so a *malandro* is at best an antihero. Someone we cheer for even when we know he is not good.

We can think about the Shakespeare character Falstaff for us to identify a similar character in English speaking countries. Falstaff is a rouge, a drunk lecherous coward who corrupts prince Henry in one play, he tries to seduce married women in a second play and leads a band of cowards to war with France in a third play. However, he is also one of the best loved characters because we can identify with him. Who would not rather drink and womanize rather than working honestly if you could get away with it? If you are forced to fight, would you not choose the back racks away from the fighting if you could choose? We love Falstaff because he speaks a truth that we can all understand, even if we know this is wrong. Brazilian likewise recognize the malandro as bad, while admiring his cunning and cheering his success. In Spanish Literature, the Malandro character is like the character of the "Picaro".

To introduce Americans to their new Brazilian allies in World War II Walt Disney created a character call Ze Carioca, who is something of a *malandro*. Ze is a nickname for Jose and Carioca is the nickname from someone Rio de Janeiro. In the film, Saludos Amigo, which Walt Disney used to introduce Americans to Brazil. Brazil was now an ally of the United States fighting the Germans and America had its large airbase in Natal. In the film, when Ze Carioca meets Donald Duck who holds out his hand to greet Ze Carioca, Ze Carioca give the Brazilian Man hug we learned in Chapter 1 in return. Ze then takes Donald around town to dance samba meet girls and drink cachaça. Poor Donald Duck has a hang over the next day. In his comics, Ze Carioca charms the girls and lives the good life. Although forgotten in the United States, Ze Carioca is seen as a sympathetic malandro in Brazil.

A visita de Disney à América Latina
Source: *El País*, 2016

What many people, Brazilians included, do not know is there was a historical person who later became a spirit in Umbanda that Ze Carioca and Malandros are based. This spirit is Ze Pilintra who is a spirit and patron saint of bars, the bohemian life, he loves gambling and fighting. The way Ze Carioca dresses, moves and talks is like Ze Pilintra who comes from the line of spirits in Umbanda.[79]

What many Brazilians do not know is that the legend of the Malandro is based on a historical person who was a black ex slave named Jose do Anjos.[80] Jose do Anjos was from the north east who was a great malandro,

---

[79] Available in: https://www.notibras.com/site/ze-pilintra-da-historia-a-oracoes-e-oferendas/#:~:text=Amante%20de%20diversos%20tipos%20de,e%20agrada%20bastante%20a%20entidade. Access in: 3/11/2021.
[80] *Ibidem*.

lover of women, great with a knife, and a gambler who loved the good life. No one would fight him, not even the police. He was a great lover of women and treated them like queens. Supposedly Jose do Anjos moved to Rio de Janeiro as a young man. Other say he was born in Rio de Janeiro. But Jose do Anjos is like Paul Bunyan or King Arthur in that you do not know where the man end or the legend begins. It is no use wondering if the man made the myth of the myth made the man, Jose do Anjos in this case became the spirit of Ze Pilantra in Umbanda and Candomblé. The characteristic to the Brazilian concept of a malandro comes from this man, or his spirit. He is well dressed in black or white suit and hat. His spirit is consulted on manners of money and his advice is usually to look at the problems of life as a game. Some of the sayings attributed to him are:[81]

"The level of my irony depends on the level of absurdities I needed to hear"

"You know you are on the right path when you lose interest in looking back."

"Sometimes the best knowledge is to look like you know nothing"

"I choose well my enemies, because I do not give the honor to cross me to just anyone"

If you bring up the name Ze Pilantra or *Malandro* in the context of a real person or spiritual being the conversation with Brazilians can turn quite serious. A friend of mine swears that she came upon the *Malandro* as a spirit at a party in the interior of Minas Gerais when she was much younger. As a teenager she practiced capoeira, and she and her girlfriend friend went with the rest of the group to a small house in the countryside of Minas Gerais. What friend did not know was the house was owned by the parents of some of the children in the group and that they practiced Umbanda in the house.

The party started off well enough, with beer drinking and dancing, and my friend was swimming by the pool. All was fine until spirits became incorporated with three of the young people one of whom was the oldest son of the parents owned the house. The spirits entered the young people who were barefooted. My friend was by the swimming pool when one of the brothers ran out the house and cried. "Put on you Sandals, Put on your sandals. The Malandro has come down and he told us he is bringing friends

---

[81] *Ibidem.*

and we need to keep the beer well stocked, or they will break up the house!" My friend stated that the brother who was possessed by the *Malandro* seemed changed in both voice and physical appearance and began playing samba on the stereo. The brother who had channeled the *Malandro* was now wearing a hat and talking with authority to the other kids and spirits. One young woman seemed possessed by a gypsy who Brazilians will recognize as one of the spirits named *Pomba Gira*. My friend could not identify the other spirit it but this one seemed to be of from a young boy that wanted candy. During the writing of this book, another friend told me that this spirit seemed to be one of the twins known as "*Cosme e Damião*" My friend and her girlfriend panicked and put on their sandals to run down the road to find a priest. Meanwhile, the younger brother called his parents to tell them what was happening.

When she reached reach the priest's house, the priest told her that he knew that that was a house of Umbanda, and they had to take care of themselves but that he was not going up there without parental permission. Fortunately, the other brother who was still unpossessed had called his parents who arrived at the house, with other members of the church who sent the *Malandro* and his friends out of the young people.

Part of being Brazilian is recognizing and respecting, beliefs and practices that are not from your own culture. Where other countries have wars and violence over divergences of beliefs, Brazilians are more tolerant and incorporate mixtures of different people into a common culture. The *Malandro* is a cultural icon central to Brazil and provides to some Brazilians a role model for life. Other Brazilians look to the *Malandro* as a petty criminal always looking for an advantage. No Brazilian will deny that the *Malandro* is part of a common Brazilian Culture. When Walt Disney visited to Rio de Janeiro, he discovered the *malandro* lifestyle in the 1940's and liked it. From this trip, Ze Carioca was born.

Gringo Advice

Jeitinho does not need to be fixed, it is a wonderful characteristic of Brazilian creativity and culture. Just like the writers of the Simpson translated, "We have Brazilian Jeitinho in Portuguese to "We can help you" in English, *Jeitinho* does not need to be changed. What needs to be changed are the rules and laws that make *Jeitinho* necessary in the first place. If Jeitinho is the way to get around the rules, Brazil needs less rules.

The confusing rules, contradictory legislation and ineffective judicial system that make *Jeitinho* a necessary resource need to be reformed. Brazilians are terrific at fixing problems and *Jeitinho* is a strategy to do that for short term problems without malicious intent. Jeitinho make life easier for the common Brazilian without access to power and lawyers. Brazilian resort to *Jeitinho* when the formal solution is too complicated or not practical.

As far as the *malandro,* he is a complicated Brazilian character. He is certainly a cultural icon of Brazil. He is neither good or bad, but he can teach us an important lesson in life. We are all responsible for our own happiness.

Chapter Ten

Corruption and Impunity

Most people in modern democracies think that their politicians get away with murder. In Brazil, they literally did. In December 1963, Arnon de Mello, father of former president Fernando Collor de Mello, murdered a colleague on the floor of the Brazilian Senate.[82] Arnon de Mello and another senator, Silvestre Péricles, had a long-standing feud. After receiving death threats, both Senators arrived armed to the Senate. During the debate on the Senate floor, Arnon de Mello thought that he saw Senator Pericles make a move for his gun. Anticipating the threat, the father of the future president took out his gun and fired three times at his enemy on the senate floor! All three shots missed his enemy, but he did hit and kill another Senator from Acre by mistake. He was arrested, tried, found not guilty for reasons of self-defense, and immediately released. Thirty years later, after his son Pedro Collor de Mello, the first directly elected President of Brazil, was impeached for corruption. His wife was suspected of stealing from a charity for the poor. Later, his campaign manager, PC Farias, and his girlfriend would be found shot under mysterious circumstances in 1993 with eight bodyguards guarding his beach house.

Fifty years later, things have at least made some improvement. Brazil's Federal Police (PF) arrested the leader of the governing party's bloc in the Senate, Sen. Delcídio do Amaral, after charging him with obstruction of justice.[83] This was not an isolated case. Former president Luiz Ignácio "Lula" da Silva, who is still one of the most powerful persons in Brazil, was sentenced to almost 10 years in prison for money laundering. However, Lula was released again along with other common criminals and politicians

---

[82] Available in: https://aventurasnahistoria.uol.com.br/noticias/reportagem/assassinato-no-senado-5-fatos-sobre-a-desgraca-do-senador-arnon-de-mello.phtml. Access in: 3/11/2021.

[83] Zavascki, Teori, "Injunction no. 4039," Supremo Tribunal Federal, November 25, 2015. http://www.stf.jus.br/arquivo/cms/noticiaNoticiaStf/anexo/Acao_Cautelar_4039.pdf. As explained later in this paper, Sen. do Amaral entered a plea deal that exempted him from further prosecution in the case in which he was involved.

when the supreme court reversed previous jurisprudence, that defendants could be freed on appeal until their case was heard by the supreme court. This gives wealthy Brazilians an almost unlimited right of appeal to be finally judged, in the supreme court. So, while the rule of law is improving there is still a long way to go to correct the impunity the rich and powerful have in Brazil.

The situation of corruption in Brazil is so disappointing that unless you are willing to take the long view it is easy to become frustrated at the lack of progress. As Homer Simpson once said, "Sometimes you have to talk bad about other people to feel good about yourself!" This is the way the *gringos* and Brazilians need to think about corruption and impunity in Brazil. No matter how horrifying and frustrating the situation of corruption in Brazil is now, from the point of view of history there is evidence of improvement.

If *jeitinho* is a Brazilian mechanism for the weak in Brazil to survive, then corruption and impunity in Brazil is for the powerful and connected. They abuse and break the law to receive and perpetuate undue economic and political benefits. A famous Brazilian comedian once said that, "Corruption is not a Brazilian invention, but impunity is truly ours." Corruption is destroying Brazil and it must stop. This is no exaggeration; corruption almost bankrupted the partially state-owned oil company Petrobras, which represents about 10% of the GDP of the country. Brazil needs to stop corruption, or it will become a failed state. It is that simple.

It is hard for a *gringo* who does not live in Brazil to imagine the scope and magnitude of corruption in Brazil. We *gringos* tend to think of corruption as involving small groups of people hiding in the shadows. It is hard for us gringos to imagine the scale and complexity that such blatantly illegal activities could involve hundreds of people and entire corporate and government departments working together to rob billions. More importantly to Brazilians is the apparent reluctance of the judiciary to punish the powerful who commit these crimes. Brazil has a long history of corruption and impunity which does not reconcile itself with the reality of most Brazilians, the overwhelming majority of whom are hardworking and law-abiding people. The scale of corruption in this century has awakened the population to the imbedded corruption in Brazilian society and what appears to be vested interests of the political and, at times, the judicial establishment to maintain the status quo. Brazil is now facing a struggle for law and order which has been delayed by history. Brazil's history of corruption came to Brazil with the arrival of the Portuguese monarchy in 1808. Only due to the economic crises brought upon the country in the last decades due to poor government and corruption, are Brazilians now contemplating their values. That corruption and impunity in Brazil ends, is far from clear. Brazil is at a crossroads for its future. If misgovernment and corruption continue, then Brazil will fail and become another Argentina, Cuba, or Venezuela. A state with a failed economy, massive debt, no foreign investment, and an ever entrenched and corrupt government which will become irrelevant in world affairs. A country increasingly unequal and violent. For Brazilians to stop corruption and impunity it will likely require judicial reform as well as changes in its constitution. Although there have been heroic efforts to prosecute corruption, it is far from certain if these efforts will lead to political reform. In fact, it looks increasingly clear that the Supreme Court of Brazil is more interested in releasing the corrupt and the criminal on technicalities rather than seeing justice served equally for all.

As we will see, the history of corruption and mismanagement can be traced to the Portuguese Monarchy's arrival in Brazil in 1808, and likely has never stopped. With the of democracy in 1985, one would have hoped that Brazilians would have elected politicians who supported good government after military a military dictatorship, but that was not to be. Politicians from the right, left, and center have been equally disappointing, and Brazilians are fed up and disillusioned. The greatest danger seems to be that a significant part of the Brazilian population is disillusioned with democracy itself. So, the time for reform is now. Before giving a quick review of the recent history of corruption, lets learn some of Brazilian vocabulary used describe corrupt activities.

Everything Brazilian is creative, even the language of corruption

Bagunça or mess: This is a Brazilian word that mean a mess or the fun of making a mess. The country is a *bagunça*.

Caixa dois or Second Box: This is a hidden bank account or off-books fund used to pay bribes or receive illegal funds.

Empregado Fantasma or Ghost employee: This is when you pay public employees who do not need to show up for work.

Laranja or **Orange:** This is a person or shell company used to hide a transaction that benefits the corrupt politician or businessman. Example: The penthouse that the famous politician used was owned by a *Laranja*.

Lavagem or **money laundering:** Money passes through a *lavagem* to a *caixa dois* to be used again.

Lava Jato or **Operation Car Wash:** This was the biggest corruption scandal to date that started off simply as an investigation of a money laundering using the gas station that had a carwash. This led to a multibillion-dollar investigation involving the highest levels of government including hundreds of politicians and business leaders.

Malandro é malandro e mané é mané or **city slicker and the country bumkin:** This common phrase gives insight to twisted Brazilian logic. As we know from previous chapters a *malandro* takes every advantage to get ahead. The mané are the well-intentioned fools that follow the rules. So, in the current circumstance the corrupt politicians and the justices will commonly be referred to *Malandro* while the rest of us workers and taxpayers are *Mané*.

Mensalão or **Big Monthly payment:** This refers to a practice where the workers' party would make monthly payments using state funds to politicians to vote for the workers' party program.

Rachadinha or **little crack:** This is when a politician or a public employee hires people, but they must give him part of their salary. This practice goes back at least to the Portuguese Army in the 1800's.

A Brief History of Corruption in Brazil Since the Return of Democracy

One would have hoped that politicians who were jailed, exiled, and in some cases tortured by a military government that lasted twenty years, would have learned to respect democratic government and its institutions once democracy was restored. Such was not the case with Brazil. From the resumption of civilian government in Brazil in 1984, the country has been caught up in unending waves of corruption, and in many cases with impunity. Corruption has now touched nearly every major political party from the right to the left and center. Corruption is at every level from local to national. It is destroying Brazil and must stop. Fortunately, Brazilian society is making the first steps to clean up this plague but this war against corruption is far from won. Here is brief overview of the most nefarious corruption scandals since democratic government was returned from military rule in 1985.

In 1989 Fernando Collor, the son of the senator who shot and killed a fellow senator on the floor of congress, became the first directly elected president of Brazil. By May 1992 President Collar was accused of corruption by his younger brother, Pedro Collor de Mello. Pedro Collor accused his brother of "illegal enrichment."[84] Following an investigation by a Parliamentary Commission of Inquiry (CPI) in September 1992, the CPI determined that Collor's former campaign fund raiser, Paulo Cesar Farias, controlled an extensive network that facilitated public contracts and influenced government decisions in exchange for kickbacks and 'commissions'. Members of the CPI estimate the total amount of money involved at about six and a half million dollars.[85] Due to the corruption charges, President Collor was officially removed from office by the Senate on December 29, 1992.[86]

Impunity Again

Though convicted in the Senate in 1992, the Supreme Court cleared Collor and Farias of all criminal charges in 1994, stating that the Attorney General of Brazil had failed to provide enough evidence of the corruption charges. The evidence was to the average Brazilian overwhelming with detailed files and documents but was thrown out on and legal technicalities.[87] Public outcry was loud, with a ten of thousands of Brazilians protesting the Supreme Court's decision. For these Brazilians, the decision to clear Collor was simply another example of Brazil's historic inability to rid itself of corrupt politicians.

Pedro Collar continued to serve as a senator after his impeachment, while his treasure, PC Farias, was found shot with his girlfriend in 1996. Some have claimed this was a murder suicide; other investigators speculated that the murder was just too convenient.

For former President Collor, however, the corruption allegations do not end in 1994. In 2015, he was one of the top politicians named in

---

[84] Available in: https://pt.wikipedia.org/wiki/Fernando_Collor. Access in: 3/11/2021
[85] Available in: https://memoriaglobo.globo.com/jornalismo/coberturas/impeachment-de-collor/o-relatorio-final-da-cpi/. Access in:3/11/2021.
[86] Available in: https://pt.wikipedia.org/wiki/Fernando_Collor. Access in: 3/11/2021 Access in: 3/11/2021.
[87] *Ibidem.*

the Petrobras oil scandal. Allegations were made that Collor was involved in the Petrobras scandal, but the Supreme court decided he was too old to prosecute. This is just another example of the normalization of corruption and impunity in Brazil.

The Fight Against Corruption and Impunity

In 2010 progress against corruption started with the Clean Record Act, or *Ficha limpa*. This is an interesting example of how popular and democratic movements to fight corruption get distorted by judicial interference. The Act was created by popular initiative with 1.9 million Brazilians signing a petition. The Clean Record Act decrees that a candidate who has been impeached, has resigned to avoid impeachment, or been convicted by a decision of a collective body (with more than one judge), is ineligible to hold public office for eight years, even if additional appeals remain.[88] This law was then passed unanimously in May 2010 in Congress and was signed by President Lula de Silva. This law did not make it easier for corrupt politicians to go to jail, it simply did not allow them to participate in elections.

Not allowing politicians convicted of a crime of corruption would seem to be a great idea with popular support. In a functioning democracy this might be an effective plan to reduce corruption, but in Brazil nothing is easy. Even though the entire Congress followed the will of the people, the corrupt parts of government began to weaken the legislation. Questions were raised as to whether the law could go into effect during the next elections. The Supreme Court questioned whether the law was constitutional since a politician now could be eliminated from running for office even if only one judge found him guilty of a crime and he was not allowed the politician all the levels of appeal. This argument temporarily worked to stop the effect of the law, and only in 2012 with an appeal to the Supreme Court did the law take effect. Corruption is so widespread that more than a thousand politicians have been made ineligible to run for office due to this law.

In 2014, what started out as an investigation of money laundering through a carwash, *Lava Jato* in Portuguese, soon became the largest corruption scandal in Brazil. For perhaps the first time, people and politicians were going to go to jail for corruption. A formally unknown Judge in Curitiba, Sergio Moro, sentenced politicians and business

---
[88] Wikipedia. "Ficha Limpa". Available in: https://en.wikipedia.org/wiki/Ficha_Limpa. Access in: 2 jun. 2020.

executives to prison and the Brazilians loved it. Most of these judgements were confirmed upon appeal and the sentences enforced. *Lava Jato* soon encompassed billions of dollars of bribes to hundreds of politicians, almost bankrupting the state oil company, and even imprisoned of the former President of Brazil, Lula de Silva. In the end, all the major political parties were involved and executive from major Brazilian corporations were also arrested and forced to implicate even more politicians from all the major political parties. The size of the scandal shocked Brazil and millions of Brazilians went to the street to protest.

Big protests in Brazil demand President Rousseff's impeachment
Source: *BBC*, 2015

The depth of the corruption continued, with not only the President being impeached but the Vice President Michelle Temer, who assumed the office of president soon found himself at the center of corruption accusations. Shortly after taking office after the impeachment, President Michelle Temer was also implicated with phone evidence of taking bribes. Brazil's political scandal, *Lava Jato*, reached an astonishing scale. The corruption was widespread; no fewer than 20 different political parties have had members implicated. More than 200 people have reportedly been charged with crimes. Two former Brazilian presidents, the heads of both houses of Brazil's Congress, more than 90 lawmakers, and one third of Temer's cabinet have been implicated. The value of bribes paid as part of this scandal is estimated at about US$2 billion. That is billion with a B.

Corruption Fights Back. The Supreme Court, and Congress

Brazilians were shocked and angered at the scale of corruption and voted out many in Congress who had taken bribes, so you would expect Brazil to be reformed. But the reforms are stalled from an unexpected suspect, the Supreme Court. Unlike the supreme court in other countries, the Supreme Court in Brazil does not just interpret laws but actively gets involved in ruling in administrative processes of the other two branches of government. This gives the Court great latitude to make policy or contradict policies of the Executive Branch and generally gum up the works of government.

The Supreme Court, who you would expect to uphold law and order, makes decisions that are hard for the common Brazilian to believe. Many times, they seem to favor the corrupt politicians. It is bizarre, but you can ask any Brazilian and they will repeat the same names of judges that seem to favor the corrupt politicians. I am not a lawyer and I am sure that these great legal minds are following established jurisprudence, but to the common Brazilian the decisions do not seem just. To the common Brazilian it is all too familiar, the poor go to jail without access to defense and the rich and well connected are never punished.

In one famous example in 2019 the Brazilian Supreme Court freed the imprisoned president Lula, who had been convicted on bribery charges related to *Lava Jato*. The Supreme Court argued that convicted criminals have an almost unlimited right of appeal. The prisoners who had been convicted in a lower court and then convicted in an appeals court could continue to appeal until finally decided by the Supreme Court. This was a stunning decision for it not only allowed Lula to be released from prison but hundreds of other corrupt politician and regular common criminals were also released pending appeals. Since the legal process is slow in Brazil, if you have money you likely will not see jail time because the legal process will take longer than the statute of limitations. Because the Supreme Court ruled that this was to protect the presumption of innocence that is part of the constitution, it is not even clear if a law could be passed to correct this ruling.

Another decision that the Supreme Court made the appears to hamper the investigation of political corruption. It decided that cases in which even part of a bribe went to an electoral campaign could be taken out of the hands of the regional courts, which had proven highly effective at pursuing them.

Any case involving elections, even including criminal bribery would instead be decided in Brazil's electoral courts, which have fewer resources. These election courts are not criminal courts. Sending criminal bribery to electoral courts is like sending a major criminal scandal to the county election commission for a legal decision. Rulings such as these add to a growing perception that some of the country's top Justices see themselves as untouchable, and many Brazilians question the ethics of some of them. You can ask Brazilians and they will all name the same judges that raise eyebrows due to the decisions they make that appear to support the corrupt status quo. Politicians get excused from jail by judges because they are too old, too sick, or the process took too long, and the list of technicalities goes on.

Interference by Congress and the Judiciary in corruption investigations is commonplace and justified on unusual technicalities. When one politician was followed and taped while receiving a suitcase of money, and subsequently arrested by the federal police, the judge overseeing the case famously said that "only one suitcase full of money may not be sufficient evidence of a bribe." In most countries the legislative branches of government exclude or stay away from members under investigation. In Brazil, the congressional leadership actively interferes in investigations of its members. It is typical for congressional leadership to protect corrupt politicians, claiming parliamentary immunity. The leadership does not cooperate with investigators, refusing to give access to documents or technology on the basis that the politician can claim as part of their legislative job. The courts, especially the higher courts, instead of ruling for the prosecutors and the police, largely rule in favor of the corrupt politicians upon appeal or review. Several previously guilty high-profile criminals and politicians who had been declared guilty in multiple courts, are strangely subsequently freed on technicalities. When this happens, it diminishes the image of the Supreme Court and Brazilian justice. Calls for overthrowing the Supreme Court are clearly undemocratic, but considering the continued abuses of power, completely understandable. One day in 2018 on a commercial flight, a lawyer told one of the Supreme Court Justices, what an embarrassment the court was for the Brazilian public. Upon arrival the Supreme Court Justice Lewandowski had the lawyer arrested.[89] The lawyer was only released after public, media, and social media protests. So much for upholding free speech!

---

[89] Available in: https://g1.globo.com/df/distrito-federal/noticia/2018/12/04/advogado-e-detido-em-voo-apos-dizer-a-lewandowski-que-stf-e-uma-vergonha.ghtml. Access in: 3/12/2021.

Now I can hear you say, where is the presumption of innocence? Are you not innocent until proven guilty? Brazilians will tell you that the amount of evidence collected in most of these cases is overwhelming. They have seen these cases of political impunity for their entire lives and until *Lava Jato* and the public's outcry to stop fraud, it seemed that very few politicians ever went to jail. What was different in the *Lava Jato* case was prosecutors began to use plea bargains to reduce the sentences of business executives who paid the bribes to testify against the politicians who asked for the bribes. The use of plea bargains was relatively new to Brazil. Once the prosecutors used plea bargains and threats of jail time, executives cooperated and provided overwhelming evidence against the corrupt politicians.

What the federal police and prosecutors did with the *Lava Jato*, and other investigations was to plea bargain with the businessmen caught making bribes, who were not so well protected as politicians, to give evidence against the politicians that received the bribes. Both the bribe payors and the bribe receivers had enormous organizations and departments that organized the payments and the distribution of millions of dollars to hundreds of people. An operation this large requires organization and records. When the businessmen were forced to cooperate with law enforcement, all the records of payments of bribes were handed over to the prosecutors of *Lava Jato*.

Although there are four levels of appeal in criminal courts, jurisprudence and past practice was that a criminal would go to jail after losing his first appeal. This was not just for cases of criminal corruption, but for violent crimes as well. President Lula was imprisoned not when he was convicted by Sergio Moro, but only after he lost again in the court of appeals. The next levels of appeal were not intended to review evidence, but only points of law in cases suspected of having some form of procedural negligence. To let the former President out, the Supreme Court reinvented its understanding of the Brazilian Constitution, interpreting the presumption of innocence to now extend to all levels of the court until reaching the Supreme Court. When the supreme court reinterpreted the constitution to allow, everyone the right to appeal to the supreme court, President Lula was able to get out of prison but also other common and many violent convicted criminals were release as well. This decision as well as the decision allowing campaign bribery cases to be tried by the Court of Elections instead of criminal court has caused the Supreme Court to be held in disgust by most Brazilians. It certainly is a setback to the fight against corruption.

Gringo Advice

It is easy to be discouraged with the state of corruption in Brazil, unless you can look back in though history to realize that much progress has been made. With competitive exams and high pay, the judiciary has become more professional, especially in the lower courts. The population now no longer tolerates or admires corrupt politicians. The federal police are largely independent of the Minister of Justice and outside political influence. The tactics and professionalism of the federal police have improved, and with it the esteem and support by the Brazilian population. Perhaps most importantly the federal police are largely popular with the prosecutors. Serio Moura, the famous prosecutor of *Lava Jato,* and former minister of justice is perhaps the most popular public figure in Brazil. He must be supported by the Brazilian people.

There are two roads that Brazil can take. It can reform corruption and grow, or it can continue with its current system. If corruption is not controlled the economy and debt will cause some sort of political upheaval. Brazilians are already highly taxed with poor services for the amount paid. Today there are protests asking for military rule. People are taking to the streets asking for the supreme court and congress to be closed. This would be a horrible idea! Brazilians do not want military rule and even the military look back on the period of military dictatorship as a stain on their reputation.

So, the only road that Brazil can take is reform. This may need a new constitutional amendment, or congress could change the law so that the right of appeal is not unlimited. The judicial process is slow, and it is reasonable to expect criminals to go to jail if they have lost upon first appeal, assuming there is no gross negligence in the judicial decision. At the time of this writing, there seemed to be some effort in the Brazilian congress to write a new law or even change the constitution define this practice. If we realize that progress has been made in cleaning up corruption it gives us hope that the next generations of Brazilians will make even more progress.

Ideally Congress would also eliminate or modify criminal immunity that politicians currently hold while in public office. The idea of parliamentary immunity in other countries is to protect politicians from attacks for their ideals. In Brazil, unfortunately, politicians are arrested for common crimes and avoid prosecution by using their political immunity.

Brazilians are more knowledgeable and less tolerant of corruption now. The national demonstrations against corruption in 2017, the economic crisis, improved education, and access to news has changed Brazilian attitudes. The 2018 elections forced out many of the politicians suspected of corruption. There is still resistance to change in every branch of government. The best we can hope for are long-term changes that will reduce corruption over time. We can only hope that future generations of Brazilian will push for clean government.

Chapter Eleven

Social Inequality and Racism

Favela do Vidigal
Source: *Wikipedia*, 2014

In the early 19th century Major Miguel Nunes Vidigal (1745-1843), was the colonial chief of police of Rio de Janeiro. Viewed as cruel in his time, he spread terror among escaped slaves and was feared by the poor of Rio de Janeiro. He was famous for his use of his police truncheon on the heads and feet of his victims. He persecuted with special attention, the torture of the Afro Brazilians, slave and free, who practiced the candomblé religion and the martial art of capoeira. Only history condemns this brute today, but at the time of the Empire he was highly decorated. Major Vidigal received the lands on the hill in 1820 as a gift from Benedictine monks to whom they had been handed down by the Viscount of Asseca, a wealthy nobleman protected by the Portuguese Crown. Major Vidigal died peacefully at the age of 93.[90] After his death his lands were invaded, ironically, by the same Afro Brazilians that he tortured during his life and the shanty town, *favela* was named *Morro de Vidigal* in his honor. This *favela* begins with shacks and tangles of electrical wires, and narrow alleys, like the favelas all over Brazil. Morro de Vidigal is situated between the beaches of Ipanema and Leblon with their luxury high rises and tourist hotels. This makes the *favela* ideal for tours for adventuresome tourist who can see wonderful views of Rio de Janeiro from the top of the hill at the Bar de Laje. The tourists get to watch the life in the *favela* while drinking caipirinhas and partying the night away from the hilltop bar. The Bar de Laje, is described in Vogue magazine as "The newest discovery of the jet set in the middle of the Vidigal community".[91] The irony of rich tourists partying in the middle of misery is sublime.

Every society must justify its inequalities for its own stability, and Brazil is one of the most inequal societies in the in the world. Other than Brazils history of slavery and treatment of freed Afro Brazilians and poor immigrants, there is no justification. When Brazil was a colony it was shielded from the thought of the enlightenment and accepted the teaching of the church that the monarchy was derived from the divine right of kings and the masses of peasants needed to accept there lot as to from the will of God. Later to justify slavery, forced conversion to Catholicism was used means to provide moral guidance to the heathens and slaves. The Catholic Church supported the institution of slavery and converted and baptized the indians and slaves to save their soul even as they toiled on this earth. Later unsuccessful rebellions by Brazilian were inspired by the ideals of the enlightenment, however none of the rebels would think about freeing slaves. The freeing of the slaves in Brazil was forced on Brazil by Great Britain, who was Brazil's most important trading partner.[92] The end of slavery caused many landowners to support a republic which helped end of the Brazilian monarchy.[93] The founding of the Brazilian Republic in 1889 was more of a military coup and certainly was not a popular movement. The sudden elimination of the monarchy reduced the number of masterful

---

[90] Available in: https://pt.wikipedia.org/wiki/Ficheiro:1_vidigal_favela_rio_2014.jpg. Access in: 3/12/2021.
[91] Bar de Laje, Bar descolado no alto do morro do Vidigal, Available in: https://bardalaje.rio/. Access in: 3/12/2021.
[92] Available in: https://www.wilsoncenter.org/blog-post/slavery-brazil. Access in: 3/12/2021.
[93] Available in: https://en.wikipedia.org/wiki/Pedro_II_of_Brazil. Access in: 3/12/2021.

national institutions to one, the Army.[94] Most Brazilians had supported Dom Pedro II and did not even know that the monarch Dom Pedro II had abdicated. Dom Pedro II was against slavery and perhaps if the monarchy had not been overthrown there would be less social inequality today in Brazil. As it was, Brazil exchanged its monarchy for a military and landed oligarchy, with no ideas to justifying the inequality within Brazil or provide a vision for the future.

After alternating between republics and military government, modern Brazil has no ethos or framework to justify its inequality. For a capitalist model the government it too big and no Brazilians genuinely believes that there is equality of opportunity in Brazil. As a socialist system it would be a failure because the government programs and policies favor the well off. The Workers Party of Brazil and the other hard left parties were neither the intelligentsia nor the vanguard of the proletariat. When the hard left ran the country, instead of concentrating on addressing the poor and improving their opportunities, the Workers Party under Presidents Lula and Dilma squandered its credibility on a program of political corruption. Why would a group of idealist leftist, who suffered torture in military prisons, kidnapped the American ambassador and fought for freedom, abandon their ideals to rob the country?

Brazil has historically been unequal from its founding as a Portuguese colony. The fates of countries that were founded as colonies are differentiated depending upon the intentions of the colonizers. Most of Latin America colonies had gold and silver or other materials ready for export, so the Spanish and Portuguese colonizers had no intention of staying in Latin America. Their goal was to extract resources and return to their home countries rich. In the case of Brazil, the Portuguese needed slave labor for the export of Brazilian wood that was uses and a die for cloths. Later the Portuguese would use slave labor for sugar plantations that created wealth for the Portuguese crown prior to finding gold in Minas Gerais. Other colonies, Australia for example, had no quick path to riches, and many of the colonist were prisoners and so they had to make a society to live in Australia. There was no coming back to the home country, so you had be building the country you are your family would live in. The thirteen British colonies, as well, were setup by royal charter, but the colonist who were going to North America had no intention of returning to England. Likewise,

---

[94] Available in: https://en.wikipedia.org/wiki/First_Brazilian_Republic. Access in: 3/12/2021.

the Dutch of South Africa, the French in Canada and the colonist of New Zealand came to stay and create a new land.

When colonizers have no plans on returning to their home country, they set up institutions of local government that facilitate trade, resolve disputes, enforce contracts, and provide for the defense of the colony. Families are formed and the colonist need to provide schools and hospitals. In these types of colonies local governments created a local judicial system that had to be seen to treat all citizens fairly or the settlers would take justice into their own hands. As there are no quick riches for exploitation, the home countries governments delegate the administration to the local colonists and supervise from afar. Perhaps most importantly, these colonies provide for their own defense to support the home country.

In lands that have gold, silver, or other materials for quick riches the home government take active role in the government of the colonies. The home countries army is used first to conquer the colony, and then to enforce laws to ensure that the home country is receiving its share of riches. The Local administration and local judicial systems are subordinate to the home countries administration. When the colonial administration and judicial systems work for the benefit of the home country instead of the colonist, these administrative bodies do not develop to be independent judiciary but are subject to the whims and corruption of the home countries. Colonies without gold and silver needed long term settlers. Colonies with long term settlers set up governments for their own long-term interests. This explains the relative outcomes of these colonies as they became independent countries. Australia was a penal colony and the United States practiced slavery, but as the administrative government was created for the benefit of the settlers and not for the colonizing powers, these countries had better outcomes. As we saw in the previous chapter, the corruption in Brazil came directly from the corruption of the Portuguese government and court, and this retarded the development of Brazilian institutions.

How the Portuguese even got its claim to Brazil is bit of a historical mystery! We all know that Christopher Columbus discovered the America for the King and Queen of Spain in 1492. The Portuguese had colonies in the Azores in the middle of the Atlantic at that time. The treaty of Tordesillas divided the world between Spain in Portugal in 1494. A year earlier the original line was proposed by Pope Alexander would have excluded Portugal from South America. The great historical mystery why did and how the

Portuguese get the Pope and the Portuguese to push the line of the treaty to the west? Remember that Brazil was not officially discovered until 1500!

The Treaty of Tordesillas: How Did Portugal claim Brazil before discovering it!

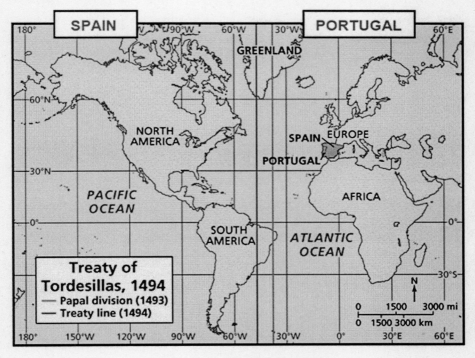

The Treaty of Tordesillas, 1494
Source: *Time wise traveller*

When Columbus returned from the new world, the news of new lands west of the Azores created political conflict between the two largest maritime nations, Spain, and Portugal. The Azores were already colonized by the Portuguese. The Portuguese claimed that a previous treaty had given them the land south of the Azores. The Spanish King and Queen wanted confirmation that the new lands discovered belonged to Spain. The Kings of Spain and Portugal asked the Pope to intercede. Fortunately for the Spanish, the pope at that time was none other than Pope Alexander VI. Not only was Pope Alexander from Spain, but he was the infamous Borgia pope, who used his position to benefit his family, mistresses and illegitimate children with lands wealth and titles.

Pope Alexander issued a Papal Bull on May 4, 1493 setting a line just west of the Azores which would in effect have excluded the Portuguese of territory in Brazil. This would have been the basis of the Treaty of Tordesillas; however, the Portuguese King was not happy with this agreement. He continued to negotiate directly with the King and Queen of Spain. As Pedro Cabral discovered Brazil in only 1500, it is mystery of history if King John of Portugal had any prior knowledge of the lands that would become Brazil. Was there an unrecorded trip to Brazil, or was a Portuguese ship blown off course and this information remained secret? The Portuguese had already reached the Cape of Good hope in Africa trying to reach India and Columbus had thought he had already reached India. The traditional explanation was that both kingdoms of Spain and Portugal were trying to protect their claims for colonizing in the future India. Independent of the underlying explanation, the King and Queen of Spain agreed with King John of Portugal to move the papal line 270 leagues westward, unknowingly giving the future Brazil to Portugal. Both Kingdoms ratified the treaty in 1494 and Pope Julius II, an Italian, sanctioned the treaty in 1506.[95]

Brazilian Resistance to early Portuguese Colonialization

King John in 1534 tried to create a system of 15 hereditary captaincies to stimulate colonization. Of these 15 hereditary captaincies, only Pernambuco and San Vincente prospered during the first hundred years. The resistance of the local Indians tribes to become slave labor for the production sugar frustrated the development of the other regions, and Indian and French resistance almost defeated the captaincy of San Vincente, an area from about Rio to Santos.

Although the Spanish and Portuguese respected this treaty other maritime nations, namely England, France and Holland were not so happy about being excluded from the new world.[96] England and Holland were already Protestant, so for these countries the treaty was largely ignored.

---

[95] Available in: https://en.wikipedia.org/wiki/Treaty_of_Tordesillas. Access in: 3/12/2021.
[96] *Ibidem.*

Becoming Brazilian

These countries sent out ships to look for opportunities in the new world. These ships came to Brazil and negotiated with the Brazilian Indians who often looked for assistance against the Portuguese. The French decided to try to settle in a part of San Vincente.

Cunhambebe
Source: Wikipédia

Cunhambebe was a chief of a confederation of tribes that had already began a resistance to the Portuguese around the present-day city of Ubatuba. Cunhambebe was a huge man who commanded a force large for of Indians. His name in Guarani alludes to the size of his chest muscles. He recognized that the Portuguese were only interested in enslaving his people and he made so an alliance with the French who were creating an outpost in what is now Rio de Janeiro. His tribe was actively resisting the Portuguese when he made his alliance with Admiral Nicholas Durand a French Knight of Malta, who from 1550 to 1567 controlled Rio de Janeiro in a French colony that was set up for protestants to settle.[97]

The tribes had untied against the Portuguese due the Portuguese habit of kidnapping and enslaving the local Indians. Cunhambebe recognized that the French colonist were different and entered an alliance with Admiral Durand and his protestant colony against the Portuguese. The history of Brazil would have been forever changed if the Portuguese in San Sebastian were expelled. Facing expulsion from San Sebastian, the Portuguese sent a group of Jesuits who spoke excellent Guaraní to negotiate a truce. The peace treaty was accepted by Cunhambebe, and the Portuguese were permitted to stay in San Sebastian. His son Cunhambebe Junior and his tribe would fight to help their French allies in 1567 when the Portuguese broke this treaty and attached and eventually expelled the French colony.[98] By the end of the century the Tamoya confederation was obliterated. If Cunhambebe had not listened to the Jesuits and just grilled the visiting Jesuits for dinner, southern Brazil perhaps would perhaps speak French today!

The Tupi Guaraní resistance to the Portuguese was not defeated militarily but from the wide variety of European diseases that the local Indians had no immunity. Just a Cunhambebe was killed by bubonic plague as he was close to expelling the Portuguese, untold millions of indigenous people were destroyed by infections and disease. Even today the immunity of the Indians found in the remote part of the amazon is a health concern.

With the decimation of the Brazilian indigenous population to disease and the growing need for slave labor in Pernambuco and San Vicente Portuguese began importing slaves from Africa around the middle of the 16th century. Brazil was largest importer of African slaves for the longest period of any country in the world. From 1600 to 1850 approximately 4.5 million slaves were taken from Africa to Brazil. This is close to four times

---

[97] Available in: https://www.curiosidadesdeubatuba.com.br/cacique-cunhambebe/. Access in: 3/12/2021.
[98] *Ibidem.*

more slaves that were sent to North America. For most of Brazil history African slaves were the biggest single group in the population. Today a 2010 census stated that 75 million Brazilians consider themselves black or of mixed race.[99]

Distribution of slaves (1519–1867)[108] [1]	
Destination	Percentage
Portuguese America	38.5%
British West Indies	18.4%
Spanish Empire	17.5%
French Americas	13.6%
British Atlantic Colonies / United States	9.7%
Dutch West Indies	2.0%
Danish West Indies	0.3%

Note: The number of the Africans who arrived in each region is calculated from the total number of slaves imported, about 10,000,000.[109] *Includes British Guiana and British Honduras

[1] Available in: https://en.wikipedia.org/wiki/Atlantic_slave_trade#cite_note-108. Access in: 26 oct. 2020.

Atlantic slave trade
Source: *Wikipedia*

Quilombos: Escaped Slave communities

These Brazilian slaves frequently escaped and set up communities in the jungle called *quilombos*. As early as 1602 Portuguese slave holders began to complain about run-away slaves, returning, sabotaging the plantations, and taking cattle and other slaves. It is hard for us to know with certainty the social and political structure of the *quilombos*. What we do know comes from European or slave owning accounts during conflicts with the escaped slaves. So, these accounts could come with some bias against these communities. What is without a doubt was that they were many of these communities. *Quilombos* provided a life of freedom for escapes slaves. Some slaves actively fought the Portuguese and, tried to sabotage the slave plantation by taking women, cattle, and other slaves. Whether *quilombos* themselves had slaves is a question that complicates a simple

[99] Available in: https://en.wikipedia.org/wiki/Racism_in_Brazil. Access in: 3/12/2021

narrative for Brazilian history. According to European accounts, within the *quilombos* if you were a runaway slave you were free, if you were born within the community you were free, but slaves could be taken from the Portuguese and kept as slaves. As slavery existed in Africa at this time, it is possible that slavery existed within the *quilombos* as well.

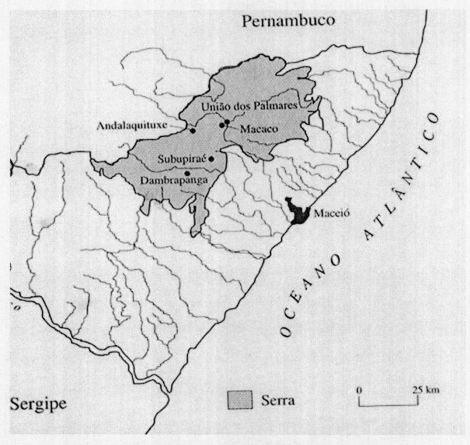

Quilombo dos Palmares: resumo, dia a dia e localização
Source: *Toda Matéria*

When the Dutch attacked Recife, in 1630 and held the city till 1654, many slaves escaped, and this began a gold age of *quilombos*. Thousands of slaves escaped and swelled the population of the *quilombos* and a period of active resistance to the Portuguese began from the former slaves. The Dutch even considered making and alliance with the quilombos, like the French and Indians one hundred years before. However, as the Dutch were also interested in sugar production which required slave labor, so this idea was discarded. While the Portuguese and Dutch were at war, there was nothing much the either could do about the quilombos.

By far the largest and most famous of these *quilombos* was Palmares. Palmares was a kingdom of Brazilian escapes slaves and as 90% of the slaves of this time came from Angola it is likely that they could communicate. Palmares was defined by the area of the current state of Alagoas in Brazil just south of the Portuguese colony of Pernambuco and the capital of Recife. Its major settlements were high on the hills which gave it some protection from the Portuguese. Other accounts by the Dutch claimed there were nine major settlements and many smaller one. At its height of power in the 1650s the territory could have been like Portugal in geographic size, with a population of 11 to 20 thousand freed slaves from Africa. During this period Palmares began to be referred to by its inhabitants as the kingdom of Angola Janga. The Portuguese authorities addressed their letters and communication to Ganga Zumba as king, and his family ruled the outlying settlements.

The Heroic struggle of Ganga Zumba and Zumbi

According to tradition Ganga Zumbi was the son of Princess Aqualtune, who was a warrior princess of an unknown African king in Kongo, she supposedly led a battalion of soldiers against the Portuguese at the battle of Mbwila. She was defeated and captured with many of her family members including Ganga Zumba by the Portuguese. As Princess Aqualtune was exceedingly strong and big, she was sold as a slave essentially for breading stock for slaves. She and Ganga Zumba and her other children arrived in Recife in 1597, supposedly the same year that 40 slaves escaped to form the *quilombo* that would become Palmares.[100] When Princess Aqualtune arrived at plantation, upon hearing of a place that slaves could be free, she organized an escape from the plantation and made the journey six month pregnant.

Upon arriving at one of the *quilombos* she was given leadership of the community perhaps because of her royal blood or her reputation as a warrior. She began to organize and consolidate the surrounding *quilombos*. Along with Ganga Zumba, she had a son Ganga Zona and a daughter Sabrina who would be the mother of Zumbi. At some unknow time, power

---

[100] Available in: https://pt.wikipedia.org/wiki/Ganga_Zumba Access in: 3/12/2021.

passed from her to her son Ganga Zumba. The date and circumstance of her death are unknown.

By 1670 Palmares had consolidated as a kingdom under Ganga Zumba. He had a palace; three wives and his relations were running the other major settlements. He ruled the kingdom from his royal compound called *Cerca de Macaco*, which served as his headquarters, and the palace was surrounded by palisades.[101] By this time, the Portuguese, however, had finally freed themselves of the Dutch intervention in Recife. The Dutch were finally expelled from Brazil in 1654, and this gave the Portuguese time and resources to make incursion to take back the freed slaves of the *quilombos*.

Zumbi was born free in Palmares in 1655 to the sister of Ganga Zumba. During one of the Portuguese raids of Palmares Zumbi was captured in 1661, when he was six years old and given to a missionary Father Antonio Mello who baptized Zumbi with the name of Francisco. Zumbi learned Portuguese and Latin. At the age of fifteen he was able to escape and return to Palmares.[102] Due to his cunning and strength he was given control of soldiers and by some accounts ran *quilombos*. Zumbi took the lead in raids against the Portuguese and these raids gave him a reputation as a great warrior.

When the Dutch were expelled from Brazil in 1654 the Portuguese began their attacks on Palmares. In the beginning these were not particularly successful. The soldiers of Palmares adopted the practice of ambushing the Portuguese soldiers in the jungle. One defeat of Palmares happened in 1663 when a black captain Gonçalo Rebelo led a force of 200 black soldiers against Palmares, was able to capture 40 escaped slaves. All the slaves were beheaded. In retaliation in 1670, soldiers from Palmares freed slaves from a sugar mill and conquered a cattle ranch.

What changed the nature of the conflict was the defeat in 1677 of Palmares, by an invasion led by Captain Fernão Carrilho which perhaps wounded Ganga Zumba and lead to the capture of some 200 former slaves including some of Ganga Zumba's family. This led to negotiations with the Governor of Pernambuco, Pedro Almeida.[103] Ganga Zumba sent a letter to start negotiations and Governor Almeida responded with an offer to recognize the freedom and the Kingdom of Palmares on two conditions. First, the settlements needed to be moved closer to the Portuguese and

---

[101] *Ibidem;*
[102] Available in: https://pt.wikipedia.org/wiki/Zumbi. Access in: 3/12/2021
[103] Available in: http://www.blackhistoryheroes.com/2010/05/zumbi-dos-palmares.html. Access in: 3/12/2021.

second only the Palmares that were born into freedom would be free, and the slaves that had escaped must be returned. Perhaps Ganga Zumba was tired of fighting but for history his reputation was ruined as he accepted these terms in 1678.

Figure of Brazilian African warrior by Albert Eckhout, *African Man*
Source: Wikipedia

Zumbi however refused these terms. By moving the mountain kingdom from the high ground Palmares would be more easily defeated, and a few of the free born Palmares that did move to the area were being enslaved by the Portuguese, who seemed to already be breaking their word. Zumbi refused to accept that he and other freeborn Palmares would be free while other blacks were enslaved. Zumbi led a revolt against Ganga Zumba and his followers. One story goes that Ganga Zumba was poisoned, another version was that he killed himself due to the disgrace of treating with the Portuguese and betraying his people. Ganga Zumba died in 1678. The followers of Ganga Zumba who moved to the coast in accordance with the agreement were enslaved as the Portuguese broke their word.

From 1678 to 1694 Zumbi was now the new King of Palmares and the Kingdom was in a constant state of war with the Portuguese. By January 1694, the Portuguese forces of mixed-race soldiers arrives at the frontier of the kingdom and wait for reinforcement. In February 1694 six cannons and 200 additional soldiers arrived to join the Portuguese forces. On February 5 the two armies faced off. Many *quilombos* were surrounded by the Portuguese forces. Some of the slaves threw themselves off cliffs to avoid capture, others ran into the jungle only to be captured and decapitated. On February 6 the royal palace, was overrun by the Portuguese. Five hundred and ten people were captured with the men put to death. Only women and children were spared, but many mothers killed their own children rather than submit them to slavery again.

With the defeat of Zumbi, the institution of slavery continued without any real resistance for hundreds of years. The impact of the slave trade was so far reaching that slavery was actively supported by most Brazilians.[104] The Portuguese and free Brazilians, largely supported the institution of slavery and no one really questioned its morality. After Brazil declared itself independent of Portugal, slavery was maintained without any question. Brazil was founded as an empire not a democracy and the monarchy needed the support of large landholders, so the question of slavery did not come up.

The End of Slavery in Brazil

It was the British Government, who was Brazil largest trading partner, and who helped the Portuguese monarch come to Brazil in the first place, who began the process to liberate Brazil slaves. The British had ended

---

[104] Available in: https://www.wilsoncenter.org/blog-post/slavery-brazil. Access in: 3/12/2021.

slavery in its own colonies in 1807 and wanted other countries to follow suit.[105] To enforce the ending of the slave trade in Brazil, the British passed the Aberdeen act in 1845 which allowed the royal navy to board Brazilian slave ships seize the cargo and try the crew in British courts. This was an outrage to the Brazilians. Brazil, however, had already previously agreed to stop trading slaves in 1820 but had never enforced this agreement. The Brazilian have a phrase, *"Para inglês ver"* which means for the English to see. This phrase came from this period where there were many promises from the Brazilian empire to restrict slavery, but never enforced. The Brazilian Empire past laws against slavery but the laws were just to show the English! The British, however, were serious about stopping the slave trade and began seizing Brazilian slave ships. In the face of these tensions Brazil was in no position to go to war with the British Empire so in 1850 Brazil enacted its own laws to stop slave trafficking and began to enforce it.

When slavery was finally abolished in Brazil in 1888, the country made no effort to assist the newly freed slaves. The freeing of the slaves may have contributed to supporting the military coup that ended the Brazilian Monarchy a year later. Rather than help the freed slaves the new Brazilian government promoted immigration to "Whiten Brazil" which was supported by theories of Social Darwinists at the time.[106] Many Afro Brazilians had no option but to starve, move to the interior, or migrate to the big cities, where they settled in many of the same shanty towns or *favelas* like Morro de Vidigal that exist today. These *favelas* are like a state separate from Brazil. There is no legal title to the land, many roads to not appear on maps. The construction is unstable and unregulated. Few public services are available, and police rarely enter. Politicians and political movements tap into these communities for support, but in other ways these *favelas* operate as parallel states to the official Brazilian government.

As an outsider, you would not enter these *favelas* without permission on the gangs or militias that run these communities. These populations of these communities speak a different dialect, than the Brazilians that live in the official Brazil. They create their own dance and music that become popular though out Brazil. They live by a set of rules and pay taxes to organizations, outside the rule of law of the Brazilian Government. People living in older *favelas* traditionally get their electricity and water

---

[105] *Ibidem.*
[106] Available in: Racial whitening – https://en.wikipedia.org/wiki/Racial_whitening viewed. Access in: 3/12/2021.

for free. You will likely notice a surcharge on your utility bill. This is a typical Brazilian solution to a difficult problem, and there is no good way to safely cut these illegal electrical connections. At times, these *favelas* violently rebel against the Brazilian authorities and at times the Brazilian Police invade the *favelas,* to remove those Brazlians and destroy their homes. The sight of these indigent families taking their few possession with them to an uncertain future is one of the hardest sights one can witness in Brazil.

Modern Inequality

"Extreme inequality breeds conflict, violence, and instability. All Brazilians, regardless of social class or race, are affected by the inequality crisis. This is what unites us."

Katia Maia

Oxfam Brazil's executive director[107]

Economist most commonly measure the inequality of a country by measuring the income distribution within a country. This measurement looks at everyone's income and comes up with a number called a Gini Coefficient or a Gini Index. This does not measure how rich one country is versus another country but the distribution of wealth within a country. A perfectly equal society where everyone would have the same income the country would have a Gini Coefficient of 0. In a perfectly unequal society where one person had all the income and no one else had anything, the Gini Coefficient would be 1. The Gini Coefficient take the total income of a country and assumes that all income is equally distributed, then it takes the actual distribution of income and measure how far the real income distribution is from the perfectly equal distribution of 0. The Gini Coefficient does not tell you how big the economy or pie is, it just tells you how fairly the pie has been cut up.

According to Index Mundi Brazil has the eighth most unequal countries in the world.

---

[107] Brazil extreme inequality in numbers, Oxfam accessible at Brazil: extreme inequality in numbers. Available in: https://www.oxfam.org/en/brazil-extreme-inequality-numbers#:~:text=28%20MBrazil%20has%20lifted,61%20percent%20of%20economic%20growth. Access in: 3/12/2021.

Rank	Country	Value	Year
1	South Africa	63.00	2014
2	Namibia	59.10	2015
3	Suriname	57.60	1999
4	Zambia	57.10	2015
5	Central African Republic	56.20	2008
6	Lesotho	54.20	2010
7	Mozambique	54.00	2014
8	Belize	53.30	1999
8	Brazil	53.30	2017
8	Botswana	53.30	2015

Countries ranked by GINI index
Source: *Index mundi*

Switzerland, Mongolia, Japan, and Montenegro are examples of more economically equal countries.

Consider that Brazil's six richest men have the same wealth as poorest 50 percent of the population; around 100 million people. The country's richest 5 percent have the same income as the remaining 95 percent.[108] In recent year Brazil implemented some plans that began to improve inequality. In the last 15 years, economic growth and government policies in Brazil lifted 28 million out of poverty. By poverty we mean the international definition of a person that live on less than $54 per month. Programs like *Bolsa Família* and *Bolsa Escola* that are conditional transfer policies that paid families for making their children attend school. For the poor, it was common to think that it was better for the family, if children to work rather than to go to school. By linking the income transfer to school attendance this program made a small impact on social inequality. *Bolsa Família* has now become one of the few government benefits that are directed especially to the poor. However, these programs are small, and though they help relieve poverty they are less effective reducing inequality. Remember there is a difference between reducing poverty which can be done by making the pie bigger and reducing social inequality which implies giving out more equal slices of the pie. During those same 15 years the top 10 percent of Brazil received for 61% of the increase of GDP.

[108] *Ibidem.*

Other government policy seemed directed promoting social inequality. In Brazil, the primary and secondary public education to university is some of the worst in the world. Brazil ranks 53 out of 65 countries in reading match and science in the PISA exams behind Mexico, Russia, and Romania. Eighteen percent of the Brazilian population if functionally illiterate. Yet the country has good public universities and spends 5.5 percent of Brazilian GDP on public university where the student that qualify pay no tuition. To enter a public university, one must pass a competitive test, usually only the children of middle- and upper-class families who have paid for private primary, secondary education as well as outside coaching schools for the exams can get into the free public universities. One third of the federal budget for education budget is spent on the public universities which as a policy for inequality is nothing more than a subsidy for the middle class and wealthy. Ironically, the working poor that can afford it, need to pay for inferior private universities to get a higher education. There has been some progress to reserve places in these universities for poor students but without improvements in the Brazilian public schools these changes will be marginal.

The tax structure also does not encourage equality. It is hard to say if the tax policy is purposefully regressive to exploit the poor but for the lower income it could be seen this way. Although income taxes are paid by the middle class and wealth are progressive. Taxes on wealth, property and land are low, while taxes on consumption items is relatively high. Taxes in Brazil are extremely complicated and change frequently so it is hard to say if there is a tax policy created specifically to exploit the poor but consider this. Most of the revenue raised by the federal government comes from consumption taxes on product. These taxes raise 53% of the federal revenue, and this does not include consumption taxes raised by local states and city. If you are poor and earn two minimum salaries, which is about R$2080 or $500 per month even though you would pay no income tax, however you would pay 26% of your income on these indirect taxes. However, if you earned 30 time the minimum wage the percent of your income for direct taxes falls to 7%. So, the landless workers and the urban workers living in Favelas or shanty towns with few public services and living in illegal communities and are still paying 26 percent of their income to a government which provided only partial services.

Brazil has no estate or death tax at the federal level. This perpetuates the concentration of wealth in a small group of families. If Brazil's six richest men pooled their wealth and spent 1 million Brazilian reals a day (around $319,000), it would take them 36 years to spend all their money. Meanwhile, 16 million Brazilians live below the poverty line.[109]

Racism in Brazil, Racial Democracy or Social Apartheid

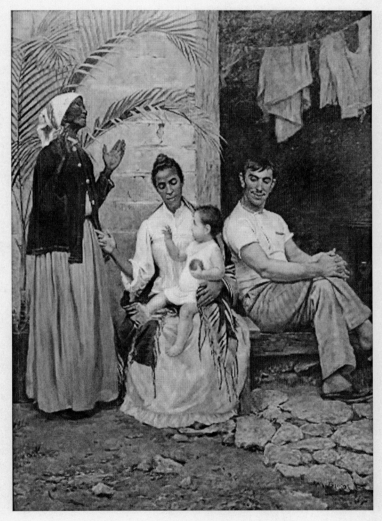

Redemption of Ham, Modesto Branco, 1895 - Museum of Fine Arts, Rio de Janeiro
Source: https://en.wikipedia.org/wiki/Ham%27s_Redemption. Access in: 4/1/2021

---

[109] Ibidem.

Brazilians have had a complex and still evolving relationship with race and Brazilian identity from the time the slaves were freed in 1888. Sometimes Brazilians will claim they live in a post racial society, but the truth is somewhat more complex. Brazilians discriminate, but it is disguised and mixed with economic inequality. Discussing race is a delicate and tricky topic, in all countries. In some ways, Brazil is very advanced in race relations and in other ways not. While Brazilians have always interacted sexually between races, you will find pockets of discrimination that would be unacceptable in other countries. How Brazilians think about race is also largely dependent on region. The following is a history of Brazilian intellectual thought about race in Brazil to try to help you understand race from a Brazilian perspective.

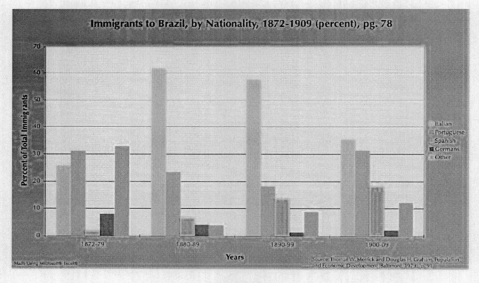

Immigration
Source: *Brown University Library*

The Brazilian version of the eugenics movement came from as sociologist, jurist, and member of the Academy of Letters in Brazil, named Oliveira Viana in the 1920s who claimed that the original Portuguese settlers who conquered and settled Brazil were descended of superior stock of the Portuguese with initiative, and promoted the idea of superior races mix with lesser races the superior genes would "whiten" the Brazilian people. In his writings and book the Evolution of the Brazilian People, "*Evolução do Povo Brasiliero,"* he was concerned with the sexual relations between the three major ethnic groups in Brazil, Indians blacks and whites. His theories were used to support Brazilian government policy to try to "whiten" the Brazilian people.

After the emancipation slavery in 1888, Brazilian landowners and government policy looked for other sources of manpower and began to promote immigration. Already underway, were a series of both public and private incentives to favor European immigration to "whiten" Brazil. These organizations would recruit European immigrants, pay, or subsides the travel costs, and relocate the Europeans when they arrived. Later government policy would try to restrict Asian immigration, who were assumed not to assimilate as easily as Europeans.[110]

Not surprisingly Oliveira Viana was against the immigration of the Japanese, these theories for racial preference were supported by government policy. The Brazilian constitution of 1934 included an article on immigration quotas which was used to restrict Japanese immigration that stated the following:

The entry of immigrants in the national territory will be subject to the restrictions necessary to guarantee the ethnic integration and the physical and legal capacity of the immigrant; the immigrant arrivals from any country cannot, however, exceed an annual rate of two percent of the total number of that nationality resident in Brazil during the preceding fifty years.[111]

Olivera Viana's theories was simply copying eugenic theory that had been developed in Europe and the United States and repackaged for Brazil. Brazil is not alone during this shameful period, the theory of eugenics was used as a basis of government racial policy, not only in Brazil but as well as Europe and the United States.

Gilberto Frye: Brazil as a Post Racial society

Into this environment, Gilberto Fryre in 1930 proposed a theory that was far more interesting and original for Brazil. With more than half of Brazilians claiming some amount of African heritage, the idea of turning Brazil into a "White" country was not going to work. These facts led Brazilian Sociologist Gilberto Frye to coin the term Racial Democracy in 1933 in his book "Master and Slaves", Gilberto Fryre made the argument that Brazil had a history of

---

[110] Available in: https://en.wikipedia.org/wiki/Racial_whitening. Access in: 3/12/2021.
[111] Available in: https://library.brown.edu/create/fivecenturiesofchange/. Access in: 3/12/2021.

mixing races and this was going to continue. Not only was mixing races inevitable in Brazil; it was good for Brazil. Gilberto took the racial ideas of the time and turned them on its head. Instead of wanting Brazil to be white, Gilberto argued that Brazil needed to embrace its mixed-race heritage as it had or would soon become the first post racial society. He called this post racial society, racial democracy where Brazilian would stop worrying about race. He did not claim that prejudice of color did not exist in Brazil but that the fraternal spirt between Brazilians is stronger than this social prejudice. His argument was that by continually intermixing the races Brazil would become the truly first post racial society. With the defeat of the Nazis in World War II, these ideas were rapidly adopted by Brazilians who took the idea of Brazil as a post racial society as a point of national pride. [112]

Racial Democracy did not mean that there was no discrimination, it just meant that interracial relations are normal to Brazil. When Pele, the black king of soccer dated Xuxa the blonde TV star, daughter of a Brazilian military family, in the 1980s, Brazilian society thought nothing was wrong with two rich celebrities going out. Sexual relations between races have, always been practiced in Brazil. This does not mean that there is no discrimination when a poor Brazilian or a Brazilian with strong African appearance tries to get a job or the same service in a restaurant.

After the defeat of the Nazis in world war II and international disgust of the holocaust, there was much international attention paid to Brazil and its claims of creating a post-race society. In the 1950's UNESCO commissioned a number of studies into the claims of Social Democracy in Brazil. Unfortunately, these studies detected that much of the claims of social democracy were myths and many follow up studies pointed out evidence of implicit and explicit racism in Brazil along with the economic inequality. Although Racial Democracy was a wonderful theory and it explains some daily behaviors of Brazilians, its claims cannot be measured in studies which point out the overwhelming inequality in Brazil.

Social Apartheid in Brazil

There is flaw with the racial democracy theory of Brazil. Bias against darks skinned Brazilians is prevalent if at times disguised. Although the middle and lower classes are mixed races, the rich tend to be white.

---

[112] Available in: https://en.wikipedia.org/wiki/Racial_democracy. Access in: 3/12/2021.

The second flaw of the racial democracy theory of Brazil is, while it is true the color of skin may not show racism, there is still a prejudice against certain racial characteristics. In advertisements for employment a requirement of needing "good appearances" to apply for a particular job was a code for Brazilians of an African profile need not apply. You cannot directly point to this racism in Brazil because it is disguised. But ask any Brazilian with strong African features if such prejudice exists and they will confirm it.

The theory of social apartheid holds that due to economic inequality the poor are segregated from the rich in Brazil much as the blacks were separated from the white in apartheid South Africa. One fact that supports this theory is that Brazil did nothing to aid the slaves to freedom in the late 19th century and left them to live in the favelas and as landless rural poor, while only a few years later, the Brazilian government would actively encourage and support European immigration. Overtime this segregation became physical with whiter upper- and middle-class Brazilians began living is secure apartments and gated communities. The children attend private schools, while the parents work in office buildings. Conversely the poor and more dark-skinned Brazilians tend in *favelas* or shanty towns far away from the city center. You will find white Brazilians in the favelas and blacks in the gated communities, but this is exceptional. The social apartheid in Brazil is similar to South Africa, but it is not just about race, it is also about economic inequality.

Gringo Advice

Reform Brazilian Government

The Brazilian State is big and perpetuates social inequality though it polices. Government salaries are higher than their equivalent job in the private sector and government pensions are more favorable than the public. As the selection for the civil service is based on exams, the poor without proper access to education do not have equal access to government jobs. According to the economist the total size of the Brazilian state is about 33% of GDP which compares to rich counties in the world. This could be used to reduce inequality, but pension and other transfers represent 23% of GDP also go to the well off and perpetuates social inequality. Of the total pensions paid only 2.3% of the payments go the poorest 20% of the populations. Legislatures and Judges are paid more than most of their peers in the rich world. Arminio Fraga, a former central bank governor estimates 9% of the government budget could be reduced by eliminating waste and closing tax loopholes.

Legalize the Favelas

Many of the shanty towns in Brazil were invaded many years decades ago and have been the homes of many generations of Brazilians. Besides building public housing, the state needs to recognize and give legal title to the de facto owners in these communities. The government must get the population of these communities into the legal sphere of the state. Legalizing the *favelas*, means, giving at no cost to the inhabitants of the property, legal title to that residence and give all benefits of the residence to the resident. This simple act creates and transfers capital into the hands of the poor in Brazil and brings these communities under the laws of the Brazilian state. The effort to legalize the favelas must be accompanied with improvements of social services and education withing the communities.

- By legalizing the property, you bring the population within the sphere of the state. This is a necessary step to remove the control of the *favelas* from the control of organized crime. I consider the militias as organized crime.

- By legalizing the property, you give incentive to the owner to improve that property.

- By legalizing the property, you are in the economic meaning creating capital for the community and Brazil immediately with the stroke of a pen! The owner for example could get a bank loan with a mortgage. He could use this to start a new business.

Overtime letting free the industriousness and creativity of the Brazilian, these communities would be transformed into working class neighborhoods. Provided state services and security these areas would reduce criminality and provide a reasonable safe environment for families. The poor would gain from the increase in worth of their homes and more importantly they would have a stake in the legal society. This transition will take time, but anything is an improvement from the current situation.

Speed Up Agrarian Reform

Agrarian reform is nothing more than taking unused land from large landowners, paying for it and giving it to the rural poor. Productive large-scale agriculture is responsible for 25% of the GDP in Brazil and is some of the most efficient farming in the world. This not the focus of agrarian reform. It is only unproductive land or land acquired illegally, that should be used for agrarian reform. The legislations have been on the books since the 1950s, but nothing ever happens. There are many reasons for these delays including a slow and at time corrupt judiciary and inefficient government along with exiting landholders willing to uses violence. Where it is possible the government should speed up the legalization of lands with existing squatting farmers.

Improve Public Education and charge tuition in Public Universities.

It is simply unacceptable for the government to subsides the wealth we free university and having failing schools for the poor. Above a certain income level tuition at a Federal university needs to be charged to wealthy students. At the same time the quality of public schools needs to be improved.

Tax reform

The Brazilian state needs to reduce its size and benefits in general to make more effective use of its funds. Brazil has a confusing mix of state and federal VAT taxes that are regressive as they are based on consumption which as a proportion of total revenue fall heavily on the poor. At the same time property taxes should be increased to fund better local public schools. These taxes would be paid by property and rural landowners who currently pay relatively small amounts.

Finally, an estate or death tax needs to be created for the richest 5% of Brazilian families to fund educational programs and directly reduce income inequality over time.

Chapter Twelve

Criminal Violence in Brazil

A friend of mine in Brazil was a professional mixed martial arts fighter and my Muay Thai teacher. He came from a working-class background. I met him because he was hired by some friends of mine who practiced Brazilian Jiu Jitsu to teach us all Muay Thai or Kickboxing. We wanted a place to learn to fight in private. A place where if you got a bloody nose, you could make sure the fighting stopped! A place without the egos that typically go along with a professional gym. We called this our "playboy fight club." The organizer of our "playboy fight club" had built a tatami behind his house. He hired two brothers who were professional fighters to teach us, and I was invited to join. A tatami is the traditional name for a place for training Judo, or the type of mats used for Judo, but in Brazil tatami used generally for any training area of all martial arts. When professional fighters from other cities came to fight, they would train with us, because the owner of the professional gym also promoted fights.

Our teacher was a professional fighter and he had won several fights in Brazil. Soon he went to Japan and won his first fight at the Pride Fighting Championships, which was the biggest event in the world at that time, bigger than the UFC. As soon as he won prize money, he wanted a new car. To celebrate his victory, I threw a *churrasco* at my house. Our teacher asked us our advice if he should use the money to buy a new car. We all told him for different reasons to get a used car first. First, our teacher had never really driven very much, so I told him he would likely get into a crash. Others told him to save his money while he was starting out because you never know how long your career would last. His brother reminded him that they both were going to buy a house for their mother.

He made up his own mind and bought himself a new car anyway. Within a few months of driving, a robber opened the unlocked car door to the back seat while my friend was stopped at a red light in the middle of the night. This thug put a pistol to my friend's head and then drove off with my friend's new car. This is only to say that in Brazil, even a mixed martial arts champion is no match for a criminal with a pistol.

Criminal Violence is more common in the poorer parts of Brazil, so if you are an expatriate or a visitor, this chapter is not to scare you about Brazil but make you aware of the problem for the Brazilian population, as well as help give you helpful hints to keep you out of trouble.

As the introduction of this book points out, many Brazilians think of their country as two different countries: a north and south, or a poor and rich, or a coastal and interior Brazil. In the case of Criminal Violence, there are also two Brazils. There is a Brazil of high-rise apartments, gated communities, and private security guards. In this Brazil, the children arrive at school with guards waiting at the entrance. The cars may be bullet proofed, with private drivers to pick up the children. In this Brazil, there are guards posted on the streets paid by the neighborhood or houses will have guard posts at the entry to the house. Security cameras are ubiquitous, and the police are welcome. In this Brazil, you will be safe.

In the other Brazil, order is kept by *militias* or criminals in a community often called a *favela* or shanty town. These *favelas* are outside the law. By far most of the people in this community are non-violent, hardworking, and poor. They work in or outside the *favela* and some have businesses within the community. No one outside the *favela* can enter without the agreement of the local criminals that run the community. Most of these criminal guards are armed. To even enter it is customary for someone within the community to introduce someone outside the community to these guards. Of, course it is impossible to generalize and classify all the *favelas* in Brazil is in category, but unlike slums in developed countries, *favelas* are not legally registered neighborhoods. As these communities exist outside the law and the formal state, they also have a higher tendency for violence. Some *favelas* like those in Rio de Janeiro are incredibly old and have traditions. The same families may have lived in these communities for generations. Other *favelas* like those that surround Brasilia are new. Of all the Brazilians that suffer from criminal violence, the poor suffer the most.

The scale of the problem

Consider this, we all know that guns are easy to purchase in the United States and in Brazil guns are hard to purchase legally. Yet the murder rate in Brazil is 29.5 per hundred thousand versus 5.35 in the United States. In other words, you are five times more likely to be murdered in Brazil than in the United States. To compare with other countries, Canada has a murder rate of 1.6 per 100,000; United Kingdom, 1.2; Switzerland, .54; Mexico 19,6; and Afghanistan 6.35.[113] This amazingly is an improvement for Brazil, which represents a reduction of 25% from 2017 when more than 59,000 people were murdered. In 2017 this big number can be explained by conflict between the two major criminal groups, the Red Command, and the PCC over a fight for territory. This year also marked the pacification of the communities in Rio de Janeiro by the army.

When you include property crimes, such as theft robbery and burglary and other reported crimes, you have a similar situation. Brazil has a 69.48 crime rate per 100,000 versus 46.73 in the United States, 43.64 for the United Kingdom. Telling Brazil lags closely behind Afghanistan which has a crime rate of 73.26.

What is going on here? How can a country filled with such great people be so violent? For us to understand why this is, we need to come back to the idea that there are two Brazils. In this case you have a legal Brazil which is part of the legal Brazilian State, and the undocumented Brazil which functions outside the law. The legal Brazil works pretty much like any other country. People live in houses that have registered titles. They can have bank accounts and get a mortgage at a bank. They pay taxes, and utility bills. The police routinely drive through these areas. The Brazilians that live in the undocumented communities or *favelas*, have no title to their houses, even if they have lived there all their lives. Electricity is sometimes improvised, and heating gas is provided by criminal gangs or militias. These same gangs provide security for the community. If the police enter these communities, it is usually for a paramilitary action against the gangs. As these communities are outside the law, for people living in the *favelas,* crime can seem like a reasonable career choice.

For those readers who are coming to live and work in Brazil, you need to learn to navigate this reality. One of the important lessons in being Brazilian is being prepared to be robbed without putting yourself in danger. When I started work in Brazil, my work colleagues told me to always keep a

---

[113] "Murder Rate by Country 2020." *World Population Review*, Available in: https://worldpopulationreview.com/country-rankings/murder-rate-by-country. Access in: 3/12/2021.

little bit of cash readily available in case of robbery. We called this "mugging money." Losing your documents and credit cards is by far a worse hassle than losing your money. Most Brazilian criminals do not want to kill you, but they are very nervous and may be on drugs, so making it easy for them to take your cash makes life easier for everybody.

Brazilians will also tell you to be wary of motorcyclists with a male passenger while you are driving. You need to be worried about two men on a single cheap motorcycle, especially when the man on the back carries a backpack. This profile represents the type of criminal who may try to rob you in traffic. Police commonly pull over motorcyclists with this profile. The following is a true story.

An American friend who lived in Brazil was driving his car. He had been told to be worried about Brazilian motorcyclists and he about the use of "mugging money." Sure enough, one day, a Brazilian on a motorcycle tapped on his car window just as my friend was stopped at a traffic light. My friend went through all the steps he had learned and was prepared for the day he got mugged. He proceeded to pull out his cash and roll down the window to give to the motorcyclist, when he noticed the Brazilian was riding an expensive 900cc BMW! The Brazilian opened his visor of his helmet and told my friend in perfect English that the back door of his car was open! The wealthy Brazilian motorcyclist and my friend shared a laugh, knowingly about "mugging money"

Later this same friend told me another story about when he really was mugged by a teenager with a gun but this time, he did not have his mugging money ready. My friend had to pull out his wallet and give the robber his money. After giving his money to the robber, but keeping his documents, my American friend asked in Portuguese, "Hey man, if you have all of my money, how am I supposed to get home?" Without thinking twice, the robber gave him back some money so that my friend could take a taxi. This is Brazil!

Hopefully, you will never face this situation as there is nothing more terrifying than being robbed at gunpoint. Somehow to be Brazilian you need to understand that while a Brazilian may rob you, and while this is a petrifying experience, this same Brazilian could interact with you under other circumstances, and everything would be OK. *Tudo Bem!*

While most of the time crime is random, other times violence is organized between major players of organized crime and the police.

It sometimes seems as if there is a simmering class conflict between rich and poor, but rarely is their criminal violence with political intent. Brazil is not heading for a revolution or guerrilla war, it just has a steady form of criminal conflict. The worst victims of crime are the poor. Sometimes it is hard to tell the good guys from the bad guys in Brazil. Here is an introduction to the organizations on both sides of the criminal violence.

The Good Guys

The Police are separated by function and by Federal, State and city administrations. If you are living in Brazil, you should have a basic understanding of the roles of the different police. While in Brazil, you need to respect its laws. Brazil is a very tolerant society, but it is also a violent society, so for your own safety stay on the right side of the law.

State Level

Military Police: Polícia Militar

Despite its name, the Military Police do not answer to the army nor are they part of the army. They are a state police that has uniforms and ranks like the military, but they are police. These are the police that are on the street arresting criminals. Most of the time the military police are relaxed and interact with the population on a friendly basis. As a Gringo, you will find the military police very friendly and charming. They have a mixed reputation, however, as some *polícia* have been involved in violence and criminal activity. This is heavily covered in the media. The *Militias* are criminal gangs, that we will see later in this chapter are frequently assembled of current or former Military Police and firemen. These *militias* have taken over shanty towns or favelas for their own use, principally in Rio de Janeiro. Some Military Police have been accused of murder, or murder for hire, but for the most part as a foreigner you will find them to be very friendly. Compared to many countries, the military police interact with the common citizen in a more relaxed way. It will be unlikely that you, as a *gringo*, should have any direct interaction with them as they do not give out traffic or speeding tickets. These police spend most of their time with serious crime. Most traffic tickets are given by automated cameras that send tickets to your house in the mail.

Unless there is an injury, Brazilians resolve traffic accidents without calling the police.

The Military Police also have unique units like SWAT units in the United States. These are the paramilitary units responsible for the invasions of the shanty towns or hostage situations. There is criticism of the Military Police due to its use of violence. While there are some also notable scandals involving Military Police, the special paramilitary units have a reputation for being incorruptible and have been the subject of movies and pop music. My advice is to avoid criminal activity in Brazil, and you will likely be able to avoid contact with the *Police Militar*.

If you are a victim of a crime in Brazil, you will need to fill out a report at any police station or by internet, with the military police for insurance or to get police help. You have nothing to be afraid of from the Military Police. As a *gringo* you will be treated well by the police as you will by the rest of Brazil.

Civil Police: Polícia Civil

The Civil Police do not wear uniforms. They are investigators of crimes. These police work in criminal investigations after a crime has occurred. You can think of it like this: the Military Police work on the streets to stop and deter crime, the Civil Police investigate crimes and criminal organizations. Sometimes it is necessary for the Civil Police to investigate the Military Police. As a result, at times there are problems with coordination between the two forces. If a military police officer is arrested for a crime, it is usually handled by the Civil Police.

City Level

Municipal Guards: Guarda Civil

This force works for the city and has evolved to a quasi-police force. Traditionally its job was to patrol parks and safeguard city property. Over time its officers have become armed and ride in patrol cars. Today the municipal guards function almost like a city police department and they report to the mayor of a city.

Federal Level

Highway Patrol: Polícia Rodoviária

The *Polícia Rodoviária* force polices the highways and railways of Brazil. Their stations are on the sides of major highways and you are required to slow down near them. You will notice Brazilians slowing down passing these stations on the highway. Occasionally you will see an officer outside of these stations. Sometimes they are monitoring all cars but more likely they will observe on their cameras a traffic any incident that requires attention. They will provide you with assistance in case of an accident on the federal highway system.

Federal Police: Polícia Federal

This agency is the equivalent of the FBI or Scotland Yard. It focuses on protection of borders, counterterrorism, and organized crime. Most notably the *Polícia Federal* are the investigators of political corruption. *Polícia Federal* are highly respected and supported by the local population due to these anti-corruption efforts. The Federal Police work with Federal Prosecutors and are mostly free of interference from other branches of government. This independence has given the Federal Police greater latitude to fight organized crime including political corruption.

Blitzes: Police Roadblocks

Any Police Department can set up a "Blitz" which mean lightning in German or a traffic stop in Brazil. A blitz is meant to be a surprise and can happen in any number of situations. If you are traveling in a border area, where smuggling is common, you may come across a blitz. Driving late at night in a major city, or driving to vacation areas, or purely at random, you may come across a blitz.

Blitzes are rare, and easy to deal with as long as you have your personal documents and automobile documents and are not breaking the law. When you come across a blitz you need to stay calm and stay in the line of traffic. Do not try to turn around or avoid the blitz, that will send the police immediately after you and you could be fined. During the blitz, the Police will look at you, ask you for identification as well as your driver's license and car certification. You need to be sure you have these documents with you in the car, if not the police may keep your car! The police will give you time to get home to get those documents, but this could be a huge hassle. If during a blitz, you are drunk you do not have to submit to an alcohol test. If you are in possession of weapons or drugs, you may be arrested and go to jail. If you have your documents, the most they may ask of you will be to open your trunk. Because they are stopping a whole line of traffic the Police will work quickly. If you do not speak Portuguese or if you have a foreign driver's license, just explain that you are a *Gringo*, and they will give you a break. They have more important things to do than hassle you.

Blitz
Source: *JM on-line*, 2020

What to do if you are in a Blitz

- Upon seeing a Blitz in front of you, slow down, do not speed up or try to avoid the blitz, this will draw attention of the police and could create problems.

- Whatever the police officer asks for, obey. If you do not speak Portuguese explain that you are a *gringo*. This will help the rest of the process. Try your best to follow his instructions.

- When the police approach you do not make quick movements and keep your hands visible. Look at the police.

- Be respectful of the police and avoid arguments, if you are in a rush to be somewhere, arguing or complaining will only make the situation worse, maybe much worse.

- Present the documents requested when requested. If you do not speak Portuguese very well explain it to the police officer. The officer will likely as you for your identification; use your passport or copy of passport if you do not have an RNE. Any photo identification from your home country can also work if needed. As stated in other parts of the book, foreigners are held in high esteem in Brazil, so if you work with the police, they will work with you to overcome any language problems.

- Do not pass the police blockade without authorization. Not only is this subject to fines but you can lose permission to drive. This is a time for calm and patience.

The Bad Guys

There are many organized criminal gangs in Brazil. For this chapter we are excluding political criminal organizations of corrupt government officials and businessmen which are included in the chapter on corruption and impunity. In this chapter we are focusing on violent criminal gangs and how they rule as a parallel state withing Brazil.

In the *favelas*, shanty towns, where the legitimate state government has no legitimate power or moral standing, criminal gangs govern. Human society cannot live in chaos. If the state does not provide a legitimate form of justice, then those communities will find another way to create stability. Even though millions of Brazilians live in these communities, their residences are not legal, they have no legal title to their homes. Though politicians will provide services in exchange for votes, the formal government remains outside the day-to-day governing of these communities. These communities live their day-to-day existence outside of the rule of law. Into this gap of power comes the criminal gangs.

Like the mafia of old, criminal gangs perform basic governing. Reports during the recent pandemic showed that the gangs would enforce curfews and limit the times outsiders could buy drugs in the community to avoid getting the community infected. However, these organizations are still criminal in nature. They sell drugs and guns, they rob banks, they kill. They are criminal gangs with a capital C. Here are a few of the more colorful and best-known gangs.

Red Command, Comando Vermelho

The Red Command is oldest organized criminal gang in Brazil. It started during the military dictatorship that ruled from 1964 to 1985. The military government mixed common criminals with leftist political prisoners. The political prisoners were taught about how to commit crime, and the criminals were taught leftist ideology and revolutionary organization structure. The Red Command operates with revolutionary cells. There is structure without a single boss. What started as a self-defense force for protection from the guards in Rios Candido Mendes prison soon spread to other prisons and to the communities in Rio.

By 1979, the group had spread out of the prison and into Rio's streets. Members who were on the outside of prison, were tasked with providing money to those on the inside through criminal activities such as bank robbery, thus allowing the incarcerated members to maintain a decent quality of life, and to finance escape attempts.

The ideas of the Red Command spread to other prisons, and the power of the organization grew. Two decades later, in São Paulo, a similar prisoners' movement would emerge — the First Capital Command (*Primeiro Comando da Capital* – PCC).

The Red Command was ideally placed to partner with Colombian cartels when the cocaine trade began to boom in the 1980s, as it had the structure and organization to reliably obtain and distribute large quantities of the drug. Members on the outside now had a clear objective: forming well-armed gangs to take over drug turf in the name of the Red Command. It gained control of many poor neighborhoods in Rio de Janeiro that had been neglected by the state, setting up a parallel system of government inside the *favelas* and providing employment to inhabitants long excluded from Brazilian society.[114]

The First Capital Command (Primeiro Comando da Capital – PCC)

I recall one day in 2006 at work when it seemed like the PCC would take over São Paulo. I was a senior manager at a multinational company with the South American headquarters based in São Paulo. The previous day's news had been about the government's plans to transfer the leadership of the PCC to prisons in the Amazon. This was the first time I had heard of the PCC, and I remember thinking how cool the name sounded.

The next day driving into work I heard on the radio that several prisons had simultaneously rebelled overnight. Later I would learn that a total of 70 prisons had been overrun and that many were holding hostages. I remember thinking it extraordinary that a criminal gang was able to coordinate simultaneous prison uprisings and take over multiple prisons at the same time. As I drove to work, I wondered how they communicated and had the leadership structure in dreadful prison conditions to pull off such an act? At that time, I was unaware that the PCC had in 1999 already pulled off the biggest bank robbery in São Paulo, stealing 32 million dollars. Nor did I know that in 2001 the PCC had staged a multi-prison riot to stop the transfer of its leaders.[115] As I worked during the day, news reports would detail, sometimes incorrectly, what seemed to be coordinated small scale attacks around different parts of the city. Everyone in my company by now had heard stories of motorcyclists riding with pistols carrying passengers, shooting the tires of cars stopped in traffic jams. We heard reports of police stations being attacked and universities and hospitals being sprayed with gun fire.

The news on the radio became more and more worrying, and by lunch this was the only topic of conversation with my co-workers. Most of my coworkers had children who were at school, and I too began to worry. Finally, at about 3:00 in the afternoon, the management of my company

---

[114] Available in: https://www.insightcrime.org/brazil-organized-crime-news/red-command-profile/ Access in: 08/08/2020.

[115] Available in: https://www.insightcrime.org/brazil-organized-crime-news/first-capital-command-pcc-profile/ Access in: 08/08/2020.

and many other companies decided it was time to let their employees leave to pick up their children at school and get home.

Traffic in São Paulo is normally bad, but with just a few motorcyclists shooting tires as well as other coordinated attacks in the city, traffic essentially shut down. I started out in the afternoon trying to give a ride to a friend of mine who was terrified, and I was trying to help her get home. As night fell, we were still far from either of our apartments, and I was not about to abandon my car and walk, so even though all businesses were closed, we arrived and a hotel that allowed us to spend the night there.

PCC
Source: *Observatório de Segurança*, 2020

Watching the news that night, we discovered that along with the prison uprising, the leaders of the PCC outside of prison had also staged multiple attacks on various parts of the city. There was chaos in the city the entire night. It took a few days for the city to return to normal. The entire uprising left more than 150 dead.[116]

The origins of the PCC can be traced to a prison football game. A group of prisoners who survived an infamous riot in the October 1992 massacre in São Paulo's Carandiru prison were transferred to Taubaté prison. There in October 1993, at the Taubate prison, a fight broke out after

---
[116] *Ibidem*.

a football game between a team of inmates from the interior of São Paulo and a team of inmates from the city of São Paulo, who won, which left two prisoners dead. Anticipating the coming repression from the prison guards and administrators the prison gangs of the two opposing teams created a mutual aid society to protect each other's members from the coming castigations.[117] As a result of the football game and the subsequent punishments, the PCC was formed to fight for justice after the massacre and to push for better prison conditions. They expressed solidarity with another prison-based gang, the Red Command, adopting its slogan "peace, justice, freedom," and advocated for revolution and the destruction of the capitalist system.[118]

The PCC like the Red Command is a criminal organization, and like the Red Commend is not really a political movement. The Red Command operates a series of cells that governs the *favelas* of Rio, but it does not organize political actions. The Red command has expanded over the years to have cells around Brazil, and even in other countries. The PCC is centered in São Paulo, but now has franchises across the country as well. The proof that they are basically criminal in nature lies in the fact that even though both organizations preach the overthrow of the capitalist society, they have made no attempt to coordinate action towards this end. Both PCC and the Red Command fortunately only use violence to further their criminal interests, not to foment political revolution.

Eventually the growth of both organizations led to conflict and rivalry. By 2016, the PCC broke a long-standing truce with the Red Command, setting off months of bloody prison riots that led to hundreds of deaths. Authorities linked the violence to clashes between the two groups over control of lucrative drug trafficking routes running through the remote northern Amazon region of Brazil. Reports also suggested that the PCC was seeking to challenge the Red Command in its home city of Rio de Janeiro, and that the PCC was fending off challenges from a rival group in São Paulo state, contributing to a spike in violence there.[119]

Milícias

Milícias is the term that Brazilian use for former or active police and fireman, who operate criminal gangs in the *favelas*. *Milícias* are most

---

[117] Available in: https://www.observatoriodeseguranca.org/imprensa/da-gangue-a-hegemonia-uma-cronologia-da-expansao-do-pcc/ Access in: 3/13/2021.
[118] *Ibidem*.
[119] *Ibidem*.

widespread in Rio and Bahia but can be found in other states as well. The Brazilian perception of the *milícias* is complicated. Brazilian citizens and politicians, tired of criminal violence, at first welcomed *milícias*. It is estimated that some 2 million people live under militia control.[120] The *milícias* took over much of this area from criminal gangs, but then proceeded to create their own criminal enterprises. *milícias* charge for their protection services and tax businesses as if they are a separate state. Recently they began the building of illegal apartment buildings in the *favelas*, some as high as ten stories tall.

On April 12, 2019 two high rise residential buildings collapsed in the community of Muzema in Rio de Janeiro, killing at least four people. A police operation quickly revealed that the buildings had been constructed illegally, without any approval from authorities. In a statement, the local government said that Muzema is controlled by militia groups and is difficult for officials to access.[121]

A further investigation revealed that one of Rio's most notorious *milícias*, the Office of Crime (*Escritório do Crime*) had financed the construction of several such buildings, selling illegal apartments off for thousands of dollars. From the outside these building look like apartment buildings you see all over Brazil, but in this case, they constructed the apartments along the boundaries of the *favela* expanding the frontier of the communities and encroaching on what is supposed to be protected jungle, deforesting the land. The entire apartment building was illegal. This proves that *Favelas* exist to all intents and purposes beyond the boundary of the legal state. There are no legal titles to property, no construction regulations, and no zoning regulations. Yet somehow roads and utilities mysteriously are extended into this parallel real estate market.

The Office of Crime, which is made up of active and former police officers moonlighting as criminals, has grabbed headlines for its connection to the murder of councilwoman Marielle Franco in 2018. Marielle Franco was an activist from the communities and elected city councilwoman who had begun investigations of the criminal activities of the *milícias*. She and her driver were murdered, and security footage of the crime was publicized on national television.

---

[120] Available in: https://www.theguardian.com/world/2018/jul/12/brazil-militia-paramilitary-wield-terror-seize-power-from-drug-gangs. Access in: 08/08/ 2020.

[121] Available in: https://www.insightcrime.org/news/analysis/milítias-become-luxury-real-estate-barons-rio-de-janeiro/ Access in: 14/07/2020.

When two former police officers and *milícia* members were finally arrested in March 2019 after much delay, this crime took a surreal path. There were multiple links between this *militia* and the Bolsonaro family, whose leader is Jair Bolsonaro, the President of Brazil. A *militia* member, former police sergeant, Ronnie Lessa, killed councilwoman Franco, incredibly Sergeant Lessa lived in the same luxury condominium as President Bolsonaro prior to Bolsonaro's election. Police raids on one of Lessa's homes in Rio found over one hundred M-16 assault rifles. The other ex-policeman, Èlcio Queiroz, who drove the car seen at the murder, had posted pictures of himself and the president on social media. The alleged founder of the Office of Crime militia, Adriano Magalhães da Nóbrega, who was a former police captain and a legal fugitive due to previous crimes. Nóbrega had close ties with the president's son, Flavio Bolsonaro. It was discovered that the president's son had hired Nóbrega's ex-wife to work in his office as a state assemblyman. To add to this bizarre drama, Nóbrega was conveniently killed in a shoot-out with police in February 2020. These close relationships between high level politicians in the official government and criminal organizations who govern the illegal state, are troubling.

If you are a gringo with a few precautions, you will be safe in Brazil. The Brazil that you will visit, and work is already prepared for your safety, you do not need to visit the other Brazil of criminality and violence. With some basic precautions in Brazil, the gringo will be safe and secure. So, my *gringo* advice on this chapter is to provide the gringo with tips on safety as well as advice for Brazil for bring its crime under control in the longer term.

Gringo Advice for day to day living and visits

If you pay attention upon your arrival in Brazil, you will notice a great deal of effort has been made to make your life safe. If you are visiting, you will likely notice security guards in your hotel, and in high-class restaurants and clubs. Security forces are the men are commonly dressed in black suits. If you visit a bank you will pass through metal detectors and bullet proof glass to enter the bank office. Your own office and the schools for your children will have similar security measures. In time this will seem normal.

If you live in an apartment you may have multiple gates and security to enter and leave. The same will apply for gated communities. If you live in a house, you will likely have guards on your street and perhaps private security patrols. All of this is to make you safe in the Brazil that you live in. All you need to do is avoid contact with "other" Brazil outside the law. The "other" Brazil can be avoided by taking the following simple steps:

1. Stay in the right areas. You need to learn to avoid going to the other Brazil by mistake. Avoid dark alleys, narrow roads, or communities that are away from public businesses, hotels, or restaurants. If you find yourself entering a dangerous area by mistake, do not drive through it, back up, turn your car around, and leave.

2. Take care of your passport and documents. Far worse than getting robbed is losing or having your documents stolen. If you are in Brazil to work, you will be issued an RNE similar to a green card. Make a photocopy of this document and passport and keep the originals safe.

3. Mugging Money. Keep some money readily available is a shirt pocket or in your car in a separate location from your wallet and documents. If you do get robbed, rapidly handing over cash is a good way to defuse the tension and can help you avoid handing over your wallet. As a last resort, get your wallet out give the cash. Your robbers understand how hard it is to replace documents and should allow you to keep them.

4. ATMs or Electronic Cash Machines have been the targets of muggings in the past so often that it is hard to find one in an open place. You can use ATMs that are either inside a shopping mall or inside a bank. The ATMs will take your Visa and MasterCard. Banks and shopping malls have security guards near most ATM machines.

5. Do not flaunt your wealth and make yourself a target. No one wears expensive jewelry or watches in Brazil. This rule goes for cameras, cell phones and other high-end items as well. If you are going into crowds, keep these items in a daypack or purse. For extra security wear the daypack backwards, on the front of your body.

6. Use taxis. Brazil has some of the best and safest taxis in the world. Avoid unsolicited people offering rides at airports and bus stations. Public transportation is safe, but it also can be crowded. If you need to use public transportation, get a Brazilian friend to show you how it works and take their advice on safety.

7. Avoid crowded streets or beaches. Muggings and pickpocketing are the most common crimes you will face in these places. If you are in a crowded beach or walk the streets in a group and keep a close eye on your stuff as you work your way through the crowd. You will see Brazilians traveling through crowds this way; follow their example. If you are caring a backpack in a crowd, wear it to the front. That is what Brazilians do.

Gringo Advice for Brazilian Crime

Brazil is a fantastic country that suffers from high levels of violence. There are a number of deep-seated problems that make criminality difficult to correct or fix quickly. First and foremost is the social inequality that leaves many people poor and poorly educated with limited alternatives. The *favelas* are essentially illegal communities and if you are born into one you have limited opportunities to find formal work or receive an education. This environment is perfect for recruiting young people into organized gangs. These gangs are large and sophisticated. Gangs have easy access to guns, even though law-abiding Brazilians do not. The continuous news of political leaders being caught stealing public funds, wears down the moral fabric of honest Brazilians and sends a message that crime is OK. The police themselves are sometimes involved in criminal activity as we have seen from the *militias*. The Brazilian Crime Association estimates that less than ten percent of murders are solved, compared to 65% in the USA and 90% in the United Kingdom.[122]

While you as a *gringo* are largely shielded by this violence, it is a terrible problem for poor Brazilians. The poor communities, the *favelas*, need to be legalized. Legal title should be given to the homeowners and services and schools should be provided for the poor. Only after the *favelas*

---

[122] Available in: http://g1.globo.com/jornal-da-globo/noticia/2014/04/maioria-dos-crimes-no-brasil-nao-chega-ser-solucionada-pela-policia.html. Access in: 3/12/2021.

are legalized is there any chance of pacification. Police attempts to pacify *favelas* though military means only produce short-term results. Both the criminal gangs and the *militias* need to be evicted but the Brazilian state must govern in its place. This is the major problem because the Brazilian state will not have the moral authority to govern if the culture of corruption and impunity continues among the political leaders. The Brazilian who live in the *favelas* need to receive the same benefits as Brazilians who live inside the formally recognized boundaries of the cities. Legalizing these communities is a first step.

The culture of corruption and impunity must end, and this will require judicial reforms, even constitutional reforms. The right of appeal should be limited to one instance and legal delays need to be eliminated. According to Brazilian federal police the biggest source of the weapons in Brazil is the United States, with many of these weapons passing through Paraguay.[123] Brazilian authorities need to stop this flow of weapons. The current government is lifting restrictions to allow more Brazilians to have access to legal weapons. This could make the violence even worse.

Brazil will only reduce criminal violence long term by addressing it problems with social inequality and reforming its weak legal system. The shanty towns and *favelas* must be legalized to become part of the formal state. This means providing ownership and titles for free to the owners that inhabit the *favelas*. Education and other social services of the state need to be provided to these communities as well. The Brazilians of these communities need to have a interest in being part of the formal state. Giving these communities ownership of their homes is a first step. If these Brazilians have legal title to their homes, they would be provided with credit if they want to improve their homes or start a business. The transition from illegal favela to legal neighborhood is a process. Legalizing these communities will not only improve the lives of the poor in Brazil, take away power from the large criminal organizations. Improving access to education and jobs for the poor is also necessary.

---

[123] Available in: https://www.reuters.com/article/us-usa-brazil-arms/u-s-biggest-source-of-illegal-foreign-guns-in-brazil-report-idUSKBN1EZ2M5. Access in: 3/12/2021.

Chapter Thirteen

Destruction of the Amazon

On August 19, 2019, the twenty million people of São Paulo metropolitan area witnessed a spectacle of biblical proportions. During the middle of the day, the skies darkened. Automatic streetlamps turned on in the middle of the afternoon. The city became eerily quiet, as if expecting some form of divine wrath. Office workers in the high rises of São Paulo crowded to the windows looking out in disbelief. Nothing like this had ever been witnessed before in the city, the largest metropolitan area in South America. Black rain began to fall.

The black rain was filled with ash from fires burning in the Amazon rainforest, some two thousand kilometers away. The rain landed on cars, houses, streets, and parks throughout the city leaving grime in its wake. Meteorologist later determined that ash from the fires in the Amazon mixed with a storm system causing the black rain to fall far from the fires. This should have been a wakeup call to Brazil to preserve the Amazon. These images of the fires were terrifying. After the storm, São Paulo turned dark under the smoke from fires in the Amazon rainforest burning thousands of kilometers away. Brazil's space research center, INPE, detected approximately 72,843 wildfires raging in the Amazon rainforest that year alone; this number has increased drastically from previous years.[124]

We, as citizens of the world, not just as *gringos,* are concerned with the destruction of the Amazon rainforest, as we should be. There no longer should be any doubt that the climate is getting hotter, and deforestation accelerates this. The Amazon rainforest is enormous. It provides the biggest source of fresh water on the planet. Finally, the rainforest has a large diversity of life. Despite what you may believe, most Brazilians share your concern regarding climate change. Most Brazilians live on the coast. They are no more

---

[124] Available in: https://www.indiatimes.com/trending/environment/amazon-forest-fire-is-so-bad-it-turned-the-skies-rain-in-sao-paulo-thousands-of-km-away-black-374136.html. Access in: 3/12/2021.

involved in what is happening in the Amazon than we are. The businesses causing rainforest destruction are largely illegal. For those of us living in Brazil, there is nothing more exasperating while traveling in Europe or North America than being accosted by a stranger who blames you personally for cutting down the rainforest. You try to explain that you feel the same way and even though you live in Brazil, you live in a city thousands of kilometers from the Amazon. Yes, you know the Amazon is being ruined, and yes, it is the lungs of the world. No, you do not personally know anyone cutting down the Amazon. As a Brazilian resident you may or may not have been to the Amazon. Even if you had, the Amazon is so big you might not have seen any of the destruction firsthand. But you have seen it in the nightly news. Most Brazilians feel about the Amazon exactly as you do, but as shown in previous chapters, they have other pressing problems in their lives that impact them more immediately and directly.

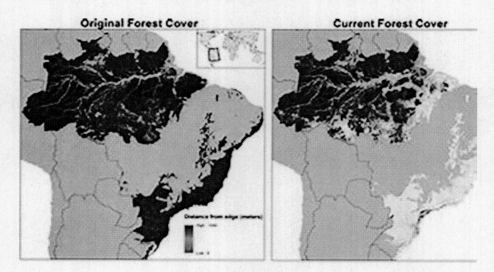

Maps of disappearing forests
Source: *Insider*, 2015

But try as they might, the efforts of those around the world to save the Amazon is certainly not getting the results. Current estimates state that 20% of the original Amazon rainforest has been destroyed. In fact, if anything, the deforestation in Brazil seems to be increasing. So, what is going wrong? I have lived in Brazil and worked in the agricultural industry for most of my career. Through the years I have witnessed Brazilians and the agricultural sector gain a greater understanding and implement better practices for protecting the environment and the Amazon rainforest. Many strategies have been implemented since I first lived in Brazil in 1998. The largest program implemented now provides agricultural companies with space imaging technology to assist in implementing sustainability programs; the Brazilian government launched this space-based system, known as DETER. It immediately notifies the government's environmental agencies of illegal deforestation in the Amazon basin. Another major attempt to control illegal deforestation comes from the private sector; multinational agricultural corporations now avoid buying cattle or soybeans from illegal farmers. So, if governments, environmental organizations, and multinational companies are working so hard to save the rainforest, why do things appear to be getting even worse for the environment? There needs to be a better approach.

One key to stopping the destruction of the rainforest is to understand why it is being destroyed in the first place. What are the social dynamics that prevent Brazil from stopping the destruction? The world has spent billions of dollars trying to preserve the Amazon. So, what is going wrong?

As mentioned earlier, most Brazilians live near the coast. Brazil has high levels of violence and social inequality. Its government institutions are sometimes weak and corrupt. Legal land holding is confusing even in the more closely monitored cities and coastal areas. Imagine how easy it would be to claim land in the Amazon under these conditions if you are willing to stay there and fight for it. Illegal squatting on land is part of Brazilian history. In many parts of Brazil if you stay on a tract of land for 30 years it is yours by law. This law does not apply to the protected areas in the Amazon rainforest. As suggested in earlier chapters in this book, perhaps the Brazilian government is simply unable to stop illegal destruction of the Amazon by itself.

Grilagem: How to legalize your illegal land grab

Legal title to land is not clear in many parts of Brazil. In many cities, legal title is the norm, but as mentioned in Chapter 13, the *favelas,* or shanty towns, have existed for decades, housing hundreds of thousands of Brazilians without legal title to their land. This has allowed organized militias to deforest areas around Rio de Janeiro and build high rise apartments to sell at low prices without any legal title and without benefit of zoning codes. Even though today deforestation in the coastal areas of the Atlantic rainforest is now severely restricted, earlier encroachments have resulted in many luxury homes near beaches that cannot produce legal title. Large tracts of land that are now established farms in the interior originally did not have clear title to land.

Grilagem in Brazil means to make an illegal land grab, the word comes from the word *grilo* which means cricket in Portuguese[125]. I will explain how the two are connected. One of the main themes of this book is that corruption in Brazil is a legacy from Portugal with the arrival of the monarchy and the aristocratic court. One of the ways the king of Portugal showed favor to the destitute, newly arrived aristocracy of Portugal, was to grant them the powers to certify legal documents in Brazil, like the powers of a notary public. *Cartórios,* as these offices are called, were created to be hereditary and given to well-connected supporters of the monarchy. *Cartórios* remained hereditary until 2016. Unlike typical notaries republic in other countries the *cartórios* of Brazil not only authenticate legal document but also register property. This provided great opportunity for fraud. In the days before computers, the land grabbers would create false documents laying claim to a tract of land. To make the documents look old, the documents would be placed in a box with crickets.[126] Chemicals produced by the crickets would darken the paper to look like an ancient manuscript, and once authenticated by a *cartório*, a real estate title could be created. The process of putting crickets (*grilo*) in a box with the papers to create an authentic-looking document to legalize land grabbing became known as *grilagem*. Obviously, this became a very lucrative business if you were well connected and owned a *cartório*. *Grilagem* is not so easy these days due to legal changes requiring approval from and payment to multiple layers of government. Computerized databases exist to register land but many times there is no cross references. Due to this lack of coordination and the additional governmental hoops and payments, land grabbing public lands still exists, but it requires more time. If this corrupt and illegal tradition from the time of the Portuguese monarchy, had not become imbedded in Brazilian land grabbing, perhaps it would be easier to police the Amazon rainforest today.

If a Brazilian is willing to squat on land, there is a good chance that if you are patient and pay the right people, the land will eventually become

---

[125] Excerpt from "Grilagem de terras na Amazônia – Negócio bilionário ameaça a floresta e populações tradicionais". Available in: https://www.wwf.org.br/natureza_brasileira/areas_prioritarias/amazonia1/ameacas_riscos_amazonia/desmatamento_na_amazonia/grilagem_na_amazonia/ Access in: 3/12/2020.

[126] *Ibidem.*

legally yours. Obviously, there is great incentive to claim protected lands. *Grilagem* has taken on a more sinister meaning over time as the process of land grabbing has become more violent and corrupt. In many cases original squatters or indigenous people are intimidated, expelled, and even murdered by miners, loggers, ranchers, and farmers willing to use violence to make their claim.

The history of deforestation and land disputes is not unique to Brazil. Both Europe and North America destroyed large tracts of native forest to promote economic development. Much of the settlement of the western United States was done with mining and land claims backed up with a pistol. Later the claims became legal. Only with the creation of national parks and forests in the 20th century did the U.S. government begin preserving the land under government control. The dynamics of Brazil today are similar to the wild west in the United States of the 19th century, including the violence, but sadly without the romance. The problem in the Amazon today is that national parks and Indian reservations are not respected. In Brazil illegal miners, loggers and ranchers actively fight the environmental police charged who are charged with protecting the Amazon and native lands.

Why is the Amazon Burning Now?

The deforestation of the Amazon has been an issue for only the last 40 years. The Amazon is being deforested not primarily for the rare tropical timber. The tropical timber is just one benefit. Burning the Amazon makes way for cattle ranching. 81% of the deforestation has taken place to make way for cattle pastures.[127] Then, only after years of grazing cattle, the land is ready to become farmland. Soybean farming is only possible after the nitrogen in the soils are reduced. Soybeans are a legume, so they are nitrogen fixing and will not grow well in freshly cut rainforest land which are already rich in nitrogen. So, it takes years to move from cutting rainforest to creating farmland. Regardless, farmland with legal title is valuable.

The Amazon burns because the world wants cheap food. Traditionally, animal protein has been rare in the diets of poor people. As the world has become richer, it not only has grown in population, but millions have been lifted out of poverty. As the poor of the world have grown richer, their diet has changed to include more animal protein. In Brazil, meat production

---

[127] World Wildlife Fund, "Why the Amazon is burning." Available in: https://www.globalcanopy.org/press-centre/why-amazon-burning. Access in: 3/12/2021

increased 1284% from 1961 to 2018.[128] During that same period the growth of meat production in China was greater than a staggering 3000%.[129] Similar increases in meat production have happened all over the world. To feed these animals requires vegetable protein, mostly in the form of soybeans.

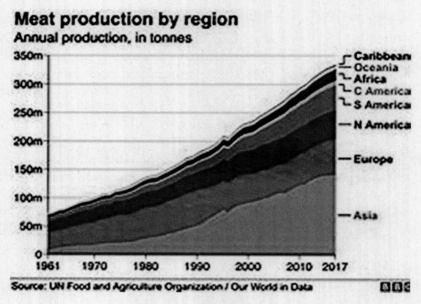

Source: *Our World in Data*, 2017

Unfortunately, the conversion rate of vegetable protein to animal protein is poor. The whole animal conversion efficiency for feed-based production is around 35 percent for chickens, 20 percent for swine, and 10 percent for beef.[130] This means that animals need to consume 10 kilos of vegetable protein to yield one kilo of beef or two kilos of pork. So, if world beef production increased 350 million tons since 1961, then you would need a multiple of 5 to 10 tons of vegetable protein, mostly from soybeans, for feed to convert to 1 ton of animal protean. Although it is fashionable to be vegetarian or vegan in some western countries, for most of the world's population, once they can afford to eat meat, there is great

---

[128] Ritchie, Hannah and Roser, Max, "Meat and Dairy Production," August 2017, Revised November 2019. Available in: https://ourworldindata.org/meat-production. Access in: 3/12/2021.
[129] *Ibidem*.
[130] A Well Fed World, "Feed to meat inefficiency ratios." Available in: https://awellfedworld.org/feed-ratios/ Access in: 3/12/2021.

resistance to return to a vegetarian diet. Fish convert vegetable protein more efficiently than other meat sources. It is reasonable to think that restricting the deforestation of the Amazon could make the price of soybeans and meat increase to the consumer; however, it is not reasonable to believe that a government, could force its population to return to its old diets. Nor could they realistically mandate that their citizens become pescatarians or vegetarians. For example, the Chinese government, realizing that it cannot feed its own population a meat rich diet without importing both meat and soybeans, invests a great deal of resources to achieve what is called "food security." Food security means one has control of food resources sufficient to cover one's needs in a time of scarcity. Fortunately for Brazil, under most circumstances it is illegal for foreigners or foreign companies to own agricultural land in Brazil.

The primary challenge to preserving the Amazon rainforest stems from economic incentives enacted to increase cattle and soybean production. While many experts will argue that improvements in yields can help meet the needs of future demand, there exists only a limited amount of unused agricultural land in the world.[131] A large portion of the world's unused arable land is in Brazil. As the world's population will continue to grow until 2050 and as global prosperity increases, so will the demand for cattle and soybeans. By 2050 the world's population will reach 9.1 billion, 34 percent higher than today.[132] An effective plan to protect the Amazon needs to consider this timeline. Most large multinational agricultural companies already employ departments of sustainability to avoid buying cattle and soybeans from regions of the Amazon that have been illegally deforested. This represents a noble effort and no doubt these companies do not knowingly buy illegal goods from the Amazon. Unfortunately, these companies' efforts fail in two important ways.

Multinational agricultural companies exist to make a profit by producing or purchasing meat and soybeans from countries where food is abundant then selling and shipping to countries where food is scarce. This is a noble mission. However, both shareholders and environmental activists want to make sure that food from Brazil is not causing additional deforestation of the Amazon. To this end, corporations have established sustainability initiatives to avoid buying produce from farmers and ranchers operating

---

[131] Janet Ranganathan, Richard Waite, Tim Searchinger and Craig Hanson - December 05, 2018. Available in: https://www.wri.org/blog/2018/12/how-sustainably-feed-10-billion-people-2050-21-charts. Access in: 3/12/2021

[132] Food and Agriculture Organization "How to feed the world in 2050" Available in: http://www.fao.org/fileadmin/templates/wsfs/docs/expert_paper/How_to_Feed_the_World_in_2050.pdf. Access in: 11/10/ 2020.

illegally in the Amazon. Even though the corporations appear sincere in their efforts, the initiatives do not work well. If anything, deforestation seems to have worsened, since these initiatives were created. So, if the goal of these sustainability policies and the departments that oversee them is to take away any incentive to deforest the Amazon, it is clearly not working.

First, it is exceedingly difficult for companies to enforce sustainability policies. Even if multinational companies have the most stringent policies and top-notch departments, they simply cannot track every truck passing in and out of the Amazon basin. Even though large companies have access to both satellite imagery and the names of illegal farmers and ranchers in the Amazon, it is easy to bypass these controls; all it takes is a willing legal farmer or rancher to issue an invoice for the goods sent to him from an illegal farm. The Brazilian government cannot inspect every truck in the Amazon basin, and if the purchasing companies receive a legal invoice from a legitimate farmer or rancher, they will complete the purchase.

It is not reasonable to expect more than this from multinational companies making agricultural purchases from Brazil, but these efforts would be a more powerful economic incentive to curtail deforesting if they could be used in conjunction with equally strong policing and enforcement of current laws. The multinational policies to support sustainability cannot replace the role of the Brazilian government to enforce laws.

Some multinational agricultural companies do bear a share of the responsibility for deforestation of the Amazon; their investments in processing facilities, roads, and port projects supporting a northern logistical solution for Brazil inadvertently have damaged the rainforest. In the 20th century most farming and ranching took place in southern Brazil. The southern transportation corridors for exports lead to the southern ports of Santos, Victoria, Rio Grande do Sul and Paranaguá. Over time both cattle and soybean production moved northward. Because the primary markets for both soybeans and cattle exports are in Asia and Europe, and both destinations are in the northern hemisphere, it became increasingly costly to truck the goods thousands of miles in the wrong direction to these southern ports, only to send the same back in the direction they originated from, then on to the northern hemisphere. This led companies to look for and invest in projects that could allow them to ship and export though northern ports that were either in or adjacent to the Amazon. These projects became viable when the Brazilian government, after many years of delay, paved highways that crossed through the Amazon River basin. With the development of northern export corridors, the Amazon River basin is under much greater threat. By now there has been more than 30 years of failure to protect the Amazon; how can the rainforest be saved when the addition of these new ports and facilities creates more threat than ever?

Satellite Data Shows Amazon Deforestation Rising Under Brazil's Bolsonaro
Source: *Voa News*, 2019

Gringo advice for trying to save the Rainforest

It is all about money, the world must lease the Amazon to preserve it

None of this is working because it does not address the central issue. The people of the Amazon are generally poor, and one way to for them make money is cutting down the rainforest as the demand for cattle and soybeans continue to grow. The demand for meat and soybeans will increase with world population until 2050, after that the world population will slowly decline. So, we need to save the Amazon until 2050 or 2075 at which time the human population should begin to decline.[133] Currently you can look at the Brazilian response to this climate emergency one of two ways: either the Brazilian government is weak and disorganized or else it is actively supporting the destruction of the Amazon!

---

[133] *Ibidem.*

The current administration, of Jair Bolsonaro will likely not accept any outside interference in the Brazilian Amazon, but a future agreement with a future administration, could be reached if Brazilian sovereignty is maintained and the economic incentives are large. Brazilians and the Brazilian government are rightfully worried about giving up sovereignty of the Amazon rainforest and usually foreigners are prohibited from owning Brazilian land in rural areas. So even any appearance of giving up sovereignty will not work for Brazil. Brazil is heading for a financial crisis and will need a bailout. This will the opportunity for the world to protect the Amazon rainforest, but the world will need to be actively managing the protecting of the rainforest as well. It is worth looking at the Amazon Fund as a potential model for a future agreement to save the Amazon for what worked but for what did not work. The failure of the Amazon fund was that was administered by the Brazilian government with little oversight from the donating countries. By soliciting donations internationally, the Amazon Fund represented an attempt to involve the rest of the world in the preservation of these valuable natural resources. The European countries stopped supporting the Amazon fund in 2019 because the fund was no longer meeting its goals to slow deforestation. The current Bolsonaro administration is not interested in slowing down deforestation. However, the economic situation in Brazil is so troublesome that in the future, donor countries could manage the project may be acceptable to a different Brazilian Administration.

Amazon Economics 101

Economists talk of public goods and externalities and we can use both concepts to justify a reasonable solution to the destruction of the Amazon rainforest. Public goods are goods that are that are shared with no cost to the community. In England's Middle Ages the towns and manors had common pastures called commons. On the commons, anyone could graze cattle at no cost. Since there was no cost, over time more and more cattle were placed on the same land, until it was overgrazed and useless. This is what is known as the tragedy of the commons. Unless supported and regulated, the commons will be destroyed because there is little to no cost in using it but great benefit to those using it up to a point. For other examples of commons, think about the lobster fisheries in Maine or the grasslands in Nepal. The problem of overfishing the oceans is another example of the tragedy of the commons.

From this concept of public goods or commons, we can extend this idea to the Amazon rainforest. Though the Amazon belongs to the Brazilian people, it benefits the world in its capacity to exchange greenhouse gasses like carbon dioxide, which increases global warming, into oxygen, which we all breath. This benefits the entire world if the rainforest remains healthy and is not cut down. It is important to note that while agriculture converts carbon dioxide to oxygen, cattle grazing on illegally cleared rainforest produces the greenhouse gas methane.

The Amazon rainforest is an asset for the world; keeping the rainforest as it is benefitting the world at no cost. The world, especially developed countries, and China produce most greenhouse gases. These developed countries typically have a higher standard of living and more wealth. On a small scale, a wealthy person produces more greenhouse gasses than a poor person. The demand for trees to produce oxygen from this increased greenhouse gas production relies disproportionately on the Amazon rainforest. To make matters worse these more developed countries already destroyed their forest for their own economic advancement. Europe, the United States and China each cut down their forests in pursuit of their wealth and development. It is quite easy for politicians outside of Brazil to say that the Amazon belongs to world; they already cut down much of their own forests! It would be like in old England if a lordly manor that had destroyed its own commons to overgrazing to then invaded another lordly manor to take over the commons and cause a war. However, if one lordly manor paid the taxes of the other lordly manor for the use of the commons, that could be an acceptable negotiated situation and avoid armed conflict.

The second concept of economics which applies to the Amazon rainforest is externalities. An externality asserts that the true cost of production of a product is not captured simply in the cost of raw materials, labor, and shipping of the product. There are many examples of externalities, but one that affects everyone is pollution. For example, airline travel is a profitable business, but the external cost is air pollution; the external cost of extracting gold is polluting rivers with mercury. The smell of turning pig iron to steel is another form of an externality; and so is the pollution resulting from extracting oil and converting it to gasoline. It is hard to think of an industrial process that does not have an external cost. The external costs are spread so far and wide that, individuals accept the cost but collectively the government intervention is required to assess the true costs. For example, the burning and cutting down of a forest could have its own externalities in the form of pollution to the nearby towns, but the collective destruction of the rainforest has a larger cost not only in terms of pollution but also reduced conversion of CO_2 and this is a cost to the world. Externalities are the justification for environmental legislation, used to capture the true cost of production, which is handled within each individual country. But how can legislation save the Amazon rainforest?

By now it should be clear that if the world wants to save the Amazon, the world will need to pay for it. The use of the economic concepts such as public goods and externalities is simply a means to justify these payments from rich industrial countries whose climates will benefit from preserving the Amazon. Of course, the Brazilian government should enforce current environmental laws, but its efforts are falling short. If the world wants to save the Amazon basin there will need to be incentives to preserve the forest that will offset the profits currently made from destroying the rainforest illegally. Even if most Brazilians want to save the Amazon, which they most certainly do, the Brazilian government is too weak, too corrupt, and too poor to effectively succeed at this goal.

Most Brazilian live near the coasts far from the Amazon. The ancestors of most Brazilians living near the coast almost destroyed another rainforest called the Atlantic rainforest. What remains of this rainforest is now highly protected. The Brazilian government effectively enforces environmental laws along the coast. So why the difference? Why does the Brazilian government effectively enforce environmental laws in the Atlantic rainforest and not in the Amazon? One reason is that the Atlantic rainforest is now much smaller, and so it is easier to police. Most of the businesses and most of the land is legally registered. A second reason is that the coastal region is richer and economically more diverse. If you are fined for an environmental crime, you or your business will pay; maybe not immediately, as the legal process is slow, but environmental crimes are still enforced, and the government receives revenue from fines.

The Amazon rainforest, on the other hand, covers a much larger area, a huge area. Those who cut down the rainforest are already operating outside the law, so there is little revenue to be gained by fining lawbreakers; they obviously will not pay. The illegal loggers, farmers, and miners are already criminals; they are ready to fight back against the environmental agencies. There are frequent violent conflicts pitting illegal miners, loggers, and farmers on one side against government environmental agencies and police on the other. The few Brazilians who are destroying the Amazon are benefiting greatly, and in the region where they operate there is little other economic activity that pays wages. As a result, for the Brazilian that lives in the Amazon there are powerful economic incentives to destroy the Amazon and little economic incentive to save it. Of course, the native Brazilian tribes want to save the Amazon and their way of life as the native reservations and health of the land rely on it, but they are not powerful enough to stop the deforestation.

Brazilian police exchange gunfire with illegal miners in Amazon as Bolsonaro begins crackdown
Source: *Express Digest*

One positive lesson learned from the Atlantic rainforest is that rainforest can regrow. Many people wrongly assume that when the rainforest is lost it will never return. There are situations in southern Brazil and in the coastal areas, where the government requires owners to reforest land with native species. Companies and large landowners who receive these penalties must replace grazing or agricultural land with native plants to essentially replant the forest. It is estimated to take 65 years to regrow a forest naturally without replanting.[134] Courts have mandated reforestation in commercial forest areas of the Atlantic rainforest. The area is replanted with native species. This practice regrows the forest even faster than waiting for natural regrowth. Of course, the replanted forest will not have all of the rich biodiversity of the original forest for many years. This replanting of the forest with native trees is expensive and labor intensive and is the result of a long legal process and court order. When you are replanting native species, not all the biodiversity can be replaced immediately, if at all. The large trees in a forest are not bought in a nursery and will take years to grow, but it is at least better than keeping the land deforested. Reforesting land is very labor intensive and should be used to employ local labor and gain support from the local communities.

The Amazon Fund: A lesson in failure but a model for the future

The Amazon Fund was unveiled by the Brazilian government during the 2007 United Nations Climate Change Conference in Bali. At the time, environmentalists all over the world were alarmed at the elevated rate of deforestation in the Brazilian Amazon rainforest. The Amazon Fund was created as a way of encouraging Brazil to continue reducing the rate of forest conversion to pastures and croplands by giving an economic incentive to preserve it. Many governments, notably Norway and Germany, contributed millions of dollars to the fund until 2019, when due to lack of commitment by the Brazilian government despite the increasing rate of deforestation, these governments and other donors decided to abandon the fund.[135]

Because the fund was created and managed by the Brazilian government's development bank, BNDES, with many Brazilian government agencies giving governance and technical advice, it should come as no surprise that eventually this fund would effectively end in failure[136] When Amazon Fund was functioning, Brazilian government agencies, such as IBAMA, Brazil's environmental agency, along with NGOs shared

---

[134] Brahic, Catherine, "How long does it take a rainforest to regenerate?" June 11, 2008. Available in: https://www.newscientist.com/article/dn14112-how-long-does-it-take-a-rainforest-to-regenerate/. Access in: 3/12/2021.

[135] Branford, Sue and Borges, Thais, "Norway freezes support for Amazon Fund; EU/Brazil trade deal at risk?" August 16, 2019. Available in: https://news.mongabay.com/2019/08/norway-freezes-support-for-amazon-fund-eu-brazil-trade-deal-at-risk/. Access in: 3/12/2021.

[136] Amazon Fund, "What is the Amazon Fund". Available in: http://www.amazonfund.gov.br/en/amazon-fund/ Access in: 3/12/2021.

its donations. IBAMA used the money primarily to enforce deforestation laws, while the NGOs oversaw projects to support sustainable communities and livelihoods in the Amazon. The management of the fund's resources stayed in the hands of the BNDES, who approved projects and fund requests. There is no proof of irregularities or mismanagement of the Amazon fund, the BNDES has been accused mismanagement of making loans to Brazilian companies that were involved in the massive frauds. These frauds were uncovered by Operation Car Wash or *Lava Jato*.

It is debatable whether the Amazon Fund ever actually achieved its goals, but it started out well. In the three years after the enactment of the fund, the rate of deforestation fell dramatically. However, after money from the fund started pouring into the Amazon, the rate remained stationary until 2014, when it began to rise once again. In general, international donors had been pleased with the fund's performance until the Bolsonaro government came to office. The program was expected to continue indefinitely, but in 2019 Norway and Germany pulled out of the Amazon Fund and large private investment funds began a boycott of Brazilian investments unless something was done by the Brazilian government to stop the continued deforestation.

The world should not give up on protecting the Amazon

Left to itself, the Brazilian state is not likely to protect the Amazon. The current legal process and enforcement of environmental laws in the Amazon region are weak, and the economic interests of those willing to profit from the deforestation of the Amazon are too strong. For the world to act, we need to remember that the world's increase in demand for meat and soybeans is fueling the decline of the Amazon. Simply put, the Amazon is burning today because it is worth the risk for those willing to break the law.

One factor working in favor of the Amazon is the precarious nature of Brazil's public finances. As we have seen is the previous chapters, Brazilians are already highly taxed and yet the cost of the state and the cost of pensions is forcing both federal and state government to run high deficits. After the pandemic of 2020, the state of Brazil's finances is precarious. The state and federal governments are in debt and have bloated administration and pension obligations. Brazilians will not support the idea of even more taxes. Given the financial stress Brazil is under, if the governments of the world want to save the Amazon now would be a good time to try.

The main failure of the Amazon Fund was that it left governance and control of the funds in the hands of the Brazilian government. When the Brazilian environmental agencies are effectively led, they can be an effective deterrent. The Amazon Fund taught us that any new fund should be governed jointly with the donor partners, and the donor partners need to be active in administration and enforcement of the fund. While it would be illegal and politically unacceptable to sell or cede sovereignty of the Amazon to other countries, a temporary solution may be acceptable. As noted earlier the world population should peak in 2050. After the population peaks, total population and total demand should begin to decline slowly. If there was to be a new fund for preserving the Amazon, then it should be based around a framework of a joint venture land lease for fifty years with the ability of that investors to help enforce Brazilian environmental law.

Creating a new fund around the framework of a joint venture designed to protect the Amazon could give the donor countries temporary power and rights, while not interfering with Brazilian sovereignty. For example, Brazil already has large national parks and Indian reservations that cover vast parts of the Amazon. The sovereignty of these areas would remain with the Indians and the Brazilian Government, but temporarily the environmental oversight of these areas would be shared with donor countries. The creation of Brazilian environmental law, national parks and Indian reservations are now and would remain areas of Brazilian sovereignty. However, for the duration of the joint venture lease, the enforcement of these laws and governance of the areas would be under the joint venture. If the joint venture between donor countries and Brazil are enforcing existing Brazilian environmental laws, it is not interfering in Brazilian sovereignty over the Amazon, it is merely helping Brazil enforce its own laws. Considered from this perspective, the "New Amazon Fund" with donor country participation could insure Brazilian environmental laws are enforced, issue environmental infractions, and collect penalties within the boundaries of the joint venture. The donor countries also could simultaneously provide technical assistance to Brazilian environmental institutions.

Of course, the donor countries in the joint venture will need to pay for this privilege. Though a large part of these funds would need to go the treasury of the Brazilian Government, a significant portion of funds need to go the local communities in the Amazon to support their development. Unless the people living in or near the Amazon are incentivized to support the efforts to preserve the rainforest, there will be continued conflict.

There is conflict already. The way to minimize conflict with the people in the Amazon region is to both enforce current environmental laws against the biggest and worst offenders, while giving economic aid or incentives to the population in general.

Currently, Brazilian forestry laws require a private land holder to preserve 35 to 80% of the native rainforest and the watershed of property in the region.[137] Modification to this law in 2017 now also requires companies who buy products from farmers to certify that they are following this law. If a joint fund was formed the funds from this joint venture should also be used to fine, enforce, and collect penalties from owners who have illegally cut forest on private property in violation of the forestry laws. The fund could then pay to reforest those lands as well as any other deforested land where proper title cannot be established. Reforesting the rainforest is very labor intensive and can provide work for local people; jobs would range from creating tree nurseries of native species to planning and maintenance of new forests. What is critical is that in addition to gaining support of the Brazilian government, the new fund needs to garner the support of the Brazilian people in the region. Most Brazilians on the coast already want to save the Amazon. However, in the Amazon region there is little economic activity and great poverty. While a fund would need to protect the Amazon under its administration it should also provide alternative economic projects for the local population. Reforestation projects to reclaim the Amazon could be one of those projects.

It is important to manage expectations. The goal here is not to preserve all the Amazon, but to preserve a great part of it until 2050 or 2070 when the world human population will begin to shrink. The current administration is unlikely to accept a new international Amazon fund as described above, but future Brazilian administrations will find its public finances in bad shape. Brazil will in the future need immediate external financial help. The Brazilian people are already highly taxed. The world's countries and investors continue to press the Brazilian government for more responsible environmental policies. Under distress, the next Brazilian administration could consider a new Amazon fund if donor countries would finance a new fund. As long as the fund enforces existing Brazilian environmental laws no one would question Brazilian sovereignty over the Amazon. The fund's

---

[137] The Nature Conservancy Brazilian Amazon The Forest Code: Using Law to Protect the Amazon. Available in: https://www.nature.org/en-us/about-us/where-we-work/latin-america/brazil/stories-in-brazil/brazils-forest-code Access in: 10/11/2020.

investors need to be partners to help the Brazilian government enforce Brazilian environmental laws, national parks, reservations, and help reforest illegal areas. If the fund can do this until 2070 when human population is in decline the most Amazon will have been saved.

Epilogue/Conclusion: Going Home

Closing this book feels like ending a voyage. We have learned and lived with Brazilians, and now we must go home or perhaps continue in Brazil as our home. For those of you who are returning home, I hope the information on how to act like a Brazilian helped you interact with Brazilians. Learning to take Brazil as it is and not force it to be like your home country is great advice to make your stay happier. The chapter on food of the regions was a way to explore the history and differences of each region in Brazil without using the same stereotypes that are sometimes used by Brazilians. If you were able to travel around the various regions of Brazil, you should have noticed the differences. Food really was just a delicious metaphor to explore these differences. As we have seen from Brazil's history, the regions were kept separate by design, and there were many forces to separate these regions into separate countries. Even today there are regional feelings that support separation; however, these feelings no longer create serious political movements. Except for a small part of what is now Uruguay, the rest of Brazil has remained unified. The chapters on Brazilian celebrations, relationships and spirituality were written for your experience in Brazil to be richer and deeper than what a tourist normally experiences.

For those of you who are staying longer in Brazil, perhaps for love, or work, the chapters on Brazilian social issues were intended to give you a historical context on major challenges facing Brazil. I recommend the histories of Laurentino Gomes, about colonial Brazil and the period of Brazilian Monarchy is an interesting way to tie today's social challenges of Brazil back to its colonial past. Besides being based in historical fact, it gives hope to a Brazilian future. It may not be fair to the Portuguese to blame them for all of Brazil's problems, but it is useful. Brazilians are a very dynamic, happy, and optimistic people, and deserve a prosperous future. The main theme in the second half of this book was that Portuguese colonial policy and monarchy retarded Brazilian development, and only today are we seeing the changes needed to strengthen democratic institutions in Brazil. It may take a generation or more for Brazilians overcome problems of inequality, violence, and education, but the trends favor Brazil. In the introduction, I modestly tried to measure up my observations of Brazil to Alexis de Tocqueville's observations on America more than two hundred years ago. In his book, "Democracy in America", Alexis de Tocqueville made some observations about the early United States, that seem both true and hopeful for the future of Brazil. The "Tocqueville paradox" is the phenomenon in which as social conditions and opportunities improve, social frustration grows more quickly.[138] He noticed in the early United States, that as communities made progress, there was more discontent for perceived injustices. We can see this same Tocqueville paradox working in Brazil today. The early history of Brazil was a history of slavery, absolute monarchy, oligarchies and military coups, and most Brazilians were acquiescent to authority. Brazilians simple accepted their lot in life. Things have changed since the most recent attempt of democracy in Brazil which began in 1984 in Brazil. Today the small improvements of law and order, social equality, improvements in educations are only highlighting the need for more improvements. Brazilians no longer accept the corruption, inequality, and impunity of the past. Brazilians now take to the street and to the ballot box to try to promote social equality and fight corruption. As the "Tocqueville paradox" predicted, this pressure for reform will only increase. If the "Tocqueville paradox" holds true, Brazil will finally become the country of the future. As Brazilians like to say, "God is Brazilian."

---

[138] Available in: https://en.wikipedia.org/wiki/Tocqueville_effect. Access in: 3/12/2021.

Bibliography

AFRICANS in Brazil: Zumbi Dos Palmares. *Black History Heroes*, 2010. Available in: www.blackhistoryheroes.com/2010/05/zumbi-dos-palmares.html. Access in: 03/13/2021.

AMAZON FUND. "What is the Amazon Fund". Available in: http://www.amazonfund.gov.br/en/amazon-fund/ Access in: 03/13/2021.

A WELL FED WORLD. "Feed to meat inefficiency ratios." Available in: https://awellfedworld.org/feed-ratios/. Access in: 03/13/2021.

AYAHUASCA puts Brazil on the shamanic tourism map. The Brazilian Report, May 9, 2019. Available in: https://brazilian.report/tourism/2019/05/05/ayahuasca-brazil-shamanic-tourism/. Access in: 3/12/2021.

BARBOSA, Kleyson. Qual a Origem Da Expressão "Pagar Mico"? *Super*, 4 July 2018. Available in: super.abril.com.br/mundo-estranho/qual-a-origem-da-expressao-pagar-mico/. Access in: 03/13/2021.

BRAHIC, Catherine. How long does it take a rainforest to regenerate? June 11, 2008. Available in: https://www.newscientist.com/article/dn14112-how-long-does-it-take-a-rainforest-to-regenerate/. Access in: 03/13/2021.

BRAZIL. Wikimedia Foundation. *Wikipedia*. Available in: https://en.wikipedia.org/wiki/Brazil. Access in: 11/13/2020.

CARNIVAL of Venice. Wikimedia Foundation. *Wikipedia*. Available in: https://en.wikipedia.org/wiki/Carnival_of_Venice. Access in: 10/31/2020.

BRAZIL: Five Centuries of Change. *Brazil Five Centuries of Change*. 2010. Available in: library.brown.edu/create/fivecenturiesofchange/chapters/chapter-4/immigration/. Access in: 03/13/2021.

CARYBÉ. Roda de Samba, 1916. Available in: https://efemeridesdoefemello.com/2016/11/27/samba-100-anos-ou-nao/. Access in: 03/13/2021.

CRONOLOGIA DO QUILOMBO DE PALMARES. *Folha Online* – Brasil 500. Available in: www1.folha.uol.com.br/fol/brasil500/zumbi_19.htm. Access in: 03/13/2021.

FEIJOADA. Receita fácil. *Recepedia,* s/d. Available in: https://br.recepedia.com/receita/graos/54649-feijoada/. Access in: 03/13/2021.

FEIJOADA Brasileira. Wikimedia Foundation. *Wikipedia.* Available in: https://pt.wikipedia.org/wiki/Feijoada_%C3%A0_brasileira. Access in: 12/07/2020

FOOD AND AGRICULTURE ORGANIZATION. How to feed the world in 2050. Available in: http://www.fao.org/fileadmin/templates/wsfs/docs/expert_paper/How_to_Feed_the_World_in_2050.pdf. Access in: 03/13/2021.

GANGA Zumba Explained. *Everything explained today.* [2009]. Available in: everything.explained.today/Ganga_Zumba/. Access in: 03/13/2021.

GOMES, Laurentino. *1808:* Como uma rainha louca, um príncipes medroso, e um corte corrupta enganaram Napoleão e mudaram a Historia de Portugal e do Brasil. São Paulo: Globo, 2014.

GOMES, Laurentino. *1822:* Como um homem sábio, uma princesa triste, e um escocês louco por dinheiro ajudaram dom Pedro a criar Brasil – um país que tinha todo para dar errado. São Paulo: Globo, 2015.

GARDIAN THE. Available in: https://www.theguardian.com/world/2018/jul/12/brazil-militia-paramilitary-wield-terror-seize-power-from-drug-gangs. Access in: 9/8/2020.

GASPAR, Lúcia. *O Carapuceiro.* Pesquisa Escolar On-Line, Fundação Joaquim Nabuco, Recife. Disponível em: Fundação Joaquim Nabuco Arquivado em 21 de setembro de 2009, no Wayback Machine. Access in: 4/2/2020.

HISTORY. Available in: https://www.history.com/this-day-in-history/president-john-adams-orders-federal-government-to-washington-d-c. Access in: 03/13/2021.

INDIA TIMES. Amazon Forest Fire Is So Bad, It Turned The Skies & Rain In São Paulo, Thousands Of Km Away, Black. Available in: https://www.indiatimes.com/trending/environment/amazon-forest-fire-is-so-bad-it-turned-the-skies-rain-in-sao-paulo-thousands-of-km-away-black-374136.html. Access in: 03/13/2021.

INSIGHT CRIME. Available in: https://www.insightcrime.org/news/analysis/militias-become-luxury-real-estate-barons-rio-de-janeiro/. Access in: 7/14/2020.

INSIGHT CRIME. Available in: https://www.insightcrime.org/brazil-organized-crime-news/red-command-profile/. Access in: 9/8/2020.

INSIGHT CRIME https://www.insightcrime.org/brazil-organized-crime-news/first-capital-command-pcc-profile/. Access in: 9/8/2020.

JANET Ranganathan, Richard Waite, Tim Searchinger and Craig Hanson - December 05, 2018. Available in: https://www.wri.org/blog/2018/12/how-sustainably-feed-10-billion-people-2050-21-charts. Access in: 3/12/2021.

JORNAL DA GLOBO. Available in: http://g1.globo.com/jornal-da-globo/noticia/2014/04/maioria-dos-crimes-no-brasil-nao-chega-ser-solucionada-pela-policia.html. Access in: 3/12/2021.

PASSION fruit (Maracujá or Fruit de la Passion). AZ Martinique. Available in: https://azmartinique.com/en/all-to-know/fruits-vegetables/passion-fruit-maracuja-or-fruit-de-la-passion. Access in: 3/12/2021.

MARECHAL Deodoro da Fonseca – Biografia. *UOL Educação*. Available in: https://educacao.uol.com.br/biografias/marechal-deodoro-da-fonseca.jhtm. Access in: 9/03/2021.

MURDER Rate by Country 2020. *World Population Review*. 2020. Available in: worldpopulationreview.com/countries/murder-rate-by-country/. Access in: 3/12/2021.

NORWAY freezes support for Amazon Fund; EU/Brazil trade deal at risk? *Nature*, August 16, 2019. https://www.nature.org/en-us/about-us/where-we-work/latin-america/brazil/stories-in-brazil/brazils-forest-code/. Access in: 03/13/2021.

OBSERVATORIO DE SEGURANCA. Available in: https://www.observatoriodeseguranca.org/imprensa/da-gangue-a-hegemonia-uma-cronologia-da-expansao-do-pcc/. Access in: 4/ 3/ 2021.

OKTOBERFEST. Dicas de viagem. Por *CVC viagens*. Available in: https://www.cvc.com.br/dicas-de-viagem/inspiracoes/centros-urbanos/oktoberfest/. Access in: Access in: 4/ 3/ 2021.

OXFAM INTERNATIONAL. Available in: https://www.oxfam.org/en/brazil-extreme-inequality-numbers#:~:text=28%20MBrazil%20has%20lifted,61%20percent%20of%20economic%20growth. Access in: 4/ 3/ 2021.

O'NEIL, Shannon K. Public Education in Brazil. *Council on Foreign Relations*. 23 oct. 2013. Available in: www.cfr.org/blog/public-education-brazil. Access in: 3/12/2021.

PALMARES (Quilombo). Wikimedia Foundation, 16 Oct. 2020. *Wikipedia*. Available in: : en.wikipedia.org/wiki/Palmares_(quilombo). Access in: 3/12/2021.

RACIAL Democracy. Wikimedia Foundation. *Wikipedia*. Available in: https://en.wikipedia.org/wiki/Racial_democracy. Access in: 3/12/2021.

SOCIAL Apartheid in Brazil. *WikiMili, T*he Free Encyclopedia. 24 oct. 2019. Available in: wikimili.com/en/Social_apartheid_in_Brazil. Access in: 4/3/ 2021.

THE NATURE CONSERVANCY Brazilian Amazon The Forest Code: Using Law to Protect the Amazon. Available in: https://www.nature.org/en-us/about-us/where-we-work/latin-america/brazil/stories-in-brazil/brazils-forest-code. Access in: 9/11/2020.

THINGS You Didn't Know About Cachaça, Brazil. *The Culture Trip*, 2018. Available in: https://theculturetrip.com/south-america/brazil/articles/10-things-you-didnt-know-about-cachaca-brazil/. Access in: 3/12/2021.

TOCQUEVILLE effect. Wikimedia Foundation, 13 June 2020. *Wikipedia*. Available in: en.wikipedia.org/wiki/Tocqueville_effect. Access in: 3/12/2021.

TRAVEL Stack Exchange, 2015. Available in: https://travel.stackexchange.com/questions/49113/what-type-of-power-outlets-should-i-expect-in-hotels-in-sao-paulo-and-rio-de-jan. Access in: 3/12/2021.

TRÊS CAIPIRINHAS DIFERENTES. Guia da Cozinha, 2019. Available in: https://guiadacozinha.com.br/receitas/tres-caipirinhas-diferentes/. Access in: 3/12/2021.

UCINI, Andrea. How Bad Will It Get?. *The Economist*, 1 Feb. 2020.

VOCÊ conhece a Cerimônia do Chimarrão? *Blog do Barão*. Available in: https://www.baraoervamate.com.br/cerimonia-do-chimarrao/. Access in: 03/13/2021.

TAXATION in Brazil. Wikimedia Foundation, 13 June 2020. *Wikipedia*. Available in: en.wikipedia.org/wiki/Taxation_in_Brazil. Access in: 3/12/2021.

ZUMBI. Wikimedia Foundation. 10 Oct. 2020. *Wikipedia*. Available in: en.wikipedia.org/wiki/Zumbi. Access in: 4/3/2021.

WILSON CENTER. Available at Slavery in Brazil: https://www.wilsoncenter.org/blog-post/slavery-brazil. Access in: 3/12/2021.

WORLD POUPULATION REVIEW. *Murder Rate by Country 2020.* Available in: https://worldpopulationreview.com/country-rankings/murder-rate-by-country. Access in: 3/12/2021.

WORLD WILDLIFE FUND. *Why the Amazon is burning.* Available in: https://www.globalcanopy.org/press-centre/why-amazon-burning. Access in: 3/12/2021.

WORLD WILDLIFE FUND BRAZIL. Grilagem de terras na Amazônia – Negócio bilionário ameaça a floresta e populações tradicionais. Available in: https://www.wwf.org.br/natureza_brasileira/areas_prioritarias/amazonia1/ameacas_riscos_amazonia/desmatamento_na_amazonia/grilagem_na_amazonia/. Access in: 3/12/2021.

Bibliography of figures

3 MOTIVOS que fazem do churrasco gaúcho o melhor do mundo. *Encantos de Santa Catarina.* Available in: https://encantosdesantacatarina.com.br/3-motivos-que-fazem-do-churrasco-gaucho-o-melhor-do-mundo/. Access in: 3/12/2021.

7 LUGARES para comer açaí em Brasília. *Blog Eldo Gomes*, 2020. Available in: https://www.eldogomes.com.br/7-lugares-para-comer-acai-em-brasilia/. Access in: 3/12/2021.

AFINAL, Cerveja ou Chopp? – O Contador de Cervejas. Bar do Jota, 16 abr. 2012. Available in: https://www.ocontadordecervejas.com.br/afinal-cerveja-ou-chopp/#:~:text=Muitos%20carregam%20ainda%20tem%20o,apenas%20a%20forma%20de%20disponibilizar. Access in: 3/12/2021.

A LAVAGEM do Bonfim é um ritual católico ou do candomblé? Por Cíntia Costa. Jornal Grande Bahia (JGB), 2012. Available in: https://www.jornalgrandebahia.com.br/2012/01/a-lavagem-do-bonfim-e-um-ritual-catolico-ou-do-candomble/. Access in: 3/12/2021.

AVENTURAS na História · Dom João VI: O assustador apetite do rei do Brasil. Uol, 2020. Available in: https://aventurasnahistoria.uol.com.br/noticias/reportagem/do-insano-apetite-a-morte-misteriosa-5-fatos-bizarros-sobre-o-monarcadom-joao-vi.phtml. Access in: 3/12/2021.

AVENTURAS na História. Biografia revela a controversa história de amor entre Lampião e Maria Bonita. *Uol*, 2020. Available in: https://aventurasnahistoria.uol.com.br/noticias/reportagem/historia-quem-foi-maria-bonita.phtml. Access in: 3/12/2021.

A VISITA de Disney à América Latina. *EL PAÍS Brasil*. Available in: https://brasil.elpais.com/brasil/2016/04/07/cultura/1460044858_011138.html. Access in: 3/12/2021.

BAIÃO DE DOIS. *Terra*. Available in: https://www.terra.com.br/vida-e-estilo/culinaria/receitas/cozinha/chef-ensina-a-preparar-baiao-de-dois-veja-passo-a-passo,9949579c10d19310VgnVCM3000009acceb0aRCRD.html. Access in: 3/12/2021.

BIG protests in Brazil demand President Rousseff's impeachment. BBC News. Available in: https://www.bbc.com/news/world-latin-america-31899507?ocid=socialflow_twitter. Access in: 3/12/2021.

BRAZIL and the World Revolutions at the Beginning of the 19th Century. JHI Blog, 2018. Available in: https://jhiblog.org/2018/03/21/brazil-and-the-world-revolutions-at-the-beginning-of-the-19th-century/. Access in: 3/12/2021.

BRAZILIAN police exchange gunfire with illegal miners in Amazon as Bolsonaro begins crackdown. Express Digest. Available in: https://expressdigest.com/brazilian-police-exchange-gunfire-with-illegal-miners-in-amazon-as-bolsonaro-begins-crackdown/. Access in: 3/12/2021.

CARNE de sol com mandioca (macaxeira). *Receita de Vovó*. Available in: https://www.receitadevovo.com.br/receitas/carnedesolcommacaxeira. Access in: 3/12/2021.

CAPOEIRA: o que é, origem, história, Angola e Regional. *Toda Matéria*. Available in: https://www.todamateria.com.br/capoeira/#:~:text=A%20capoeira%20%C3%A9%20uma%20express%C3%A3o,cultura%20popular%2C%20dan%C3%A7a%20e%20m%C3%BAsica.&text=A%20capoeira%20foi%20criada%20no,maiores%20s%C3%ADmbolos%20da%20cultura%20brasileira. Access in: 3/12/2021.

COMO ganhar dinheiro na praia: 10 ideias para te inspirar! Montar um Negócio. Available in: montarumnegocio.com. Access in: 3/12/2021.

COUNTRIES ranked by GINI index (World Bank estimate). *Index Mundi*. Available in: https://www.indexmundi.com/facts/indicators/SI.POV.GINI/compare. Access in: 3/12/2021.

CRUZ CABUGÁ, o primeiro embaixador brasileiro. Pernambuco, História & Personagens. *Diário de Pernambuco*. Available in: http://blogs.diariodepernambuco.com.br/historiape/index.php/2016/08/01/cruz-cabuga-o-primeiro-embaixador-brasileiro/. Access in: 3/12/2021.

DA GANGUE a hegemonia: uma cronologia da expansão do PCC – OSP. *Observatório de Segurança Pública*. Available in: https://www.observatoriodeseguranca.org/imprensa/da-gangue-a-hegemonia-uma-cronologia-da-expansao-do-pcc/. Access in: 3/12/2021.

DATA Magna: por que 6 de março é feriado em Pernambuco? *Canal blitz*. Available in: https://canalblitz.com.br/pe/pagina/2. Access in: 3/12/2021.

DE OLHO nas justificativas de casal de mestre-sala e porta-bandeira, por Eliane Santos de Souza. SRde, 2019. Available in: https://www.srzd.com/colunas/de-olho-nas-justificativas-de-casal-de-mestre-sala-e-porta-bandeira-por-eliane-santos-de-souza/. Access in: 3/12/2021.

DE ONDE surgiu a tradição de usar branco no ano novo? *Ceert*, 2016. Available in: https://ceert.org.br/noticias/datas-eventos/14785/de-onde-surgiu-a-tradicao-de-usar-branco-no-ano-novo#:~:text=O%20branco%20simboliza%2C%20essencialmente%2C%20a,mais%20famoso%20do%20mundo%3A%20Copacabana. Access in: 3/12/2021.

DOMINGO com costela fogo de chão. Panorama do Turismo. Available in: http://www.panoramadoturismo.com.br/programa-legal/domingo-com-costela-fogo-de-chao-2. Access in: 3/12/2021.

EM PLENA pandemia, Justiça de SP nega suspensão da Festa de Barretos. *Jornal Opção*. Available in: https://www.jornalopcao.com.br/ultimas-noticias/em-plena-pandemia-justica-de-sp-nega-suspensao-da-festa-de-barretos-269141/. Access in: 3/12/2021.

ESPETÁCULO do Bumba-meu-boi é atração na Praça Universitária. UFG - Universidade Federal de Goiás, 2011. Available in: https://www.ufg.br/n/59103-espetaculo-do-bumba-meu-boi-e-atracao-na-praca-universitaria?atr=en&locale=en. Access in: 3/12/2021.

FEIJÃO tropeiro – Fácil. *Tudo Receitas*, 12 jan 2015. Available in: https://www.tudoreceitas.com/receita-de-feijao-tropeiro-139.html. Access in: 3/12/2021.

FESTA de Iemanjá é reconhecida Patrimônio Histórico de Salvador. *Metropoles*, 2020. Available in: https://www.metropoles.com/brasil/festa-de-iemanja-e-reconhecida-patrimonio-historico-de-salvador. Access in: 3/12/2021.

FESTA de Nossa Senhora dos Navegantes se aproxima. *Catholicus*, 2020. Available in: https://catholicus.org.br/festa-de-nossa-senhora-dos-navegantes-se-aproxima/. Access in: 3/12/2021.

FESTIVAL de Parintins e a magia da maior festa folclórica do Brasil. *Raízes do mundo*, 2013. Available in: https://raizesdomundo.com/festival-de-parintins/. Access in: 3/12/2021.

FORÇAS Armadas teriam comprado 700 mil kg de picanha com dinheiro público. iG. Available in: https://economia.ig.com.br/2021-02-11/forcas-armadas-compraram-700-mil-kg-de-picanha-com-dinheiro-publico-diz-jornal.html. Access in: 3/12/2021.

FRANGO com quiabo. *Menu com Arte*. Available in: https://menucomarte.com.br/pratos/frango-com-quiabo/. Access in: 3/12/2021.

FREVO. Educa Mais Brasil, 2019. Available in: https://www.educamaisbrasil.com.br/enem/artes/frevo. Access in: 3/12/2021.

GRUPO especial encerra o 27º Festival de Bumba Meu Boi. *Tribuna Hoje*, 2019. Available in: https://tribunahoje.com/noticias/cidades/2019/09/01/grupo-especial-encerra-o-27o-festival-de-bumba-meu-boi/. Access in: 3/12/2021.

GUY Behind the Latest Big Meme You Saw Everywhere: 'I Didn't Even Know What a Meme Is'. *TIME*, 2017. Available in: https://time.com/4919007/love-triangle-meme-interview/. Access in: 3/12/2021.

HISTORY of Carnival in Brazil. *Study.com*. Available in: https://study.com/academy/lesson/history-of-carnival-in-brazil.html#:~:text=The%20pre%2DLent%20party%20was,basically%20a%20giant%20water%20fight. Access in: 3/12/2021.

HISTORY of Carnival in Rio. *Ipanema*. Available in: https://ipanema.com/carnival/history.htm. Access in: 3/12/2021.

HOME - Rio Carnival Tour. Go Carnival Rio. Available in: https://gocarnavalrio.com/en/. Access in: 3/12/2021.

HOW MUCH does it cost to visit Bonito, Brazil? Segredos de Viagem. Available in: https://segredosdeviagem.com.br/how-much-does-it-cost-to-visit-bonito-brazil/. Access in: 3/12/2021.

IMMIGRATION. Brazil: Five Centuries of Change. *Brown Library*. Available in: https://library.brown.edu/create/fivecenturiesofchange/. Access in: 3/12/2021.

LANÇA-PERFUME já foi legalizado e teve fábrica em Recife: a história da droga que se tornou símbolo do carnival. *Hypeness*. Available in: https://www.hypeness.com.br/2020/02/lanca-perfume-ja-foi-legalizado-e-teve-fabrica-em-recife-a-historia-da-droga-que-se-tornou-simbolo-do-carnaval/ Access in: 3/12/2021.

MAPS of disappearing forests. *Business insider*. Available in: https://www.businessinsider.com/r-forests-shrink-70-percent-now-less-than-1-km-from-edge-2015-3. Access in: 3/12/2021.

MEAT and Dairy Production, 2017. Available in: https://ourworldindata.org/meat-production. Access in: 3/12/2021.

O JOGO do Bicho funciona assim. São vinte e cinco animais, e cada um.... Yuri Eiras, 2016. Available in: https://medium.com/@YuriEiras/o-jogo-do-bicho-funciona-assim-bf996abefb9. Access in: 3/12/2021.

OLODUM completa 38 anos e terá acervo digital. *Agência Brasil*. Available in: https://agenciabrasil.ebc.com.br/cultura/noticia/2017-04/olodum-completa-38-as-e-tera-acervo-digital. Access in: 3/12/2021.

OS MELHORES Botecos de São Paulo. Available in: https://www.baressp.com.br/os-melhores-botecos-de-sao-paulo. Access in: 3/12/2021.

O MISTÉRIO DA MALANDRAGEM. Samba de roda, Pilintra, Zé pilintra. *Pinterest*. Available in: https://br.pinterest.com/pin/625507835724953228/. Access in: 3/12/2021.

O QUE fazer diante de uma blitz de trânsito? Jornal da Manhã. Available in: https://jmonline.com.br/novo/?noticias,8,SOBRE%20RODAS,191319. Access in: 3/12/2021.

O QUE fazer em Campos do Jordão: as melhores atrações e onde ficar. Amanda Viaja, 2020. Available in: http://www.amandaviaja.com.br/o-que-fazer-em-campos-do-jordao/. Access in: 3/12/2021

OURO PRETO. *Info escola*. Available in: https://www.OuroPretoinfoescola.com/minas-gerais/ouro-preto/. Access in: 3/12/2021.

PÃO de queijo: veja dicas, receitas diferentes e combinações de recheios. *Quem*, 2020. Available in: https://revistaquem.globo.com/viagem-e-comida/noticia/2020/08/pao-de-queijo-veja-dicas-receitas-diferentes-e-combinacoes-de-recheios.html Access in: 3/12/2021.

THE Contagious Salvador Carnival and the Difference for the Rio's Carnival. Soul Brasil Magazine, 2020. Available in: https://soulbrasil.com/the-contagious-salvador-carnival-and-the-difference-for-the-rios-carnival/. Access in: 3/12/2021.

THE TREATY OF TORDESILLAS 1494 (H7) Available in: timewisetraveller.co.ukhttps://www.timewisetraveller.co.uk/tordesillas.html. Access in: 3/12/2021.

TURISMO e viagem para Foz do Iguaçu 2021 - Férias em Foz do Iguaçu. *Tripadvisor*. Available in: https://www.tripadvisor.com.br/Tourism-g303444-Foz_do_Iguacu_State_of_Parana-Vacations.html. Access in: 3/12/2021

PARATY: Dicas de quando ir, onde ficar e comer, o que fazer. *Viaje na viagem*, 2018. Available in: https://www.viajenaviagem.com/destino/paraty/#:~:text=A%20cidade%20%C3%A9%20especialmente%20m%C3%A1gica,vai%20de%20junho%20a%20setembro. Access in: 3/12/2021.

PATO no tucupi – Receita Tradicional do Pará – As Melhores Receitas Culinárias Fáceis. Receitas.net, 2020. Available in: http://receitas.net/aves/pato-no-tucupi.html. Access in: 3/12/2021.

PIRARUCU fish Amazon's Biggest Fish Faces Threat of Extinction. *Live Science*, 2014. Available in: https://www.livescience.com/47326-amazon-fish-faces-extinction.html. Access in: 3/12/2021.

PRINCIPAIS Festas Juninas no nordeste do Brasil. *Accor*. Available in: https://all.accor.com/pt-br/brasil/magazine/one-hour-one-day-one-week/principais-festas-juninas-no-nordeste-do-brasil-c2d6c.shtml#:~:text=O%20m%C3%AAs%20de%20junho%20%C3%A9,Santo%20Ant%C3%B4nio%20e%20S%C3%A3o%20Pedro. Access in: 3/12/2021.

QUILOMBO dos Palmares: resumo, dia a dia e localização. *Toda Matéria*. Available in: https://www.todamateria.com.br/quilombo-dos-palmares/. Access in: 3/12/2021.

QUONIAMBEC – Cunhambebe. *Wikipédia*. Available in: https://pt.wikipedia.org/wiki/Cunhambebe. Access in: 3/12/2021.

REVOLUÇÃO Pernambucana. Wikiwand. Available in: https://www.wikiwand.com/pt/Pernambuco#:~:text=A%20chamada%20Revolu%C3%A7%C3%A3o%20Pernambucana%2C%20tamb%C3%A9m,mar%C3%A7o%20de%201817%20em%20Pernambuco. Access in: 3/12/2021.

RESUS REWIEW, 2012. Available in: https://resusreview.com/2012/infectious-disease-reading-list/. Access in: 3/12/2021.

SATELLITE Data Shows Amazon Deforestation Rising Under Brazil's Bolsonaro. Voice of America - English, 2019. Available in: https://www.voanews.com/americas/satellite-data-shows-amazon-deforestation-rising-under-brazils-bolsonaro. Access in: 3/12/2021.

SAGU DE VINHO. Coisas da Léia. Available in: https://www.coisasdaleia.com.br/tag/receita-de-sagu-de-vinho. Access in: 3/12/2021.

SAMBA Howto. *Howtowiki*, 2019. Available in: https://howtowiki91.blogspot.com/2019/03/samba-4-howto.html. Access in: 3/12/2021.

UM dia no pantanal mato-grossense. *All accord live limitless*. Available in: https://all.accor.com/pt-br/brasil/magazine/one-hour-one-day-one-week/um-dia-no-pantanal-mato-grossense-2ec97.shtml. Access in: 3/12/2021.

VERDADES sobre o candomblé, 2016. *Carlos Lima Jornal on-line*. Available in: https://www.cljornal.com.br/destaques/verdades-sobre-o-candomble/. Access in: 3/12/2021.

VENETIAN Carnival is a painting by Vincent Stiepevich, 1879. Available in: https://fineartamerica.com/featured/venetian-carnival-vincent-stiepevich.html. Access in: 3/12/2021.

VIDIGAL. Favela do Rio. 2014 – Vidigal. *Wikipédia*. Available in: https://pt.wikipedia.org/wiki/Ficheiro:1_vidigal_favela_rio_2014.jpg. Access in: 3/12/2021.